THE ECONOMICS
OF NATURAL
RESOURCES

THE ECONOMICS OF NATURAL RESOURCES

Ferdinand E. Banks

The University of Uppsala
Uppsala, Sweden

PLENUM PRESS · NEW YORK AND LONDON

Library of Congress Cataloging in Publication Data

Banks, Ferdinand E
    The economics of natural resources.

    Bibliography: p.
    Includes index.
    1. Natural resources. 2. Raw materials. 3. Economics. I. Title.
    HC55.B25   333.7   76-25583
    ISBN 0-306-30926-2

© 1976 Plenum Press, New York
A Division of Plenum Publishing Corporation
227 West 17th Street, New York, N.Y. 10011

Printed in the United States of America

To my teachers

PREFACE

This is a reference and elementary textbook on the economics of natural resources, with the emphasis being on the economics of industrial raw materials.

Considerable efforts have been taken to make this book suitable for three categories of reader. The first is the reader with an elementary course or two in economic theory somewhere in his or her background. For this category the present book can be looked upon as a continuation of the elementary course in economics, with the pedagogical vehicle being an exposition of the markets for certain raw materials. Together with a few of the more important articles in this field, there should be enough material below for one semester's work. Where these articles are concerned, I recommend Solow (1974), Nordhaus (1973 and 1974), and Pearce (1975).

The next category of reader, and equally as important, will consist of individuals largely without any previous training in economics, but seeking an essentially nontechnical introduction to the economics of raw materials. Approximately 50 to 60 percent of this book is directed toward these readers: most of Chapters 1 and 2; at least half of Chapters 3 and 5; most of Chapters 4 and 7, and all of Chapter 8. My belief is that after one or two readings, this category of reader should find no difficulty in following the debate on natural resource and energy problems that is going on in almost every country in the world. In addition, I hope that he or she will get a glimpse of the power—and the excitement—of elementary economic theory.

Finally, the advanced student or professional economist should also find this book to be of interest, since, as far as I know, a considerable amount of the material presented below is unavailable in this form elsewhere. What I have attempted to do is to introduce many of the topics that I have found to be of particular importance for my own work with copper, aluminum, and iron and steel, taking into account the need to stress certain aspects of microeconomics that I feel have been given insufficient attention in the pedagogical literature. The emphasis below, however, is on *informa-*

tion; and I hope that the reader will come to understand that excursions into abstract theory are taken with the greatest reluctance.

In those few cases where relatively advanced mathematical economics, or econometrics, seemed necessary, I have resorted to footnotes and four short appendices in the rear of the book. Although there has been a growing tendency to think of mathematical economics as a kind of Grand Guignol for a certain elite within the profession, the simple truth is that once analytical economics, like physics and engineering, develops channels for getting rid of unsound and unusable ideas and techniques, it will have a crucial role to play in the battle for the future.

The same is true of the gentle art of econometrics. Despite a great deal of wishful thinking on the subject, there is *no* econometric model of *any* commodity market in existence today that is capable of giving the kind of forecasts promised by the model builder when he was negotiating the price of his services; and for reasons best known to these and other econometricians, such models are unlikely to appear in the near future. On the other hand, econometrics, when used in conjunction with economic theory, economic history, a study of the institutional aspects of various markets, and a liberal dose of common sense, might conceivably provide a basis for making realistic forecasts, as well as to clarify some of the mysteries of the international economic system.

At this point I should like to thank the superb economists and statisticians whom I have consulted in the course of my work, both personally and through their publications. In particular I can cite John Cuddy, M. J. Colebrook, Bryan Chambers, and Joseph Shaw of the UNCTAD Commodities Division; Aziz Taj of the UNCTAD Research Division; Paul Rayment of the Economic Commission for Europe; Luis Correo Da Silva of UNIDO; and H. Timm of the HWWA Institute for Economic Research, Hamburg. Also my colleagues at the Universities of Uppsala and Stockholm: Ragnar Bentzel, Göran Ohlin, Villy Bergström, Anders Kristofferson, Per Wikman, and, especially, Erland Holmlund and Christian Nilsson.

I must also acknowledge the help of Hildegard Harlinger of the IFO Institute for Economic Research, Munich; Alan Lamond of UNCTAD; Kenji Takeuchi of the World Bank; O. Andersson of the International Iron and Steel Institute; Barbro Gyllenhammar and Sonia Axelsson of Uppsala University; the librarians of the UNCTAD-EEC reference room, Geneva; the UNIDO library, Vienna; and, especially, the director and staff of the magnificent library of the Institute for World Economics, Kiel. Finally, I would like to thank the Ford Foundation and Statens Råd för Samhällsforskning for grants that enabled me to write this book.

Ferdinand E. Banks

ACKNOWLEDGMENTS

The following acknowledgments are in order: to *Zeitschrift für Nationalökonomie* for permission to use material from my article "An Econometric Note on the Demand for Refined Zinc"; to *Econometrica* for permission to use material from my article "An Econometric Model of the World Tin Economy: A Comment"; to the *Journal of Economic Theory* for permission to use material from my article "A Note on Some Theoretical Issues of Resource Depletion"; and to *Jahrbücher für Nationalökonomie und Statistik* for permission to use material from my article "Elementary Investment Theory: An Optimal Control Approach." I have also employed considerable statistical material from United Nations documents that have been placed in the public domain, and, in accordance with the wishes expressed in some of these documents, I should like to point out that I appreciate the access that I have had to various material from UNIDO, UNCTAD, The International Bank for Reconstruction and Development, the FAO, and the ILO. Finally, to Claes Brundenius and Universitetsforlaget, Oslo, for permission to reproduce material from the article "The Anatomy of Imperialism: Multinational Mining in Peru."

CONTENTS

THE ECONOMICS
OF NATURAL
RESOURCES

BACKGROUND AND INTRODUCTION

1

Historians in general have yet to commit themselves on such matters as the cosmic significance of the October (1973) War in the Middle East, but it does seem appropriate at even this early date to make some observations on what the immediate aftermath of this event—in particular the "energy crisis"—has meant for the international economy in general, and the market for raw materials in particular. First, in concert with the forecasts of such aggressive purveyors of doomsday as the Club of Rome, it has helped to fix in the minds of many people in the industrial countries an image of immediate geologic and other limitations to natural resource availability. This, in turn, has led to some rather unpleasant suggestions about the possibility of having to scale down material aspirations for the present generation and its immediate successors. In one form or another this notion has been gaining ground for at least a decade, but the October War gave it a special urgency.

In examining this topic, one of the first questions that comes to mind is whether the severe economic downturn that began in 1974 could have been mitigated had this pessimism not been present. This may, of course, be one of those unanswerable questions that economic history has a way of posing from time to time, but the author is convinced that the level of tolerance by the general public for any economic crisis at the present time is to an overwhelming extent conditioned by psychological considerations, and the really important factor is how economic phenomena are presented and interpreted. I therefore propose, at this point, to take some notice of the large number of academics and journalists, many of whom normally reside well beyond the outskirts of productive economic life, who have recently come forward to analyze the sad state into which 20th-century man is apparently falling. In particular, their indictment of science and technology as the main conspirator against the well-being of humanity deserves some comment.

The complaint, in brief, runs about as follows: Science and technology, which might be described as the locomotives of economic growth, have promoted an insatiable appetite for the finite resources of the globe.

As a result, if we enlarge the emphasis placed on these scourges, and maintain the prominence that the scientific method has been given in the scheme of things, then we will increase the rate at which our limited supply of raw materials will be depleted, or "plundered" as the expression sometimes goes. The outcome of this type of behavior is an increase in the risk that the bulk of the world's population will someday dramatically find themselves without the resource base needed to maintain a positive rate of growth, and will instead experience a cataclysmic and definitive fall in their standard of living. In the case of the less developed countries this will mean mass starvation; and for the rest of the world social upheaval, wars, dictatorships, and such. Various rich, but erratic, variations can be immediately spun from this theme. For instance, the position has been advanced that nuclear technology should be rejected since, if it proves superior from the cost point of view to other sources of energy, and if it is safe, then it will intensify the demand for raw materials.

It goes without saying that science and technology have many sins to answer for, but so, for that matter, has ignorance. The trouble with the kind of speculation reviewed in the above paragraph is that it gives no clues as to just when natural resources should be exploited. If we look at the situation for such items as coal and copper, we indeed find that seams have been growing thinner and thinner over the past 50 to 100 years. Yet, if we take the case of copper, the former chief economist of CIPEC, Marian Radetski, assures us that raw copper can be won from ore with a copper content of 0.5 percent at a cost that, measured in goods and services, is not higher than it was more than a hundred years ago, when ore content was between 5 and 7 percent.[1] And this is true even though consumption has increased 150 times in this period. Actually, Radetski's testimonial underestimates the gains that should be accredited to technology, considering that a hundred years ago a large part of the manual work associated with mining was carried out by children in their early teens working twelve hours a day, six days a week. In fact, if we limit ourselves to technical matters, it could be argued that it has never been easier to obtain raw materials than at the present time, nor have they been used with greater efficiency in the promotion of the general welfare. Moreover, thanks to the impetus given science by the so called energy crisis, we are going to see resource-saving

[1]CIPEC (Intergovernmental Council of Copper Exporting Countries) is the name of the producer organization of the less developed of the copper producing countries. See Radetski, M., "Koppertillgångarna—ett fallstudie i resursuttömning," *Ekonomisk Debatt* 8, 1974. In the same vein, Barnett and Morse (1963) have argued that costs and real prices of almost all extractive output in the United States have been falling from 1870 to 1957; while V. K. Smith (1974) has extended this result up to 1972. Smith's work indicates, however, that this fall may now be taking place at a diminishing rate.

devices and measures pressed into service at an appreciably faster rate than would have been possible had earlier attitudes and expectations prevailed. However, it does no harm to admit that the general welfare could probably be equally well served if even a fraction of the ingenuity that has gone, or will go, into extracting mineral wealth from the substrata of the earth could be applied to some of the social problems of the major industrial countries.

At the same time that various scholars have been sacrificing precious sleep and energy in their investigation of the long-run prospects for the physical survival of mankind, a large and growing number of journalists, politicians, economists, and others have been busy analyzing recent market phenomena in hope of being able to chart the short-run course of the international economy. Many of these researchers and thinkers (among whom the President of France deserves particular attention) have come to the conclusion that the above-mentioned scarcity of raw materials is not coming, but is here; that the balance of economic power between the developed and less developed worlds is in rapid transition—to the disadvantage of the former; and that the citizens of the industrial world had best heed the writings on the wall and make haste to repent.

Now, repenting is a noble art, and certainly one that many of us should practice from time to time; however the truth of the matter is that this kind of gospel might be a little more palatable if its advocates were better able to conceal their own pronounced tastes for the more exotic offerings of the consumer society. It should be emphasized, however, that "palatable" does not mean acceptable. Even if these idealogues were to leave the corridors and salons of power, take up the life style of Trappist monks and chant their message from the dungeons of Kabul, the fact remains that if we attempt to interpret the history of the early 1970s with the help of a very small amount of undergraduate economic theory, we get an entirely different set of results from those reached by the publicists of the Apocalypse.

To see why this is so, we can begin by observing what happened to the price of some of the more important industrial raw materials between 1969 and the beginning of 1975.

The story in Figure 1-1 is as follows. As the war in Vietnam, in particular the United States's involvement, began to wind down, the slow rise in the price of raw materials that began in the mid 1960s was arrested and a slight downturn began. At almost the same time, however, the international business cycle gained a new impetus, and so this downturn was quickly reversed. Even so, underlying expectations at this time pointed to a return to "normality" on the world commodity markets—that is, a situation in which the basic metals and other primary commodities were freely available for prices that were, in comparison with other factors of production, relatively low.

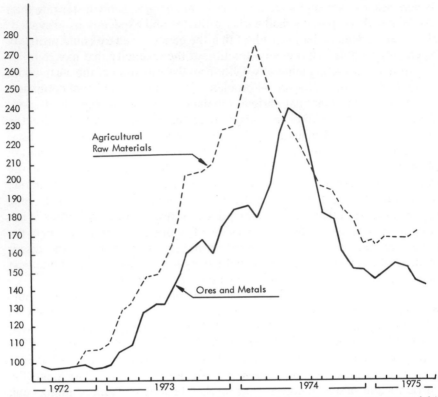

Figure 1-1. Monthly indices of market prices of ores and metals (and agricultural raw materials) exported by LDCs (1968 = 100). Note: Indices calculated on the basis of dollar prices or the dollar equivalent of prices expressed in other currencies that have been converted at current exchange rates. Source: UNCTAD monthly commodity price bulletins.

The reason for this is easy to understand. The demand for industrial raw materials is of an input–output nature, by which we mean that when industrial production goes up or down, raw material demand goes up or down almost proportionally.[2] Assumptions were thus that when the busi-

---

[2] Price has almost no role to play in demand here—except for the degree that it influences the demand for stocks. The reason for this is that, in the *short run,* very little substitution is possible for most commodities, and thus a price rise, for example, will not dampen demand for the particular input. In addition, manufacturers producing items that utilize only a small amount of an input—such as automobiles, which contain only a small amount by weight and value of such things as copper and aluminum—usually reason that, if it is necessary, they can pass these price increases on to the final consumer. For instance, a tripling of copper prices would result in a scarcely noticeable price increase for an automobile, even if the entire price increase were added to the original price of the car.

ness cycle crested in late 1973 or early 1974, and the rate of growth of demand for raw materials fell while, presumably, the rate of growth of supply remained unchanged, prices would begin moving toward their pre-Vietnam War level.

There was still another factor influencing raw material prices during this period that had never been encountered before to any significant extent. A large percentage of the international transactions for raw materials takes place in dollars and, due to the excessive increase in the global circulation of dollars caused by budget deficits used to finance the war in Vietnam, the value of American currency vis-à-vis other currencies deteriorated substantially. Among the things to which this led was a widespread speculation against the dollar in favor of some other currencies, and also of various primary commodities.

A large part of this speculation for primary commodities went through the *futures* market. The operation of this market will be taken up in detail in Chapter 5; however, it is primarily a market for paper titles that are manipulated in such a way that physical delivery of the commodity rarely takes place. On the other hand, prices in this market are sometimes taken as an indicator of what actual prices are going to be. What happened was that speculation against the dollar (and some other currencies) caused an increase in the price of futures contracts, which in turn reflected on the price at which spot (or cash) and *forward* sales were being made. (The forward "market" can be thought of as the market on which goods are sold for future *physical* delivery.) Thus, in 1973, in addition to the "hausse" (rise) on the world commodity markets caused by the upswing of the business cycle, there was a large positive speculative component that was completely unrelated to the availability of many of these commodites relative to their demand as inputs in the same period.

The correction of this situation was in progress, principally via some major currency alignments, when the war broke out in the Middle East. This war, and the oil embargo that followed it, raised the specter of a general shortage of raw materials that led to the following unusual situation: although the oil shortage and the rise in oil prices caused a slowing down in industrial production and a fall in the demand for industrial raw materials to be used as current inputs, there was a large increase in the demand for these materials by inventory holders. This demand, which was of a precautionary and speculative type, sufficed to drive the price of several commodities up to record heights.

About the middle of 1974, with the inventories of most industrial raw materials at or close to the desired level, and with businessmen, politicians, and even economists beginning to comprehend the simple mechanics of the energy crisis, the demand for raw materials began to assume reasonable proportions. This could only mean a sharp downward pressure on the price of these materials. What the reader should note here is the complex role that *expectations* play in determining demand, and how on occasion higher prices—instead of mitigating the demand—only caused further increases in demand.[3]

The basic difference between oil and the other industrial raw materials should also be stressed. The important thing in this respect is not the structure of the oil cartel, nor the various cultural or political ties between some of the members of this cartel, but the sheer quantitative importance of oil as an industrial input in comparison with other raw materials. In addition, there is the well-known short- or medium-run impossibility of substituting other materials for oil in many of its uses. The simple truth of the matter is that, given the economic status of the commodity as a wasting (i.e., nonrenewable) asset, and its ubiquity as an industrial input, it was inevitable that its price was going to increase. The tragedy of the situation was the lack of foresight displayed by the governments of the major consuming countries in not initiating or increasing the exploitation of alternate energy sources years ago—particularly when they realized that the owners of Middle East and African oil were not, in fact, subject to the statutes of North American or European antitrust legislation. Moreover, the situation was hardly ameliorated by the aggressive insistence of certain pillars of the academic community that the price of oil actually belonged back at the one or two-dollar level, and it was only a matter of time before so called "market forces" contrived to put it there—unless by market forces they meant massive unemployment in the consuming countries.

---

[3] As an example we can postulate that demand is a function of the present price *and* the price expected in the next period. Obviously, we are now considering a demand for a commodity to be used as a current input and in inventories. We might then have for our demand equation

$$q_t = q_t(p_t, p^e_{t+1}) = a_0 + a_1 p_t + a_2 p^e_{t+1} \qquad a_1 < 0, a_2 > 0$$

We must now say something about how expectations are formed. One possibility is extrapolative expectations, which means that $p^e_{t+1} = p_t + \lambda(p_t - p_{t-1})$, with $\lambda > 0$. In other words, we assume that if price increased from the last period to this, we will get an increase in price in the next period. Thus we get for the demand equation

$$q_t = a_0 + [a_1 + a_2(1 + \lambda)]p_t - a_2\lambda p_{t-1} \qquad \lambda > 0$$

We now see that we can have $a_1 + a_2(1 + \lambda) \gtreqless 0$, depending upon the size of a_1, a_2, and λ. If, in fact, this expression was positive, we would have $\partial q_t/\partial p_t > 0$. Another possibility would be some kind of reverse extrapolative expectations, where we have $\lambda < 0$. The thing we would expect, of course, is to have a nonconstant λ that was positive on some occasions and negative on others. This arrangement, however, would complicate things considerably.

An interesting approach to the problem introduced above is that of Varon and Takeuchi (1974), who imply that a gradual increase in the price of oil, and perhaps some other minerals, would have led to a more rational allocation of global resources of important raw materials over the last decade or so. The technical argument here is far from elementary, but applied to the topic under discussion it might go as follows: If the price of oil, relative to the price of other factors of production, has been too low over the past 10 or 15 years, then there have been investments in machines, structures, and durable goods (e.g., automobiles) whose utility or profitability has declined considerably now that there has been a drastic rise in the price of fossil fuel. The present price rise, of course, had a political rather than an economic motivation to begin with; but even so there is no escaping the fact that since global reserves of traditional fuel are limited, the price system will have to take this into account sooner or later. The same type of argument can perhaps be presented for some of the nonfuel minerals, but not with the same urgency as oil. Not only are efficient substitutes available for most of these other minerals but, while the burning of oil dissipates its energy beyond hope of recapture, such things as copper and aluminum can be economically recycled.

The previous discussion has provided an introductory explanation of commodity prices as they have developed over the past few years, and further comments are presented below. The reader should note, however, that despite occasional departures from the idiom of orthodox economic theory, the underlying presentation is along conventional economic lines, and at no point has it been necessary to go into such exotic topics as the imminent decline of industrial man, or the "tribute" (presumably in goods and services) that the 20th century must pay the 19th, despite the considerable amount of wishful thinking on this subject that is in circulation these days.

Sweden, for example, is a country that is heavily dependent on imports, being, in this respect, one of the most "open" economies in the world; yet in recent years annual imports (from all sources) of nonfuel raw materials came to only about 1–1½ billion kroner, while Swedish aid to underdeveloped countries has climbed to well over two billion kroner. (It should be mentioned also that a part of the "tribute" here went not to the 19th century, but to the pretentious and corrupt drones who have come to dominate both the giving and receiving side of the aid business.) Similar observations seem to be valid where other industrial countries are concerned; and, in fact, if we look at the average of the total value of imports from the underdeveloped countries into the industrial countries of copper, iron ore, tin, bauxite/alumina/aluminum, phosphate rock, zinc, silver, lead, and manganese for the period 1967–69, we see that this was slightly less than $5 billion per year.[4] There are, of course, a large number of corporations and other enterprises in the developed countries with sales or turnover figures far in excess of this amount. As for the short-term export prospects of the countries trading these materials, Varon and Takeuchi have pointed out that the expected increase in foreign exchange earnings for these countries of about $10 billion for the period of 1967/69 to 1980 will be less than one-tenth of the growth in revenue from oil exports during the much shorter period from 1973 to 1980.

In considering this somewhat sobering fact, one might be tempted to view sympathetically the argument of Professor Harry Johnson (1967) that it might be a good idea for countries anxious to industrialize to attempt to maximize their profits from primary production over the short run "in order to secure their development objectives," even if this short-run strategy should reflect negatively on long-run earnings. Some, and perhaps many, people have interpreted this advice to mean that it would be a good idea for LDCs to form OPEC-type cartels and raise prices now, even if it resulted in consumers finding "safe" sources in the future, and making various types of substitutions (such as aluminum for copper). The problem here is that economic development and maximizing profits from mineral development are not the same thing. Many LDCs have large reserves of raw materials, but there is no clear-cut proof that these have made noticeable contributions to the raising of the general standard of living in those countries. On the other hand, countries such as Singapore, North Korea, South Korea, Cuba, and Taiwan have experienced important economic and/or social development without a particularly impressive raw materials base.

In fact, what seems to be the case is that rapid increases in income derived from the markets for primary commodities have a way of being used to purchase expensive weapons systems and to promote the luxury consumption of the few, to the highly noticeable exclusion of the many. Large-scale capital formation and the genuine modernization of social and

---

[4]The approximate values per commodity are as follows for the period 1967–69:

Copper	2,280	Zinc	130
Iron ore	812	Silver	132
Tin	565	Lead	113
Baux./Alum.	450	Manganese	98
Phosphate rock	220		
		Total	4,800

These figures are in millions of dollars. During the same period, the average annual receipts for the oil exporters of the LDCs was about $14 billion. In 1975 the anticipated oil income of these countries is from 70–90 billions of dollars, while income from the items listed in this footnote may reach $7 billion.

economic institutions are conspicuous by their almost total absence, although there is no shortage of systematic corruption, bureaucratization, and high-flown rhetoric. Everything considered, it is probably safe to claim that it would be extremely difficult to alter the international balance of economic power on the basis of some geologic advantages in the production of primary commodities, although, needless to say, there will always be individuals who find it to their advantage to claim that the opposite is true.

PRICES AND SCARCITIES: SOME GENERAL OBSERVATIONS

In the production of industrial goods, the three principal inputs are labor, capital, and raw materials. Labor, and sometimes capital, are called primary factors, while raw materials (which are themselves produced with the aid of labor and capital, and perhaps other raw materials) fall in the category of intermediate goods. On occasion, raw materials are called primary commodities but, strictly speaking, primary commodities are unprocessed natural resources such as bauxite, copper ore, etc. As the reader will soon observe, no great attempt is made in this book to emphasize the differences between processed and unprocessed commodities, although it can hardly be denied that important differences exist. Instead we concentrate, as much as possible, on those problems of price formation, investment, and so on that are common to all stages of processing and, for that matter, vary only slightly as we go from one industry to another.

The question is often raised as to the importance of raw materials in the production process in relation to other inputs. This topic will be considered later, but Wohlin (1974) has estimated the average raw material content of industrial goods to be on the order of 10–15 percent by value. Financially this is a small, though not an insignificant, amount; but from the technical point of view it is crucial in that, physically, many of these inputs must be available or the entire production process would break down.

Where the price relationship between raw materials and industrial goods is concerned, a number of conflicting opinions are available. During the 1950s and 1960s the economists of GATT (the United Nations General Agreement on Tariffs and Trade) maintained that the prices of industrial goods habitually climbed faster than raw materials prices, and those countries whose exports are basically primary products (of all types) were placed at a disadvantage when they traded these goods for industrial commodities. Wohlin, and others, are not so certain, noting that while the prices of raw materials have climbed at an explosive rate on some occasions, and slumped on others, the long-run perspective indicates that the prices of raw materials have kept pace with industrial prices. UNCTAD (the United Nations Conference on Trade and Development) would seem to take issue with this vision of the world, since the various stabilization devices considered and analyzed by Dr. John Cuddy and his associates at that organization use as their starting point the inherent weakness of primary commodity prices. Some justification for the latter point of view is provided by the situation of the international economy at the time of writing of this book: a high rate of inflation *and* a downturn in the business cycle in the major market economies that has resulted in a sharp fall in the price of primary commodities relative to industrial goods.

In line with the objectives of the present chapter, a brief empirical treatment of some aspects of this topic is in order. To begin with, we can look at both the world commodity trade and the trade in manufactures.

Table 1-1 is designed to provide some general insights into the order of magnitude of world trade and how this trade is divided between primary commodities and manufactures. In considering all primary commodities, however, we become involved with many that are outside the scope of this book, such as agricultural commodities. It might thus be a good idea to look at Table 1-2, the share of the less developed countries, or LDCs as they will be called in much of the sequel, in the total world output and the reserves of some of the more important industrial raw materials in 1974.

The material presented above indicates that, at least in the short run, the LDCs as a group have an important position on the world's commodity markets. This may be true in the long run also, however here the situation is less clear. The LDCs are strong in copper, but the dependence of the industrial countries as far as this metal is concerned could diminish considerably if more recycling were practiced and there was a more rapid substitution of aluminum for copper. As for aluminum, bauxite—the basic raw ingredient of aluminum—is to be found in very large quantities in the crust of the earth. In addition, it is possible to produce aluminum without bauxite, and several nonbauxite technologies are available in pilot form and have shown considerable promise. Similarly, the potential supplies of iron ore are tremendous; and this is true even in the United States, a particularly large consumer of this commodity. Natural rubber can be replaced to a great extent by synthetic rubber; and even concerning oil it is difficult to say just what the possibilities are for production from nontraditional sources (shale, tar sands, the processing of coal, etc.).

Another perspective on this problem can be gained by examining the production, consumption, and exports (and imports) by LDCs of the nine major nonfuel minerals (bauxite, copper, iron ore, lead, manganese ore, nickel, phosphorous, tin, and zinc). Table 1-3 presents this information in relation to the developed market economies and the centrally planned economies.

Table 1-1. World Trade in Commodities and Manufactured Goods (1971)[a]

Exports to — Exports from	Developed market economies		Developing market economies		Centrally planned economies[b]		World total	
	Primary commod.	Manufac.	Primary commod.	Manufac.	Primary commod.	Manufac.	Primary commod.	Manufac.
Developed market economies	45.2	144.8	7.6	36.6	2.1	8.4	55	190,6
Developing market economies	34.7	8.3	8.2	3.4	2.8	0.2	46.2	12.4
Centrally planned economies	4.9	4.7	1.4	3.5	5.5	15.0	12.1	23.6
World total	85.1	157	17.2	43.5	10.4	23.0	114.4	226.7

[a] Manufactures: chemicals, engineering products, etc. SITC 5–8. Primary commodities: all food items (including beverages, tobacco, edible oils), agricultural raw materials, crude fertilizers, crude minerals, metalliferous ores, metal scrap, etc. SITC 0–4.

[b] Albania, Bulgaria, Czechoslovakia, German Democratic Republic, Hungary, Poland, Romania, U.S.S.R.

Note: The expression "Developing Market Economies" is taken to be equivalent to LDCs in general, although, strictly speaking, this designation may not be true.

Source: U.N. Monthly Bulletin of Statistics, 1973. All figures in billions of U.S. dollars.

Table 1-2. Output and Reserves of Less Developed Countries, 1974

Material	LDCs share of	
	World output (%)	World reserves (%)
Nickel	2	22
Lead	12	21
Zinc	13	23
Copper	34	47
Bauxite	43	57
Iron ore	24	29
Tin	69	79
Manganese ore[a]	60.5	—
Raw phosphate[a]	60.2	—
Natural rubber	99.0	
Oil[a]	75.3	—

[a] Export figures.

This table indicates that since 1950 LDCs have supplied the world with about a third of its most important nonfuel minerals. Moreover, given the fact that a large part of the financing of any industrialization that might take place in these countries would be via the sale of raw materials, the possibilities are that these exports will continue to be in the vicinity of this level.

Although it might be desirable, no attempt will be made at this time to initiate a serious attack on the relationship between the export and import prices of LDCs. The reason for this is that methodological problems are involved in the construction of terms of trade indexes that would cause *any* index that could be presented to be open to serious criticism. The only device that will be used here is a simple diagram showing the average annual rates of change of the prices of primary commodities as compared to manufactured goods. Figure 1-2 is based on the UNCTAD index of primary commodity prices and the United Nations index of export prices of manufactured goods (estimated in 1974).[5]

[5] An introduction to the problems encountered in preparing terms of trade and other indexes can be found in Habeler (1961), Rayment (1970), and Wilson, Sinha, and Castree (1969). Another problem that will not be considered in detail here is the "productivity" of raw materials, but it must be mentioned. For the United States, real GNP doubled between 1950 and 1970, while the consumption of primary and scrap iron increased by about 20 percent, so the productivity of iron (GNP per ton of iron) increased by about 2.5 percent a year during these 20 years. In the United States consumption of manganese increased by 30 percent, so the productivity of manganese increased by about 2.25 percent a year. The consumption of nickel doubled (as did GNP), and so its productivity went unchanged. Consumption of copper in the United States increased by a third between 1951 and 1970, and so GNP per pound of copper increased by about 2 percent a year. The productivity of lead and zinc also increased by 2 percent a year during this period, while the productivity of bituminous coal increased at about 3 percent a year.

Table 1-3. Production, Consumption, and Net Imports and Exports of Nine Major Raw Materials, 1950–80[a]

Area	Production				Consumption				Net exports (imports)[b]			
	1950	1960	1970	1980[c]	1950	1960	1970	1980[c]	1950	1960	1970	1980[c]
Developed market economies	3.1	4.4	7.3	10.0	4.6	7.0	11.6	17.6	(1.5)	(2.6)	(4.3)	(7.9)
LDCs	1.8	3.5	5.3	10.3	0.2	0.5	0.8	2.2	1.6	3.0	4.5	8.1
Centrally planned economies	0.8	2.5	4.4	7.0	0.9	2.6	4.6	7.1	(0.1)	(0.1)	(0.2)	(0.1)
World	5.7	10.4	17.0	27.3	5.7	10.1	17.1	27.1	—	—	—	—

[a] In billions of U.S. dollars.
[b] Imports in parentheses.
[c] Estimated.
Source: Various United Nations documents.

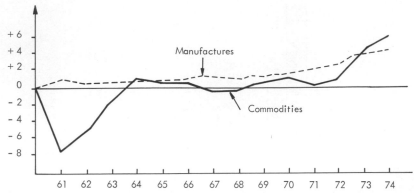

Figure 1-2. Comparison of changes in price of primary commodities and manufactured goods (average annual change in percent).

Though on the basis of the material presented in Figure 1-2 we see that it would be difficult to make a case for or against any advantages held by the producers of industrial goods over the producers of primary products, two issues must still be faced. The first is that the above diagram contains information concerning all raw materials—nonindustrial (such as coffee, cocoa, etc.) as well as industrial. In addition, Figure 1-2 contains the effect of the production of manufactured goods by LDCs. This problem is not so serious as it might seem at first glance, since a very short statistical exercise would show that for the greater part of the last 10 or 15 years the market prices of ores and metals, agricultural raw materials, vegetable oilseeds and oils, and foods and beverages have had a tendency to move together. In addition, the production of manufactured goods in LDCs is not very extensive and, moreover, a considerable part of this production does not enter into international trade. Still, for the purpose of this book, a less-aggregate analysis is desirable, and, while it would be possible to construct another index that would isolate the effects of industrial raw materials in the diagram given above, it is probably just as instructive to look at the prices of some important industrial raw materials over the past twenty or so years.

Table 1-4 shows the price situation on the markets for the major industrial raw materials up to the October (1973) War in the Middle East. In taking these figures at face value, the obvious contention would have to be that the laws of supply and demand have not blessed the exporters of such items as aluminum, natural rubber, lead, iron ore, and, until recently, oil. While the prices of these commodities have been almost constant over this period, the general world price level of the consumer and investment goods for which these commodities would be traded have increased at a rate of between 2½ and 4 percent per year.

Table 1-4. Price Information for Some Important Industrial Raw Materials, 1951–75

Year	Aluminum ingot[a]	Natural rubber[b]	Lead[c]	Zinc[d]	Copper[e]	Iron ore[f]	Tin[g]	Oil[h]
1951	18.0	60.7	17.5	18.0	24.2		127.0	
1952	18.4	38.8	16.5	16.3	24.2		120.4	
1953	19.7	24.2	13.5	10.9	28.8		95.8	
1954	20.2	23.6	14.1	10.7	29.7	12.3	91.8	
1955	21.9	39.2	15.2	12.3	37.5	13.0	94.7	
1956	24.0	34.2	16.0	13.5	41.8	14.4	101.4	
1957	25.4	31.2	14.7	11.4	29.6	15.1	96.2	
1958	24.8	28.1	12.1	10.3	25.8	14.5	95.1	
1959	24.8	36.6	12.2	11.5	31.1	11.5	102.0	
1960	26.0	38.1	11.9	12.9	32.0	11.5	101.4	1.91
1961	25.5	19.5	10.9	11.5	29.9	11.5	113.3	1.86
1962	23.9	28.6	9.6	11.6	30.6	10.8	114.6	1.78
1963	22.6	26.1	11.1	12.0	30.6	10.1	116.6	1.79
1964	23.7	25.2	13.6	13.6	31.9	10.1	157.6	1.74
1965	24.5	25.7	16.0	14.5	35.0	10.1	178.2	1.81
1966	24.2	23.6	15.1	14.5	35.1	9.9	164.2	1.72
1967	25.0	19.9	14.0	13.8	33.2	8.7	153.4	1.85
1968	25.6	19.9	13.2	13.5	41.8	8.4	148.1	1.76
1969	27.2	26.2	14.9	14.6	47.5	8.4	164.5	1.51
1970	28.7	21.0	15.6	15.3	57.7	9.3	174.2	2.70
1971	29.0	17.4	13.8	16.1	51.4	10.5	167.3	2.50
1972	26.5	17.1	15.0	17.7	50.6	10.8	177.5	2.50
1973	27.1	33.1	16.3	20.7	59.4	9.8	227.5	2.50[k]
1974	34.7	34.0	22.5	36.0	77.0	10.4	396.2	10.80
1975[m]	40.4	25.1	21.0	38.7	64.0	11.8	324.0	11.90

[a,b,c,d,e,f,g]Cents/pound.
[h]Rotterdam Heavy Fuel, dollars/barrel.
[k]September, 1973.
[m]Estimated.
Sources: World Bank Statistical Summaries; UNCTAD documents; oil price estimates by Mr. Aziz Taj.

It should be noticed that the above paragraph merely says something about the price of some industrial raw materials in relation to other goods: it is not a statement about economic growth or development. For instance, if it were the purpose of this book to expound at length on these particular topics, the argument would be that economic growth and/or development is largely a matter of cultural and social factors, and, in essence, has little to do with such things as prices or price ratios. In examining the Swedish mining sector, for example, a reasonable explanation for its prosperity would deal largely with the technical skill of its workers, technicians, and managers; the progressive outlook of Swedish society as a whole; and the interest of the productive elements within that society in raising their standard of living and expanding the professional and educational opportunities of themselves and their families. Strangely enough, such things as the terms of trade for Swedish mining products would play only a minor role in the discussion. This is because forward-looking societies—that is, societies with a future—have a way of accepting the terms of trade, whatever they are, and finding some way of making the best of them. More important, if they cannot make the best of them, they find some way of changing them to their advantage in the long run. The way this is done is by producing a different selection of commodities.

SOME ASPECTS OF RESOURCE AVAILABILITY

The above section leads almost directly into a consideration of mineral reserves. The approach taken here is that the key factor determining the accessibility of natural resources over the coming years will be scientific and technological advance, although, beyond any shadow of a doubt, there are enormous quantities of resources waiting to be discovered whose exploitation would be profitable employing techniques of the distant past.

In discussing availability the concept of upper-layer profusion (or total availability) provides a good starting point. What this approach does is to take into account the not very well known fact that almost all rocks are ore-bearing rocks. Admittedly, at the present level of technology, this category of availability is of little practical importance, but it should not be forgotten. What it does is to say something about the goal toward which mineral retrieval technology should and may be working.

More to the point is the concept of maximal recoverable resources, which will be taken here as approximately 0.01 percent of total availability down to a depth of 500 meters. The reader may be able to suggest other depths, but it should be remembered that at present the deepest mines have penetrated only somewhat beyond a mile, and then at great expense. At a much lower level of availability we have figures that organizations such as

Table 1-5. Some Indices of Resource Availability in Years

Material	Average concentration in earth's crust, grams/ton	Annual consumption		
		Known reserves	ULP[a]	MRR[b]
Copper	63	45	121,000,000	170
Iron	58,000	117	907,500,000	1,328
Phosphorus	—	481	435,000,000	801
Molybdenum[c]	1,000,000	65	211,000,000	315
Lead	12	10	42,500,000	81
Zinc	94	21	204,500,000	309
Uranium	—	50	927,500,000	422
Aluminum[d]	83,000	250	19,250,000,000	34,033

[a] ULP = Upper Layer Profusion.
[b] MRR = Maximal Recoverable Reserves. This figure does not take price or technology changes into consideration.
[c] The average concentration figure for molybdenum is measured in parts per million.
[d] This entry is for bauxite as well as many other silicates.
Note: Many of these figures do not take into account the possibility of mining lower grade ores as prices increase or technology advances. Similarly, it should be appreciated that the above indices are approximate.

the Club of Rome have employed as part of the background for their arguments that present usage rates of resources are laying the foundation for a massive human tragedy sometime in the next century.[6] These three concepts of reserves, together with some other material, are presented in Table 1-5. Resource availability in years has been calculated by dividing one of the concepts of reserves by present annual consumption.

The first comment on Table 1-5 deals with the concept "known reserves." Known reserves are those that have been charted in one sense or another; but there is little reason to consider this a more important category of supplies at the present time than, say, probable reserves. The reason for this is that national geological surveys are incomplete for many developed countries, and have hardly begun for most LDCs. Italy, for example, provides an example of a developed country driven to the rim of bankruptcy by the energy crisis, but where substantial amounts of natural gas, as well as some oil, have just been discovered about 20 kilometers from Milan. Ireland can report a similar experience. Recently, what may be the largest zinc deposit in Western Europe has been discovered only a few miles from Dublin. If we take an underdeveloped country, the Spanish Sahara contains the largest deposit of phosphate rock in the world: an

[6] Where massive human tragedies are concerned, we are in fact seeing these all the time: starvation in the Sahel and Bangladesh are two examples of the present day. It should be appreciated, however, that events of this type can be directly attributed to stupidity and corruption on the part of some politicians and officials in the countries concerned, as well as the almost astonishing incompetence of some international organizations.

estimated 1.7 billion tons of the material, with much of this less than 20 feet below the surface of the earth. There is no idea, however, as to how much titanium, vanadium, copper, and zinc this area may possess, although it is common knowledge that these minerals are present and possibly in great abundance. The reason for the uncertainty in these matters, it should be added, undoubtedly turns on a great deal of bureaucratic mismanagement and misjudgment—conduct that in certain parts of the world is the rule rather than the exception.

In a similar vein it might be interesting to examine the information given above that deals with the availability of copper. According to the known reserves/annual consumption estimate presented in Table 1-5, this amounts to 45 years, which corresponds to a figure for world reserves of about 340 million tons.

There is, however, nothing sacred about these figures. Taking the situation in the United States, it is estimated that at present prices exploitable reserves amount to 85–90 million tons; and expectations are that with the technology of the immediate future this figure can be increased to about 135 million tons. To these supplies it might be possible to add "hypothetical" resources, or resources believed to exist in districts containing copper deposits; and "speculative" resources, which are resources that may be discovered in localities that are broadly favorable from a geological point of view, but in which as yet there have been no discoveries. The U.S. Geological Survey places 145 million tons in the first of these categories and 110 million in the second. Thus it is not inconceivable that the United States possesses an amount of exploitable reserves of copper within its own borders that is almost equal to present known global reserves. Of course, it should be recognized that this copper, as well as other resources, will not be located just by talking about it, nor, once located, will it come to the surface by itself. For these things to happen, energetic and imaginative exploratory programs and mining policies will have to be formulated by both the mining companies and the authorities. If, by some chance, these programs are not forthcoming, there may be more of a clue to the future of civilized man in the Club of Rome report than many of us imagined. At the same time it should be emphasized that there is no economic sense in spending huge sums of money now to locate resources that will not be used for 40 or 50 years.

Thus far the discussion has been concerned with the technology of the immediate or near future. In the case of commodities that are obtained by mining, this involves equipment and techniques that are exploiting today's grades of ore. In the 19th century only ores containing 4 to 6 percent copper were of interest, while at present ores are being worked that have a copper content of as little as 0.4 percent; and it is almost certain that in 20 or 30 years ores down to 0.25 percent can be profitably exploited. The energy needed to produce a pound of aluminum has decreased from 12 kilowatt-hours in 1939 to a low of 6.5 for the most modern processes. The coke input of blast furnaces has fallen from 5 tons per ton of pig iron during the first half of the last century to less than 1 ton of coke today. In 1945 an output of 1000 tons of iron required, on the average, 500 tons of limestone. Today only 150 tons of limestone are used.

In tandem with a kind of core technology that has remained pretty much the same over the past generation, such things as flotation methods of enriching various polymetallic ores have been developed, together with hydrometallurgical and other processing techniques, that have made it possible to extract copper, zinc, lead, silver, nickel, cobalt, and many other metals from very low grade ore. Until recently, for example, the mineral nepheline was considered to be of little or no value, but now a technique has been developed for extracting its small aluminum content, and so nepheline has been reclassified a valuable raw material. Taconites are at present an important source of iron ore, although before World War II there was no way to achieve a commercially successful extraction of iron from these rocks. Technological advances of this type should become much more common as governments and firms put more time and energy into securing and conserving their supplies of industrial raw materials.[7]

The time may also have arrived to do some speculating about the amount of raw materials that could become available as we move to a higher level of technical development. To begin with, it is interesting to consider the possibilities that will be broached when minerals can be extracted at deeper levels than can be worked today. At depths of greater than 5 kilometers there may be very large deposits of coal, oil, gas, bauxite, and so on. In addition, some of the rock formations at this depth are thought to contain sizable amounts of iron, manganese, chromium, cobalt, nickel, uranium, copper, gold, etc. In order to reach these resources, however, a great deal of highly sophisticated scientific and engineering work is going to be necessary, particularly for the design of instruments and equipment that can be used at great depths under extreme pressure and heat. Just when this matériel will be ready cannot be predicted, of course, since an estimate cannot be made of the incentives that firms and governments will experience that will cause them to finance the necessary research and development.

On the other hand, the mining of various portions of the ocean's floor may be a realizable enterprise before the end of the present century.

---

[7] A similar example involves the burning of water with oil. Research stimulated by the energy crisis has led to the development of a device in which water replaces air as a source of oxygen in conventional combustion processes. Based on an ultrasonic reactor first patented by E. Cottell, it apparently has fewer waste products, and the oil gives off much more heat. Notice that here the improvement did not involve the fuel, but the way in which the fuel was used.

Interest in operations of this type has been growing since the early 1960s, and the basic technology for mining to depths of from 10,000 to 15,000 feet below the surface of the ocean is almost ready. Estimates of just what mineral wealth is to be found on the floor of the oceans vary. The manganese, nickel, cobalt, copper, tin, etc. found in the depths of the Pacific and Indian oceans would, if it could be brought to the surface, increase the global supply of some of these items by very large amounts. Where the actual mining of these nodules is concerned, several large international firms have already begun deep ocean exploration programs. The lessons that should be learned in these and similar operations may result in an important flow of minerals from this source before the end of the century.

Other possibilities include extracting ores from seawater and breaking up rocks and processing them. If we take the first of these, it can be noted that every cubic kilometer of seawater contains approximately 37.5 million tons of solids in solution or suspension. The greater part of this is sodium and chlorine, but there are also large amounts of magnesium, together with some iron, gold, copper, nickel, silver, etc. There is also a great deal of uranium in seawater. It has been calculated that if only one percent of the uranium in the sea could be extracted, it would provide an amount of energy more than nine times the highest estimate of that available in coal—which in energy units comes to several hundred years. Some estimates indicate that the commercial extraction of uranium will be possible if, or when, the long-term price of uranium reaches $20/pound.

As for the breaking and processing of rocks, it has been estimated that one cubic kilometer of granite or shale contains 230 million tons of aluminum, 130 million tons of iron, 260,000 tons of tin, 7,000 tons of uranium, 13,000 tons of gold, etc. Of course, the scientific work that must be carried out before we have actual access to these supplies is formidable, and it hardly seems likely that it will be completed until well into the next century or, most likely, later; but if we can make the heroic assumption that some day this work will be done, then the problem of running out of minerals will probably cease to be relevant for several thousand years, after which time we can begin considering what movable resources are available on the moon.

SOME ELEMENTARY ECONOMICS OF ALUMINUM AND RUBBER

This section will introduce, at a very elementary level, some aspects of the markets for aluminum and rubber that can be used to illustrate several of the more important problems in commodity economics: price formation, investment, and substitution.

Almost everyone who has picked up a basic textbook in economics is familiar with the simple supply–demand model. The model takes the following algebraic form, with supply and demand a function of price:

$$s = f(p) \qquad s = \text{supply}$$
$$d = h(p) \qquad d = \text{demand}$$
$$s = d \qquad p = \text{price}$$

The three variables s, d, and p are called endogenous variables; and normally they can be solved out of this system of three equations. We should observe the *units* being employed here: both demand and supply are in "units" per time period. With aluminum, for example, we might have long-tons/year. The price is measured in some relevant monetary unit. Diagrammatically we would have a situation as shown in Figure 1-3.

We have in Figure 1-3 an equilibrium at $(\bar{q},\bar{p})$ in that, at this point, the market is cleared—that is, the same amount demanded as supplied; and the price is immobile. If we specify that d is strictly current demand—that is, being used in the production process in the present period; and s involves only current production, then we have a *pure flow model*. Most textbooks, however, do not make this specification. For them both d and s are, true enough, flows; but d can involve a demand for goods to go into inventory as well as for current use, while s can represent supplies that originate in inventories as well as current production.

As the reader will come to realize in the next few chapters, neither a pure flow model nor the usual textbook "flow" model suffices to give us all the answers we require in order to understand price formation in most of the raw material markets. A certain amount of aluminum produced today was not used for current consumption, but went into inventory; just as a

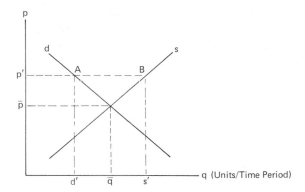

Figure 1-3. Typical supply–demand model.

certain amount used in the present period was not produced during this period, but came out of inventory. (For instance, if the above diagram were a pure flow model, and if price were p', then supply would be s' and demand d'. Thus $s'-d'$ would be added to inventories in the present period.) Most important, inventories—or, more specifically, the relation of inventories to demand—play a key role in determining the market price of a commodity. It seems to be a statistical fact that the price of most industrial raw materials is a function of the ratio of inventories to demand, and, since this concept cannot be conveniently fitted into a flow model, this type of model cannot be regarded as completely suitable for the investigation of the markets for raw materials until it is augmented.

A simple alternative to the model presented above will be given later in this section, and the full scale extension of this model in Chapter 3. At the present time some aspects of the pricing of aluminum in the United States will be taken up. The pricing of aluminum follows a scheme known as *producer pricing*. What this involves is producers, often after getting permission from the authorities, setting what they believe to be a long-run equilibrium price; and on the basis of this price making their production decision. Together with this producer price we can identify another price, which is called a "free market," "open market," "dealer," or a "merchant" price. If, for instance, during a certain period, demand is larger than production, then this demand will be satisfied by new production *and* a decrease in stocks. Some of these stocks will usually be held by producers or consumers, but normally a large part of them will be in the possession of individuals or organizations that are designated *merchants,* or *dealers*. These merchants do not sell at the producer price, but at a so-called free market price which, unlike the more inflexible producer price, is highly responsive to the total market supply and demand. This topic will be treated further in Chapter 5, but the reader should appreciate now that the key element in this discussion is stocks: if, for example, stocks are falling very rapidly in relation to current consumption, price has a tendency to rise.[8] Figure 1-4 shows the movement of price on the world aluminum market in relation to the change in some other variables.

[8]Two conceivable pricing rules are

$$P_t = P_{t-1} - \lambda\Delta I_{t-1} \qquad \lambda > 0$$
$$P_t = P_{t-1} - \lambda(I_{t-1} - \bar{I}) \qquad \lambda > 0$$

In the first of these, price is increased if stocks in the previous period fall, with the amount of the price increase being proportional to the fall in stocks. Here, consumption is not involved. In the second equation price is raised by an amount proportional to the difference between the level of stocks in the previous period and a given level. This given, or desired, level can, of course, be proportional to consumption or some other variable.

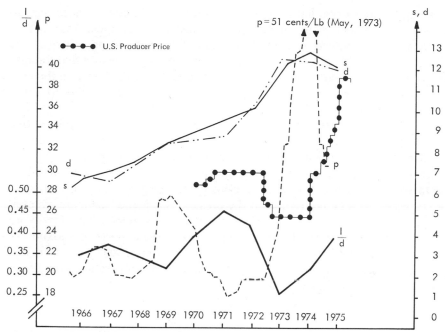

Figure 1-4. The demand for and supply of aluminum (nonsocialist countries); inventory/demand ratio; and the price of aluminum. Where s = supply, millions short tons/year, d = demand, millions short tons/year, I/d = inventory to demand ratio, and p = price, U.S. cents/pound. Source: various publications.

It is fairly easy to see in Figure 1-4 that when supply (s) was larger than demand (d), there was a tendency for inventories to rise relative to demand, and price to decline. The price shown is the "free market" price. As indicated, the producer price is much less volatile and generally moves in steps. Another point of interest where this industry is concerned has to do with investment. During the period 1970–72, when there was considerable excess supply in this industry, many plans for new plants and equipment were canceled. Then, when the upturn came in 1972–73, there was insufficient capacity to meet demand, and had it not been for large releases of metal from the United States government strategic stockpile, the price might have gone higher than the 51 cents shown in the figure.

More will be said about producer pricing and its relation to free market prices later in this book. Investment and the investment decision will also be examined, but it is no secret that the key elements, where this matter is concerned, are the cost of new plant and equipment in relation to the expected price of the product. At the present time the cost of a 150,000 ton/year smelter in the United States may be as much as $400 million, and producers are saying that an aluminum price of 50–55 cents is necessary to justify investment in the industry. By "justify" they mean that with a median rate of return on capital of about 10–11 percent prevailing in the United States, this price will have to be forthcoming to ensure that the rate of return on aluminum capacity is at least equal to the median, and thus the aluminum industry remains an attractive proposition relative to other industries.

This is of course a valid argument; however, it should be realized that at the present time the amount of unused capacity in the industry is on the order of 25–30 percent, as compared to a normal 8–10 percent. Thus it seems likely that despite earlier prognoses saying that the long-run aluminum problem would turn on a lack of processing capacity instead of a shortage of bauxite ore (which at the present time is the basic raw material input for aluminum), this particular dilemma is postponed for a few more years. On the other hand almost 80 percent of the exports of bauxite ore originate in the LDCs, and thus, in the short run at least, the principal manufacturers and consumers of aluminum may be vulnerable to unilateral price increases initiated by producers.

Natural and Synthetic Rubber

The purpose of this section, as well as this chapter, is to introduce as gradually as possible some basic analytical concepts that are indispensable for the understanding of the economics of natural resources. Aluminum was important in that through devices such as Figure 1-4 it was possible to see the role played by inventories in price formation, and thus the inadequacy of the simple flow model. Another commodity that it might be useful to examine at this junction is natural rubber, of which the production share of LDCs is about 99 percent. It should be appreciated, however, that any discussion of natural rubber automatically involves the consideration of synthetic rubber, since, in many uses, these commodities are excellent substitutes for each other. In fact rubber—or "elastomers," which is the designation of natural *plus* synthetic rubber—is important for our discussion in that it can give the reader a good insight into some problems of replacing an industrial input by another that, structurally, is very much the same, but that is produced under entirely different circumstances.

Most natural rubber (about 70 percent) originates in four Asian countries: Malaysia, Indonesia, Thailand, and Ceylon; with Malaysia and Indonesia responsible for about three-quarters of world exports of natural rubber. But there is also natural rubber in other parts of Asia, as well as in Africa and South America. Table 1-6 says something about the production of this commodity in 1969.

Table 1-6. The Production of Natural Rubber by Regions

Country[a]	Production[b]	Yearly rate[c] of change	Share in total
Asia:			
Malaysia	1267.9	3.5	43.9
Indonesia	790.6	0.4	27.4
Thailand	281.8	4.8	9.8
Ceylon (Sri Lanka)	151.0	3.4	5.2
Vietnam	26.2	−4.9	0.9
Cambodia	51.8	5.0	1.8
India	80.0	9.1	2.8
Other Asia	24.8	1.9	0.9
Africa:			
Liberia	66.9	4.0	2.3
Nigeria	56.8	4.3	2.0
Zaire	35.0	−0.2	1.2
Others	22.8	14.4	0.8
Latin America:			
Brazil	24.0	−0.1	0.8
Others	7.0	1.3	0.2
Total	2886.2		

[a] Excludes centrally planned countries.
[b] 1000 metric tons, for year 1969.
[c] For approximately a 10-year period.
Source: FAO Production Yearbook World Bank Reports.

Natural rubber is shipped to manufacturers mostly in the form of rubber sheets. Of late, many shipments are taking the form of blocks, and this is thought to be the form that will predominate in the future, since blocks are easier to handle and store, and for various reasons quality control is facilitated. The most important market for rubber is the automobile industry, but it is also used in the manufacture of numerous household and industrial goods. Over the postwar period the world demand for rubber has been expanding at an average rate of about 7 percent per year, while it was only in the period 1960–70 that the rate of production of natural rubber was able to exceed 4 percent for a sustained period. The difference has been made up for by synthetic rubbers, the most prominent of which is styrene-butadiene rubber. Polybutadiene and polyisoprene rubbers have also become quite important.

As mentioned earlier, synthetic rubber is an excellent substitute for natural rubber in many uses, and we have observed the share of natural rubber in the total elastomer market steadily decreasing over time. One of the reasons for this is that in many countries (in particular the United States) the users of synthetic rubber (e.g., the large tire and rubber goods manufacturers) are also large producers of synthetic rubbers, and by using more synthetic, as compared to natural rubber, they free themselves to a considerable extent from the vagaries of weather and international conflict. It has been estimated that as much as 25 percent of elastomer demand is specific to natural rubber, and probably will not be displaced by synthetic rubber in the near future. It happens, however, that polysoprenc rubber is "almost" a perfect replacement for natural rubber, and if some method were discovered to produce it more economically, or if the price of natural rubber were to rise above that of polysoprene and stay there for a few years, natural rubber would probably find its market share reduced even further. Moreover, it seems to be the case that once consumers have switched to synthetic rubber, it is almost impossible to switch back. The reason for this is that production and handling plants and facilities for the two types of rubber are completely different.

On the other hand, there are various factors mitigating against a faster rate of substitution. Research on natural rubber has driven up present yields per acre in some places to three times as much as 25 years ago, and these yields might eventually increase by five or six times as much. These developments definitely tend to maintain, or even press down, the price of natural rubber. On the other hand, the price of many production factors going into the manufacture of synthetic rubber, in particular energy and labor, is increasing at a rapid rate; and even though technology is making considerable advances in the synthetic rubber industry, it is uncertain as to whether the industry as a whole could better its competitive advantage relative to natural rubber at the present time if the new yields that are technically possible for natural rubber could be introduced on a widespread basis.[9]

As already mentioned, important changes in yields (measured in pounds/acre) have been recently achieved on a pilot basis. This has mostly involved replanting and planting new areas with the recently developed high-yield clones. At the same time, increases in the yields of existing trees have been realized by the application of yield stimulants, of which "Eth-

---

[9]Representative tapping and collection costs (U.S. cents/pound) in terms of yield (pounds/acre) in Sri Lanka and Malaysia:

Sri Lanka (Ceylon)		Malaysia	
Yield	Cost	Yield	Cost
500	14.3	250	10.0
500–750	13.6	250–500	8.9
750–1000	12.1	500–750	8.0
1000–1250	11.3	750–1000	7.0
1250–		1001–	6.3

Source: World Bank documents International Rubber Study Group.

rel" is perhaps the best known. Some experiments indicate that yields can be increased by up to 100 percent if these yield-stimulating chemicals are applied to older but well-tended trees. Among other things this type of chemical may make it possible to increase the output of rubber trees in the short run (without resorting to destructive techniques such as "slaughter tapping"). Finally, some progress is being made in reducing the "gestation period" of rubber trees—that is, the period between the planting of the tree and its maturing to a point where it can be tapped. (At the present time rubber trees come into production after a period of from five to seven years from the time of planting. They reach their maximum capacity after twelve years, and once matured, produce for at least twenty years without any considerable variation in output.)

In the case of synthetic rubber, the major part of research and development funds has gone toward getting a product that can replace the so-called indispensable share of natural rubber; but it is also true that considerable effort has gone toward reducing the cost of existing synthetic rubbers. It may be possible, on the one hand, to get industry costs down via economies of scale—that is, building larger plants that employ the most modern equipment. At the same time, it should be remembered that the cost-of-production factors have shown a tendency to rise very rapidly of late; and, in addition, new types of expenditure, such as for the suppression of pollution, must be taken into consideration.

This chapter will be concluded by considering an amendment to the simple flow model presented earlier in this section. Kolbe and Timm (1972) have employed a model of the following type for forecasting the price of natural rubber:

$$
\begin{aligned}
s &= f(p_{t-i}, Y) \\
d &= h(p_{t-j}, X) \\
p_t &= g(I_t) \qquad \text{or} \quad p_t - p_{t-1} \equiv \Delta p = z(\Delta I) \\
I_t &\equiv I_{t-1} + d - s
\end{aligned}
$$

This is obviously a step in the right direction. Notice that price is now related to the level of stocks—with an alternative formulation taking the *change* in price (Δp) as a function of the change in stocks (ΔI). Where supply and demand are concerned, these are a function of price in the present period ($i, j = 0$), *or* in some earlier period—it is impossible to say *a priori;* and also a function of the exogenous variables X and Y. Where X is concerned, the variable that we would most expect to find would be industrial production or some "proxy" (such as gross national product). There is, of course, no reason why we should just have one exogenous variable, and so X could be a vector; and certainly we would expect to find the price of synthetic rubber in this vector. The final expression is simply an identity; but it does tell us that if flow demand (d) does not equal flow supply (s), then $I_t \neq I_{t-1}$. That is, we would have changes in stocks. Ertek (1967) has constructed a model of this type for the world copper market.

Later in this book the theoretical background to this type of model will be discussed in detail, but a modification of this model can be suggested right now. This modification will be based on the discussion earlier in this section, in which price was taken as a function of the ratio of inventory to flow demand—or, alternatively, the change in price is a function of the ratio of the change in inventory to the change in price. Our model now has the following appearance:

$$s = f(p_{t-i}, Y)$$
$$d = h(p_{t-j}, X)$$
$$p_t - p_{t-1} \equiv \Delta p = g\left(\frac{\Delta I}{\Delta d}\right)$$
$$I_t \equiv I_{t-1} + d - s$$

Again it should be emphasized that X need not be just one variable, but can be a vector. On the other hand, supply might easily be just a function of price, and so $Y = 0$. These matters will be pursued more thoroughly in the sequel.

ELEMENTARY ECONOMIC THEORY 2

This chapter continues the elementary economic theory that was begun in the last portion of the previous chapter. Perhaps the best way to pick up the discussion is to draw a diagram showing the "costs" and "benefits" of producing, over time, a typical industrial raw material. The commodity chosen here is oil. For instance, the scheme shown in Figure 2-1 would be valid for a North Sea oil field, or the exploitation of deposits off the continental shelf of the United States, or in the Gulf of Siam.

The reader should notice the sequence portrayed in the above. First the seismographic investigation to establish the presence of oil. Then prospecting to find out how much oil there is, so that the profitability of exploiting the deposit can be determined. This is followed by the emplacing of the platforms on which the oil rigs and other equipment will sit. As shown here, the purchasing of these platforms, their emplacing costs, as well as those costs associated with the purchase and laying of pipelines and such things, are called investment costs. After some of the platforms are in position and pipelines run ashore, production is begun. This is shown in Figure 2-1 at t_c. A variable cost is associated with this production in the form of wages, salaries, fuel, spare parts, drills, etc. Later on, at t_e, as the source begins to be exhausted, there may be investment in equipment and facilities that will allow a higher level of exploitation to take place than would otherwise have been possible. Whether this investment in equipment for secondary exploitation will take place or not, of course, depends on a number of factors, both technical and economic. A discussion of some of the problems connected with North Sea oil will be found later in this chapter in the section on discounting and capital values.

In the next section some aspects of exploration will be discussed. Following this we will look at the processing and distribution of industrial raw materials. Once this is seen it will be possible to begin a serious examination of the costs of production, investment, pricing, and so on. This investigation will occupy the greater part of the next four chapters, and its purpose is to give the reader the background to make a systematic attack on the problem of analyzing production processes in which costs and benefits

Benefits

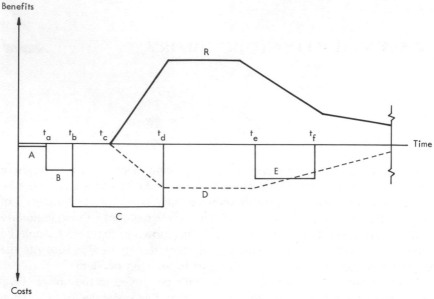

Figure 2-1. Cost-benefit diagram for a North Sea oil field. A = seismographic investigation, B = prospecting, C = investment in production equipment, D = variable production costs, E = investment in equipment for secondary exploitation, and R = revenue.

are distributed over time. In this chapter the raw materials industries from which examples and data are drawn are oil, copper, tin, aluminum, and lead.

EXPLORATION

The economics literature dealing with mineral exploration is neither extensive nor distinguished. Despite enormous advances where the techniques of mineral survey are concerned (and at the present time these include a wide range of aerial, geophysical, and geochemical methods), luck seems to continue to play as important a role in the location of natural resources as technical or organizational factors. At the same time, it remains true that Dame Fortune usually intrudes on him who is most persistent in seeking her.

Although we are far from having a complete insight into the extent of the globe's mineral wealth, it does no harm to admit that certain portions of the earth's crust are more generously endowed geologically than others. North America and the U.S.S.R. come easily to mind when this topic is broached; but being highly or less highly favored is largely a relative thing and depends on what historical period we are talking about. In the years just prior to World War I, Western Europe was often thought of as being adequately furnished with natural resources, since the emphasis during that period was on the making of steel and fairly large supplies of coal and iron ore were available. Today, on the other hand, journalistic fashion often encourages its inhabitants to think of themselves as being on the brink of pauperdom, thanks largely to their overzealous utilization of natures afflu-ence. One way of viewing this situation, however, involves recognition that it was through the transformation of mineral assets into various forms of capital assets that the technical and organizational skill of today's Europe was created. Moreover, technical skill is still, by any sensible measure, the most precious resource at the disposal of the industrial or of the less developed world. Europe and North America, for example, will be employ-ing their accumulated pool of technical and scientific knowledge as the basis of new types of industries (such as the breaking up and processing of rocks, or the mining of the ocean's floor) long after many of the traditional sources of minerals and fuels have been relegated to the level of historical curiosities.

At the present time the global pattern of mineral endowment roughly appears as follows: most of the metallic minerals are found on huge blocks or shields that have been relatively stable components of the earth's geological structure for about 400 million years. As examples we can cite the Canadian Shield; the Femo-Scandia Shield, which stretches across Scandinavia and a large part of Eastern Europe and Russia east of the Urals; and the Siberian Shield. Other shields can be found in the highlands of Brazil, Africa, and most of Western Australia. In Paleozoic times these last three were conjoined, and the name that geographers have given this union is Gondwanaland. The breaking up of Gondwanaland is sometimes connected with the phenomenon called *continental drift,* and is interesting for a number of reasons. For instance, given the mineral riches of Brazil and Australia, it might be deduced that Antarctica is one of the most attractive regions in the world from a geological point of view, since in the time of Gondwanaland it was apparently sandwiched between the other two. In fact, at the present time, there are extensive plans being made all over the world to commence investigating the mineral wealth of this area. Other shields that seem due to come in for considerable attention in the future are the Precambrian Shield, south of the Amazon River, and the Arabian Shield—sometimes called the Arabian-Nubian Shield—which has many similarities to those of Canada and Australia. This shield is about 1200 miles long and 1000 miles wide, and apparently stretches across the Red Sea into Egypt. At the present time it is known to contain at least 20 minerals, located in more than 300 places. These include iron, silver, gold, copper, phosphate, and uranium.

It is interesting to conjecture that, even at the existing level of technology, important discoveries could be made within even the highly prospected shields. The casual observer, whose interest in minerals can hardly be expected to provide the incentive for more than a few minutes reflection on the topic per decade, has only a vague appreciation of the enormous efforts required to obtain enough information to commence actual mining operations. The mapping of the Zambian copper belt required almost eight years, and similar efforts were necessary in neighboring Katanga (Zaire). Even so, it is the case in Zaire that large deposits of ore are just being located in the vicinity of mines that have been in operation for almost a century. In a sense this is only natural, since the cost of discovering a single mineral deposit of copper, lead, or zinc could range up to $500,000 in regions with a good mineral potential; and even then there is only a one-in-50 chance that it will prove worth exploiting.

However the reader should remember that it is pointless to spend money developing reserves too long in advance of when these reserves will be required. For instance, if one dollar is used today to create a unit of reserves that will not be used for 20 years, and the discount rate is 10 percent, then the profit in money terms from extracting the commodity must be at least $(1 + 0.10)^{20} = \$6.72$ after the 20 years to justify this investment, otherwise the dollar should be invested in a financial asset. On the other hand, small ratios of reserves to production may be uneconomical because a large part of the useful life of the recovery equipment could be wasted if the stock of reserves was used up too soon.

Science and technology are also playing a major part in exploration. In 1965 an aerial survey employing magnetometer and scintillometer cost about $6,000 per 1000 square kilometers. If an electromagnetic survey was added, the total cost increased by approximately $15–20,000 for the same area. As expensive as this might sound, it is only a fraction of what a similar investigation would cost if it were done on the ground. Photogeology, or the interpretation for geological purposes of aerial photography, seems to be in an explosive stage of development. Similarly, geochemical and geomagnetic devices are making it possible to avoid much of the expensive and time-consuming test drilling that formed the core of most exploratory programs of the past. Various radioactive measuring instruments and probes, whose readings or wave patterns can be analyzed and interpreted by computers, are being introduced into exploratory work at a very rapid rate. Devices of this type were instrumental in discovering and charting uranium deposits in the Northern Territory of Australia in recent years.

At the present time geophysical investigation appears to be the most rapidly expanding type of exploratory activity. Mining geophysical techniques have their origin in the northern part of the Soviet Union and Canada, and in Scandinavia, in the 1930s and 1940s. In the case of Scandinavia and Canada, the search was for copper, nickel, zinc, and other base metals employing the airborne magnetometer. The airborne scintillometer was introduced in the hunt for uranium, and it registered important successes not only in Canada and the U.S.S.R., but also in Brazil and Africa.

Where the financing of exploration is concerned, both industry and government sources are involved. Paterson (1974) has examined this and many allied topics in an important article, and he points out that governments seem to be supporting an increasing part of these expenditures in recent years. This is particularly true for Canada, Brazil, Venezuela, Iraq, Zambia, Mexico, Saudi Arabia, Sweden, South Africa, the United States, Japan, and West Germany. With countries like Japan and West Germany, much of this exploration takes place in other countries as a form of bilateral aid. For instance, the West German Geological Survey is doing a magnetometer/radiometric survey in Brazil. Also, in the past 25 years, the United Nations Development Program and its predecessor (the United Nations Special Fund) have carried out more than 50 mineral exploration projects, with a total cost of more than $90 million.

A by no means minor advantage of these new techniques is that quantitatively, as well as qualitatively, more exploratory work can be done in a given period; and, to a certain extent, exploration can be divorced from the remainder of the mining operation by the use of consultants or by local personnel working with minimal capital equipment. Thus, many of the funds allocated by the United Nations for exploration went to consulting companies. As for the financing of ground geophysical programs, this is, for the most part, undertaken by the mining industry, but with increasing participation by local governments or national corporations. Some expenditures on geophysical surveys in 1972 is shown in Table 2-1.

The last point to be made in this section is that airborne geophysical surveys involve a ground follow-up that, under certain circumstances, can be fairly expensive. A situation does not yet exist where deposits of a mineral can be indicated by airborne survey, and mining can begin directly.

MINERAL PROCESSING

Most of the industrial raw materials being considered in this book pass through a number of stages in going from ore to refined products or semifabricates. In the case of metals we begin with mining, or ore removal, and this involves such things as separating, blasting, and loading. Then we

Table 2-1. Airborne and Ground Geophysical Expenditure for Mineral Exploration, by Percent and Total Expenditure, 1972[a]

Area	Ground	Air
Africa Middle East Far East	29.6	39.8
Canada	26.0	21.9
United States	18.6	10.9
Australia New Zealand	3.9	10.3
Europe	10.4	5.9
Mexico Central America South America	11.5	11.2
Total percent	100.0	100.0
Total expenditure	$12,950,000	$18,950,000

[a]Non-centrally-planned economies.

have the first state of processing, which includes such operations as crushing, grinding, and concentrating (often combined with one or more stages of separation), and which, with some commodities, is called milling. Next comes smelting and/or refining, involving the use of equipment such as furnaces, converters, and electrolytic-type units. Finally we have semifabricating, in which the output of the smelter or refinery is rolled, drawn, and extruded into highly usable shapes such as sheets and rods. If the reader desires he can add fabrication to the cycle, where this is production of the particular finished product; but since doing so involves consideration of products that may display an extreme heterogeneity, there is some doubt as to whether this stage logically belongs to the discussion.

At each step of the above we are also dealing with a different "purity" of the relevant commodity. Take copper as an example. The first stage, mining, results in the production of an ore with a copper content of less than 6 percent. (In the United States in 1970, the average copper content of raw copper ore was 0.6 percent). The next stage, milling, results in an aggregate of 30 percent copper, and is obtained by crushing the ore into pieces the size of walnuts, introducing it into a grinder with the help of water, and there turning it into a power; and then transmitting this powder (in solution) into a concentrator where waste products and water are siphoned off and some reagents introduced.

Smelting involves first roasting the concentrate (to remove sulphur), and then introducing it into a reverberatory furnace where the roasted concentrate is smelted and a matte containing about 32 percent copper is produced. A converter then transforms the matte into blister copper with a purity of about 99 percent, following which the blister is turned into refined copper. This is done first through fire refining (in a refining furnace), and in those cases where the fire-refined copper meets the specifications of semi-fabricators, it is used without further processing. Otherwise, where special properties are required (e.g., when the material is to be used for the conducting of electricity, or when precious metals are available to such an extent that their recovery is economically feasible) the copper is electrolytically refined—with precious metal recovery being a part of this process. Finally, the refined copper goes to brass mills, wire mills, etc., where it is turned into sheets, tubes, rod, and wire.

The above discussion has involved what is known as primary copper. There is, however, another important type of copper that, on the basis of its origin, is called secondary copper, or scrap. Secondary copper comes either from the reduction of finished goods containing copper, or from some of the stages of processing (in the form of shavings, etc.) Forty percent of the total copper consumption of the nonsocialist world has its origin in scrap.

Copper is alloyed with zinc and tin to make brass and bronze, which are probably the best known of the many copper alloys; and a large part of the input of brass mills consists of unprocessed old and new scrap. What the reader should be careful to note here is that only a part of scrap goes to the refinery. In the United States in 1965 this amounted to 403,000 metric tons. On the other hand 775,000 metric tons was used without refining—or, perhaps we should say, rerefining—for such things as the input of brass mills. Moreover, it is the case that a large part of the copper mined in the last 100 years could still be made available, via recycling, for use today. At present the average scrap recovery ratio is about 75 percent—that is, on the average, about 75 percent of the copper in items containing copper can be recovered—and given the attention now being paid to recycling technologies, this percentage should show a significant increase. Figure 2-2 illustrates some aspects of the above discussion.

Figure 2-2 is intended to show the circulation of an industrial raw material only in broad outline. What we really need are expository devices that show movements in and out of inventory, as well as exports and imports. This type of material will be provided later on, both in this and ensuing chapters.

As noted above, it is possible to make a sharp distinction between a primary material, such as copper ore, and the same material after it has

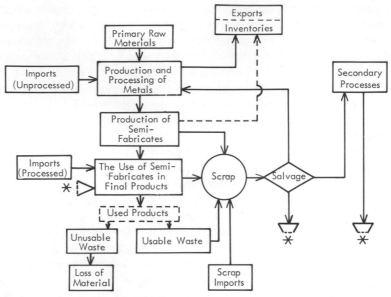

Figure 2-2. Typical circulation diagram for various metals. The asterisks indicate direct input into the manufacture of final products. Inputs from secondary processes can be such things as various brass products, castings, etc.

gone through one or more stages of processing. This distinction, of course, need not be along geographic lines, but it often works out this way. Theoretically it is possible—and it happens in many cases—to have processing facilities directly adjacent to, or at least in the near vicinity, of the mine or pit; and thus the transformation of the raw ore to smelter or refined product, or even perhaps to semifabricate, would hardly be noticeable from outside the boundaries of the installation. At the very least it might be expected that such things as smelting and refining the raw material would show a tendency to take place in the same country as its mining.

It seems to be so, however, that a large part of the mining and rough processing of raw materials takes place in less developed countries, while the advanced stages of processing tend to localize in the major industrial (or consuming) countries. In the case of copper, almost 40 percent of ore production takes place in the so-called CIPEC group of countries (Chile, Zambia, Zaire, and Peru), and at present they smelt and refine about 50 percent of their output. Semifabrication and further transformation is hardly practiced at all in these countries.

Aluminum, which on the basis of the physical quantities now consumed must probably be regarded as as important an industrial input as copper, presents a more striking example of geographical diversity so far as its various stages of transformation are concerned. Where the technical side is concerned, we have roughly the following: bauxite mining; alumina preparation; the production (in a smelter) of primary aluminum; aluminum shaping (semifabrication); and aluminum end use. Most of the major aluminum producing countries are completely dependent on outsiders for their bauxite—the only important exceptions being France and the U.S.S.R. The bauxite production of the European Economic Community (EEC) was about 3.6 million tons in 1972, while its aluminum output was 1.3 million tons. Since from four to six tons of crude bauxite are needed to produce one ton of aluminum, this aluminum production represents between 5.2 and 7.8 million tons of bauxite. Thus about 4.2 million tons (or 55 percent of requirements) had to be imported. By the same reasoning, North America's present bauxite deficit can run as high as 80 percent; while Japan's is, for all practical purposes, 100 percent.

Table 2-2 below has been constructed to provide an insight into the production of bauxite, alumina, and aluminum. Almost half of the world bauxite output originates in three countries (Australia, Jamaica, and Surinam), with Australia showing the most dynamic expansion during the last 10 years. There is also a rapidly growing production in the U.S.S.R., where there has been considerable experimentation with the production of aluminum without using bauxite. These production processes employ clays that are fairly common in many industrial countries but that have been ignored due to the comparatively low price of bauxite. Similar experiments would appear to be underway in France. Considerable potential for bauxite production also exists on the west coast of Africa, and at least one country, Ghana, may have sufficient energy potential to produce a considerable amount of primary aluminum.

The imbalance between production and consumption does not show up in Table 2-2, but it exists just the same. A factor that will be emphasized later, but that can be mentioned now, is the profound influence of the cost of electrical power (as well as the possibility of achieving economies of scale) on determining where aluminum is to be produced. A census of worldwide production operations seems to indicate that on the average from 15–20,000 kilowatt-hours of electricity are required for every ton of aluminum. Since experience indicates that a plant having a capacity of less than 60,000 tons/year of aluminum shows rapidly increasing unit costs, it would appear that less developed countries desiring to enter the aluminum manufacturing business must reckon on making huge investments in electrical power alone. On this point it can be noted that it is still considerably more profitable to ship African ore to Norway, and Australian ore to Japan, than to build up processing capacity in the ore-producing areas just named—despite their not inconsiderable energy potential.

Our discussion of aluminum will be continued later after some elementary cost theory has been introduced. The following scrutinization of the way in which a country disposes of its copper, however, can easily be applied to other raw materials; and the reader who is particularly interested in aluminum might find it instructive to perform the same exercise for aluminum in Australia or Jamaica. This exercise centers around Table 2-3, which provides a simple introduction to raw material flow accounting, showing movement of the commodity from ore to semifabricate, and introducing at the same time stocks and exports. Peru is the country providing the basic data for the construction of Table 2-3, and the reader can observe the comparatively small percentage of primary ore that gets to, and past, the refining stage.

Some detailed comments will now be made on Table 2-3. Ore production here is shown as 212,500 metric tons. This is copper content! By that it is meant that with the percentage of copper per unit of raised ore (or the *ore grade*) in Peru averaging out at about 1 percent, it is necessary to mine and

Table 2-2. Some data on Bauxite, Alumina, and Aluminum (1973): the Reserves of Bauxite; the Production of Bauxite, Alumina, and Primary Aluminum; Scrap Recovery; and the Production of Semimanufactures

Country	Bauxite reserves[a]	Prod. of bauxite[a]	Alumina prod.[a]	Primary aluminum prod.[a]	Scrap recovery[b]	Prod. of semis.[b]
Rep. of Guinea	4,064	3.7	–	–	–	–
Australia	4,064	17.6	3.58	–	–	–
Jamaica	813	13.5	2.51	–	–	–
Surinam	610	6.7	1.40	–	–	–
Yugoslavia	203	2.2	–	–	–	–
Greece	91	2.7	0.48	–	–	–
Guyana	81	3.6	–	–	–	–
France	71	3.1	1.12	0.36	123.5	360
U.S.A.	46	1.9	6.29	4.11	1,116.0	4,828
U.S.S.R.	–	5.8	2.90	1.95	–	–
Hungary	–	2.6	0.66	–	–	–
Japan	–	–	1.99	1.10	536.5	1,296
Germany (FR)	–	–	0.93	0.53	370.6	771
Canada	–	–	1.13	0.93	–	281
Norway	–	–	–	0.62	–	–
Ghana	–	–	–	0.15	–	–
U.K.	–	–	–	0.25	212.5	398
TOTAL[c]		73.0	26.18	12.71	2811.8	

[a] Millions of metric tons.
[b] Thousands of metric tons.
[c] World total, and not total of columns.
Note: The amount of secondary aluminum production as compared to total production (= primary + secondary) has remained approximately 22 percent over the last decade. Where the future of secondary production is concerned, it is expected to increase. The leading consumers of primary aluminum are the U.S., U.S.S.R., Japan, Germany, U.K., and France.

Table 2-3. The Disposition of Peruvian Copper[a]

Stage of processing	Production	Exports	Export destination
Ore	212,537	2,258	Japan
		758	Sweden
		222	Others
−Stocks	0		
−Exports	3,238		
Concentrates	209,269	16,884	Japan
		4,729	U.S.
		1,348	Sweden
		1,544	Others
−Stocks	0		
−Exports	24,505		
Blister	186,853	79,217	U.S.
		24,460	Belgium
		18,345	W. Germany
		16,956	Others
−Stocks	9,375		
−Exports	138,978		
Electrolytic copper	38,500	24,154	U.S.
		3,110	Japan
		5,823	Others
−Stocks	2,109		
−Exports	33,807		
Semis	3,340	68	Denmark
		33	Others
(Residual . . . 3230 = Domestic Use + Stocks + Unknown)			

[a] Source: *Annuario Minero del Peru,* 1968; and World Bureau of Metal Statistics.

treat approximately (212,500/0.01) metric tons of material to obtain 212,500 metric tons of copper ore.

We also see that 3,238 metric tons of ore was exported. It is usually a very uneconomical matter to export completely unprocessed ore, and it is difficult to deduce the exact economic motivation for such a transaction. The same hold true for concentrates—of which a total of 24,505 metric tons were exported, principally to Japan, the United States, and Sweden. It might be the case, of course, that in Peru there was a shortage of milling and smelting capacity, while during the same period there was an excess of this type of capacity in the importing countries; in which case a low selling price in Peru, and low processing costs in the importing countries, combined to make it economically feasible to ship these bulky items rather than stockpiling and processing them later.

When we come to blister we see that we have large exports, and some stockpiling. (The stockpiling figure is a net figure—that is, during the relevant period more blister went into stock than came out.) It should be remembered that in the next period some of these stocks will be exported, and others will continue on to the next stage of processing, while the rest will remain undisturbed. Thus we see the possibility of a situation in which more copper will be processed (i.e., milled, smelted, refined, turned into semifabricates) then was dug up as ore in the same period. For this to happen some of the commodity would have to come out of inventory at one or more stages of processing, and in a table such as Table 2-3 this decrease in stocks would be indicated by a positive sign. Here the reader might do well to work through and consider, in Table 2-4, the implications of the two following (imaginary) situations: (A), in which there are no stock changes, and (B) a situation in which there are decreases in stocks.

In the case of (A), the situation is clear: everything not exported moves on and is processed at the next stage. Total exports are 10,000 + 40,000 + 100,000 + 50,000 = 200,000; and this is also the amount of ore (copper content) produced during the period. In the case of (B) however, although 200,000 units of ore was produced during the period, total exports (again copper content) was 10,000 + 40,000 + 100,000 + 55,000 = 205,000. Where did these extra 5,000 units come from? As the reader will notice, 10,000 tons of blister came out of inventory, as well as 5,000 tons of electrolytic copper. Of the 15,000 units (copper content) taken out of inventory, at least 5,000 were exported. (It may be possible to argue, for instance, that all 15,000 units were exported—in which case the 10,000 units shown as going to domestic use would have come from current production. As far as the accounting side of the discussion is concerned, this is an unimportant issue. What is important is that 200,000 units were produced, and 215,000 used. The total decrease in inventories must therefore be 15,000.) At this point the reader will be given a warning. Statistics dealing with stock movements should always be handled with considerable care and a certain amount of skepticism. In addition, it is essential to ascertain, in the context of the problem being examined, the exact significance of the sign attached to inventory movements. In the present scheme a negative sign means movements into inventory; and a positive sign means withdrawal from inventory.

THE DEMAND FOR INDUSTRIAL RAW MATERIALS: SOME ELEMENTARY THEORY

For various reasons, the topic of the demand for industrial raw materials is much simpler than a number of other topics that will be treated in this book—such as price formation. Still, despite its simplicity, it involves a number of aspects that are habitually misunderstood in both the "scientific" and the trade literature.

Table 2-4. Two Examples of the Disposition of an Industrial Raw Material (Copper)

Stage of processing	Production (A)	Production (B)
Ore	200,000	200,000
±Stocks	0	0
−Exports	−10,000	−10,000
Concentrates	190,000	190,000
±Stocks	0	0
−Exports	−40,000	−40,000
Blister	150,000	150,000
±Stocks	0	+10,000
−Exports	−100,000	−100,000
Electrolytic copper	50,000	60,000
±Stocks	0	+5,000
−Exports	0	0
Semis	50,000	65,000
±Stocks	0	0
−Exports	−50,000	−55,000
Residual	0	10,000 (= Home Use + Unknown)

The first thing that must be stressed is that when the demand for a raw material is a demand for a *current input,* then it is of an input–output nature. By input–output we mean that raw materials are an intermediate good, and are demanded as the result of the demand for a final good: the greater the output, the greater the demand for input. As an example we can take automobiles, which are probably still the most important consumer durable. Increasing the demand for automobiles in a given period means increasing the demand for copper, aluminum, steel, etc, in that period. Moreover, in the short run, producers of automobiles do not tend to react to changes in the prices of these inputs since, among other reasons, the amount of a given input is determined by the design of the final good, and this is often invariant in the short run. (Also, of course, the increase in price of an input can very often be passed on to the final consumer). There is, in other words, a simple relation between input and output of the type $X_{ij} = a_{ij}T_j$, where X_{ij} is the total amount of input i going into output j. (For instance, i might be aluminum and j automobiles). T_j simply gives the total amount of output j, while a_{ij} is the input of i per unit of output j. a_{ij} can be called an input–output coefficient.

The next matter of importance is the expression *current input.* A current input is defined here as one that is to be used in the near future, or the current production period if the reader prefers this terminology. This point must be brought out because, as we know, many thousands of tons of various industrial raw materials are purchased each year for inventory.

They are purchased as a buffer against unexpected increases in future demand, or because producers think that prices in the future might increase in such a manner as to justify the cost of purchasing and holding stocks, and so on. Put another way, in every period so and so much of a commodity is produced, but only a part of this production is "consumed," or goes into a final production process. The rest goes into the inventories of producers, consumers, and merchants.

It is here that price enters the discussion. Even if the demand for current inputs is not sensitive to price, the demand for inventories is. If the price of an input should increase by 25 percent, there would probably be no decrease in the buying of this input for use in current production processes, at least not in the short run. It might be, however, that less of the item would be bought for inventories; although if it was thought that the future would involve price increases of a similar magnitude, more of it might be bought for inventories.[1] A situation of this type apparently prevailed on the markets for copper and oil in the last part of 1973, and throughout most of 1974. However, in a normal situation even small differences between the present price and the forecasted value of the future price can cause movements in and out of inventory.

In the previous section we examined the situation as we move from stage to stage in the ore to semifabricate cycle. In both theoretical and econometric work the demand that we are usually concerned with is that for refined material: refined zinc, tin, copper, aluminum, and so on. Refined copper is, after all, copper of great purity and in only a few shapes. Smelter products, on the other hand, are too impure; while semifabricates are too special—instead of the demand for semifabricates it would be more appropriate to look at the demand for tubes, sheets, etc. Thus, if we are interested in the demand–supply scheme for a typical industrial raw material, we might have the arrangement presented in Figure 2-3.

Here we have the supply of refined tin in the United States, composed of domestic refinery production; imports of refined tin; secondary refined—that is, tin scrap that has been reprocessed and, for all practical purposes, is

---

[1] In Banks (1972) an equation has been fitted for the consumption of primary + secondary refined tin in the United States. In the equation C is consumption, p price, Δg the change in inventories of durable goods in the United States, while D is a dummy equal to unity for 1953. Annual data was employed, and standard deviations are in parentheses:

$$C_t = 54.56 + 0.563\, C_{t-1} - 0.13246\, p_{t-1} + 0.050\, \Delta g + 9.97\, D \qquad R^2 = 0.667$$
$$ (0.186) \qquad (0.057) \qquad\quad (0.014) \qquad (4.279)$$

This equation indicates that the consumption of tin is price sensitive. As it happens, however, the consumption here involves buying for both current inputs *and* inventories.

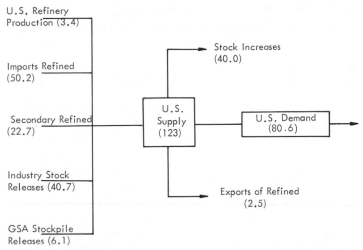

Figure 2-3. The supply and demand for refined tin in the U.S. (1966). The units are in thousands of long tons. Source: U.S. Government Stockpile Reports.

identical to primary refined; releases from the inventories of merchants, consumers, dealers, etc.; and releases from the United States Strategic (GSA) Stockpile. This makes a total supply, or availability, of 123,000 long tons. The current input, or current demand, by domestic consumers is 80.6 thousand long tons. Exports came to 2.5 thousand long tons, while 40.0 went into inventory.

What we should note here is the very small change in private stocks: approximately as much went into inventory as came out. It is, of course, rather remarkable that we have information on both inventory releases and increases. In many situations we would only have a net figure—that is, we would know whether domestic inventories increased or decreased during the year, or the period in which we were interested. It can also be observed that only a small portion of domestic refined supply was provided by domestic refiners of primary materials, while there were heavy imports of refined tin. With copper, for instance, we have precisely the opposite arrangement.

Finally it should be pointed out that the GSA stockpile is an inventory of raw materials that was originally established as a reserve to be made available in the case of national emergencies. After a while, however, it was used occasionally as a price stabilization device—particularly in the case of tin. It would be extremely difficult, if not impossible, to formulate a behavioral rule for the actions of the managers of the GSA stockpile; but at the same time it must be acknowledged that the policy, or lack of policy, of this authority has influenced the market for tin to a fairly high degree, particularly by influencing expectations as to the availability of the metal.

SOME ELEMENTARY COST AND SUPPLY THEORY

The supply of a commodity in the market is generally related to the price at which the commodity can be sold. But whether more or less of a commodity will be offered at a given price depends upon the cost of producing the commodity. Given his estimate of the market price, and assuming that he can sell as many as he wishes of the units that he manufactures, it is the cost of the product, which is determined by the cost of the inputs, that settles for the producer the number that he will manufacture during a given period. A drastic increase in the cost of energy, with all other costs and the price of the product unchanged, will cause the producer of an energy-intensive product to reduce, or to start planning to reduce, his output. Equally as important, if he is thinking about expanding his output by making some major purchases of equipment, and if the new equipment is not "energy saving," then he will hesitate to order this equipment.

It is customary to divide costs into two classes. The first contains fixed costs, or costs whose magnitude is independent of output during a given period. Here we have such things as the rental for leased property, the salaries of various officers and other personnel engaged on a contract basis, some insurance and advertising costs, bonded debt, and so on. A very important fixed cost that will be taken up later in this chapter is depreciation cost. This is a cost that is associated with owning and maintaining a fixed productive capacity (such as a plant, mine, etc.), and which must be honored regardless of the status of output. It should also be easy to deduce that when capacity is expanded by increasing plant or mine size, fixed costs increase.

Variable costs, on the other hand, are costs that vary with the annual rate of production. Labor cost is of course the best-known variable cost, since with a given installation of a given size it takes more or less labor to produce more or less output. When considering a product such as aluminum, however, it should be remembered that energy costs are at least of the same order of importance. Other important variable costs are raw material inputs, certain indirect taxes, and so on. Before going to a concrete example, the following elementary situation might prove to be of interest.

A product is manufactured that has a annual fixed cost (FC) of $4,000. Its variable cost (VC) is $1,000 per unit up to five units, where variable costs are payments to the variable factors mentioned above. Between five and eight units the variable cost is $2000 per unit. A reason for the increase in variable cost might be that the rated, or normal, capacity of the equipment being used is five units/year, and although more can be produced, it cannot be produced as efficiently. For instance, the additional units of labor employed would be engaged in activities that were subsidiary to those of the machine operators, mechanics, and so on. By the same token more raw materials would be required per unit of output due to wastage connected with having to feed the machines faster. (Remember that we are talking about a larger output in the same time period, one year, in which we maintain the same length of working day and week.) Maintenance costs might also be higher, and so on. Continuing, it is physically impossible to produce more than eight units per year. We then have the situation shown in Table 2-5, with Q-output, AFC-average fixed cost, TVC-total variable cost, AVC-average variable cost, TC-total cost, ATC-average total cost, and MC-marginal cost.

The reader should check a few values in Table 2-5 if he is out of practice working with this kind of material.[2] In examining this table we see that the marginal cost curve, which can also function as the supply curve, is constant up to and including five units, at which point there is a "step." The curve then goes vertical at eight units, which simply indicates the impossibility of producing more than eight units in one period. The average fixed cost decreases as production is increased and the total fixed cost is spread over more units; while the average variable cost is constant up to five units, after which it increases. The average total cost first decreases, and then begins to rise. Diagrammatically this situation is shown in (A), Figure 2-4.

We also have, in (B), Figure 2-4, some curves of the shape that you are probably familiar with if you have taken the first course in economics. Now remember that the curves in (B) and (A), Figure 2-4, are short-run curves: they are applicable to a situation where some of the inputs are fixed. As will be shown later in this book, in the long run, when all inputs are variable and the fixed costs can no longer be regarded as fixed, we might also have cost curves with this general shape. It is the case that Johnston (1960) and others have examined this matter rather carefully, and they seem to feel that the shapes shown in (A), Figure 2-5, resemble long-run curves that many producers consider relevant for their operation.

Given cost curves of the sort shown in (A), Figure 2-5, it may be reasonable to regard the situation shown in (B), Figure 2-5, as a satisfactory approximation. In any event, in the normal range of operation, it is quite

[2] Some of the costs in Table 2-5 are computed as follows: $AVC = TVC/Q$; $ATC = TC/Q$; while marginal cost (MC) is $\Delta TC/\Delta Q$. For instance, in going from 5 to 6 units of output we have increased cost from 9000 to 11000. Thus the change in output (ΔQ) = 1, while the change in total cost (ΔTC) = 2000. Marginal cost is then $\Delta TC/\Delta Q = 2000/1 = 2000$.

Table 2-5. Sample Calculations: Average Fixed, Variable, and Total Costs

Output (Q)	Total fixed cost (TFC)	Average fixed cost (AFC)	Total variable cost (TVC)	Average variable cost (AVC)	Total cost (TC)	Average total cost (ATC)	Marginal cost (MC)
0	4,000		0	0	4,000		
1	4,000	4,000	1,000	1,000	5,000	5,000	1,000
2	4,000	2,000	2,000	1,000	6,000	3,000	1,000
3	4,000	1,333	3,000	1,000	7,000	2,330	1,000
4	4,000	1,000	4,000	1,000	8,000	2,000	1,000
5	4,000	800	5,000	1,000	9,000	1,800	1,000
6	4,000	667	7,000	1,170	11,000	1,830	2,000
7	4,000	571	9,000	1,290	13,000	1,860	2,000
8	4,000	500	11,000	1,370	15,000	1,880	2,000
9	4,000	442					

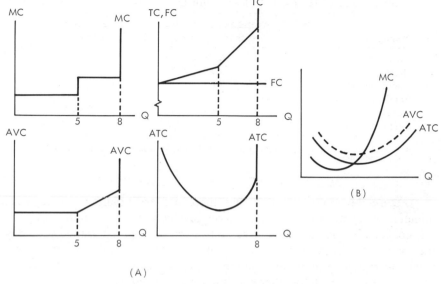

Figure 2-4. Various cost curves.

common to represent costs by an average value. If we look at the U.S. lead industry, we have in Table 2-6 the following average figures for 1955–59.[3]

The next step will be to look at some actual inputs for the production of aluminum and bauxite. To start, Figure 2-6 shows the raw materials and processes necessary to produce one pound of aluminum, assuming that four pounds of bauxite suffices to initiate the process. (The input ratio of bauxite to alumina ranges from 2:1 to 3:1, while experience has shown that the input ratio of alumina to aluminum has been stable at about 2:1.)

[3]It can be mentioned here that the Lead and Zinc Study Group publishes excellent statistics dealing with production, consumption, and inventories in these industries. This organization has its secretariat at the United Nations, New York.

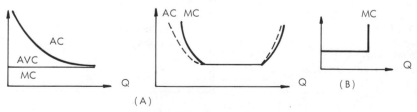

Figure 2-5. Various cost curves.

Table 2-6. Cost Figures, U.S. Lead Industry, 1955–59[a]

Mining method	Average direct mining costs (dollars/ton)	Labor as percent of total cost
Open pit	0.32	36.4
Block caving	1.41	54.2
Room and pillar	2.05	43.7
Sub-level stoping	2.37	56.9
Cut and fill	6.69	56.7
Square setting	10.20	71.2

[a] Source: United States Department of the Interior, Bureau of Mines, Information Circular No. 8325 (1967).

Figure 2-6 makes it clear that there are essentially three separate manufacturing processes involved in the production of aluminum, although it is conceivable that continuous systems exist or will be designed someday that permit the production of aluminum from bauxite to be regarded as a single operation. It might also be interesting at this stage of the discussion to examine Figure 2-6 together with Figure 2-2. What we have in Figure 2-6 are the components "primary raw materials" and "production and processing of metals." If, however, the primary raw material is imported, then it would be represented by the component "imports unprocessed."

We can now go to some average figure for aluminum costs in cents per pound in the United States, together with the fixed capital cost of one metric ton of new aluminum processing capacity.

As can be seen from the right-hand side of Table 2-7, capital costs in

Table 2-7. Average Estimated Costs, in Cents per Pound, of Aluminum Production in the United States in 1974; and Average Estimated Fixed Capital Cost in U.S. Dollars of One Metric Ton of New Aluminum Processing Capacity, 1970 and 1975

Average costs (U.S.), cents/pound		Fixed capital cost, dollars/metric ton		
			1970	1975
Bauxite	2.7[a]			
Alumina	4.7[b]	Bauxite facilities	150	250
Transportation	1.9	Alumina facilities	450	870
Other raw materials	3.95	Smelting facilities	760	1,800
Electricity	4.0	Power generation	300	650
Labor	3.6	Total cost	1,650	3,570
Capital costs	4.8			
Selling and administration	1.05			
Total costs	26.70			

[a] Based on 4 tons bauxite to give 2 tons alumina.
[b] Based on 2 tons alumina to give 1 ton aluminum.

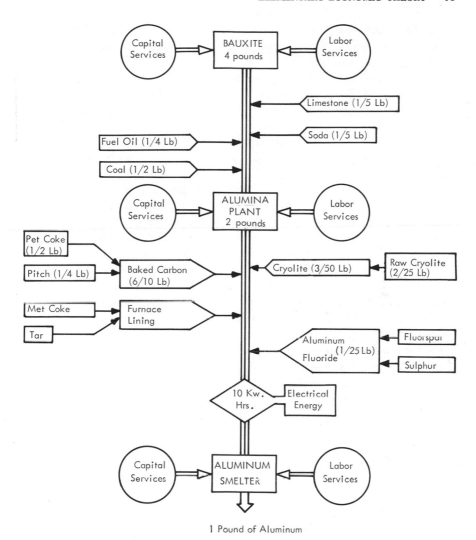

Figure 2-6. Inputs and processes in the production of one pound of aluminum.

this industry are increasing at an unusually rapid pace—at least as fast as the average rate of world inflation. But so, for that matter, are other costs. Jamaica, for instance, has put a tax on bauxite that is a percentage of the U.S. producer price, and has supplemented this with a royalty on each ton of bauxite mined. Given the increasing cooperation between the bauxite producing countries, it seems likely that these taxes, in one form or another, will be imposed by almost all producers.

Since aluminum is one of the most energy-intensive of the major industrial materials, the increase in energy prices is going to result in extremely large increments in production costs. Japan, for instance, has followed a policy of reducing its dependence on foreign countries for aluminum, and as a result faces a huge power bill in order to keep its expensive aluminum capacity operating at close to rated output. The same thing is true to Western Europe, with the notable exceptions of Norway and Iceland. To the above costs must be added the extensive modifications to plants and waste dumping processes that will be necessary if environmental standards are to be met.

Still another dilemma for the major producers of aluminum is the agitation being raised by many of the LDCs that produce bauxite in favor of more alumina production being located in their countries. Alumina yields considerably larger local outlays for supplies, labor, and various services than bauxite. On the average, alumina provides four times the employment per ton as bauxite, and foreign exchange benefits would be comparable for a country producing and exporting alumina. There is no evidence, however, of any great enthusiasm on the part of consumer firms or countries to transfer alumina production closer to the source of bauxite, and the huge growth in the size of ore carriers, as well as the technical advances characteristic of these ships, are reducing haulage costs in such a way that it is becoming extremely difficult to justify large increases in alumina capacity in the bauxite-producing countries on the basis of direct economic considerations. However this may be precisely one of those situations in which so-called direct economic considerations will have to be ignored, since here it may be the case that indirect economic and social considerations are more important. After all, it hardly makes sense for the governments and taxpayers of the consumer countries to give financial aid to underdeveloped countries, with all the waste and corruption that this inevitably leads to, instead of granting these countries some priority in the development of their industrial structures.

The cost of producing alumina has also increased rapidly, with the big factor here being the near quintupling of the price of caustic soda in recent years, as well as the *indirect* rises in the cost of power. To recognize this the reader should understand that about 16 percent of the cost of producing aluminum is due to the direct cost of power; but there are other energy inputs in the form of coal, petroleum, coke, and fuel oil, and in addition there is the energy needed to produce other inputs. All together, the energy cost might exceed 30 percent. Moreover, even those developing countries that have access to cheap power run up against the returns-to-scale problem: as the size of plant decreases, the unit cost of production increases. In

1966 the U.N. published the following figures having to do with production costs as related to the size of installation:

Annual capacity (tons)	Production cost (dollars/ton)
20,000	502
30,000	492
60,000	463
100,000	450

If we consider the Caribbean region, where about 35 percent of the world's bauxite is produced, the financing of aluminum production facilities would fall to a considerable extent on foreign investors from the main consuming countries. Just how appetizing they would find this task is difficult to say, given the risks of expropriation, the tariff barriers erected to discourage the import of aluminum ingot by both the United States and the EEC (which amount to about 8 percent), and the fact that, even if they did build in this region, they would probably end up with plants of less than optimal size. Still, on occasion, financing is available—even for the most expensive projects. The Trombetas complex being constructed in Brazil by a Brazilian-North American-European consortium has an estimated capital cost of $4200/metric ton at the present time, and before it is completed this figure will be much larger.

THE ELEMENTARY THEORY OF CAPITAL VALUES

Although many readers of this book undoubtedly have an acquaintance with discounting and the elementary theory of capital values, the topic is of such great importance for our discussion that a short review is in order.

The crux of the matter is the following: 100 monetary units—or, for that matter, 100 units of any asset—is worth more today than the same amount of the same asset at some point in the future.[4] If we look at monetary assets, then 100 monetary units now can purchase a bond, bank account, or a similar asset that will be worth $100 (1 + r)$ monetary assets in a year, where r is the prevailing rate of interest. This $100 (1 + r)$ monetary units in a year is the alternative to 100 monetary units (which is the situation

---

[4]Given no change in prices, an automobile or washing machine today is worth more than the same automobile or washing machine at some point in the future, since if possessed now its services could be enjoyed for a longer time.

if no asset is bought), and all things equal, the one that a rational person would choose. Also, the interest rate on a financial asset, in a "perfect" market, sets the lower limit on the acceptable rate of return of a physical asset: if the rate of return on a physical asset (e.g., a machine) is less than the rate of interest on a bond or bank account, then a rational man will buy the financial asset.

Continuing this discussion, let us take a situation in which the rate of interest is 10 percent. If you buy a one-period (i.e., one-year) bond for 100 dollars you get, after one year, $100 (1 + 0.10) = 110$ dollars. The rate of return is $(110 - 100)/100 = 10$ percent $=$ the rate of interest, of course. Next, take the case of a two-period bond. If you buy this asset for 100 dollars you have, after one period, 110 dollars, and after two periods $100 (1 + r)^2 = 100$ $(1 + r) (1 + r) = 110 (1 + r) = 121$ dollars. Now reverse this process. One hundred ten dollars a year from now has a *present value* of $110/(1 + 0.01) =$ 100 dollars. One hundred twenty-one dollars two years from now has a present value of $121/(1 + r)^2 = 121/(1 + 0.10)^2 = 100$ dollars. Put still another way, 110 dollars a year from today, or 121 dollars two years from today, is the same as 100 dollars today. In a perfect market these values are interchangeable.

Before going to physical assets, let us examine one more arrangement. Take a bond that never matures—a so-called perpetuity. Let us assume that this bond gives us an income of 10 dollars per year, every year. The problem is: what is the present value of this bond—that is, how much would a rational man pay for an income stream consisting of ten dollars per year, every year in the future? Diagrammatically we have the following situation, where the assumption is that the rate of interest is 10 percent.

$$\frac{10}{1.1} \quad \frac{10}{(1.1)^2} \quad \frac{10}{(1.1)^3} \quad \cdots \quad \frac{10}{(1.1)^n} \quad \cdots \quad \text{Present value}$$

$$
\begin{array}{cccccc}
& 10 & 10 & 10 & \cdots & 10 & \cdots & \text{Return} \\
t = 0 & \downarrow & \downarrow & \downarrow & & \downarrow & \\
\uparrow & t = 1 & t = 2 & t = 3 & & t = n & \text{Time} \\
-100 & & & & &
\end{array}
$$

The present value of the income stream of 10 dollars every period is obtained by the summation of individual present values. The 10 dollars that we get at the end of the first period has a present value of $10/(1 + 0.10) = 10/1.1 = 9.09$ approximately. The 10 dollars that we get at the end of the second year has a present value of $10/(1 + 0.10)^2 = 10/(1.1)^2 = 8.3$, and so on. We have in fact

$$PV = \sum_{1}^{\infty} \frac{10}{(1 + 0.1)^i} = \frac{10}{1.1} + \frac{10}{(1.1)^2} + \frac{10}{(1.1)^3} + \cdots + \frac{10}{(1.1)^i} + \cdots = 100$$

When this series is summed it gives 100. And this makes sense! If you buy a bond (a perpetuity) for 100 dollars, and the interest rate is 10 percent, you get as your return 10 dollars every period you have the bond, regardless of how many periods that may be. (A variant of a perfect bond might be a bank account in a "safe" bank that, for deposits left long enough, pays a guaranteed fixed rate of interest.)

At this point we turn to a physical asset. A physical asset (such as a machine) is for our purposes about the same as a bond, with one big difference—labor is required to cooperate with the machine, and this labor must be paid. At first, however, the assumption will be made that the wage rate is zero. Thus if you buy a one-period machine—that is, a machine that can only produce for one period—and produce and sell 110 dollars worth of goods, after which the machine depreciates completely, and you have no labor costs, then you have a return of 10 percent if you paid 100 dollars for the machine (and the rate of interest was > zero).

A certain attention should also be paid to terminology. The *cost* of the machine is 100 dollars. Now, assume that you borrow money to buy this machine, and the rate of interest is 10 percent. The 110 dollars that you obtain for the goods you produce can be called *revenue,* or *income.* Repaying your debt is sometimes called *amortizing* the debt.

Next assume that with a rate of interest of 10 percent, you borrow 100 dollars to buy a machine that produces 120 dollars worth of goods. Again assume that there are no labor charges, and that the machine falls apart after one year. Amortizing your debt takes 100 dollars, and the *interest charge* is 10 dollars. You therefore have 10 dollars left. This ten dollars, discounted back to the beginning of the first period, or $10/(1 + 0.10) = 9.09$, is a *profit,* or an increase in *wealth.* Two things should be stressed here. The first concerns discounting: in a situation where we are dealing with revenues and expenses at different points in time, it is necessary to put these revenues and expenses on a common basis. This is done by discounting back to a single point—usually the beginning of the first period. Thus, in the example above, where the machine was purchased for 100 dollars and produced 110 dollars worth of goods, with an interest rate of 10 percent, there was no profit. For the economist, a positive profit on a physical asset means that the asset shows a return that is greater than the return obtainable from a bond or a safe financial asset.

What, then, is the situation if instead of borrowing money to buy a machine, you use your own money. Assuming again that the rate of interest is 10 percent, you buy the same physical asset, produce and sell 110 dollars worth of goods, and as before the machine falls apart. Again you have 10 dollars more than you started with. The problem is that you have it one period later, and there is no difference between 100 dollars now and 110 dollars one year from now—if the interest rate is 10 percent. Thus, once again, the profit is zero. Similarly, take a situation where you use your own money to buy a machine for 100 dollars, with which you produce and sell 120 dollars worth of goods. With a rate of interest equal to 10 percent, this income discounted back to the present gives $120/(1 + 0.10) = 109.1$ dollars. Profit, which is measured at the initial point, is $109.1 - 100 = 9.1$. Put another way, your profit is the sum of discounted costs and benefits, with the benefit in this case being 120 dollars—with a discounted value of 109.9; and the cost being 100—with a discounted value of $100/(1 + 0.10)^0 = 100$.

Does having a positive labor cost change anything? The answer is no— at least in principle. Take a situation where we buy a machine with our own money that costs 100 dollars. We produce and sell a product for 120 dollars; and at the same time as the product is sold, pay labor charges of 5 dollars. Again assume that the rate of interest is 10 percent. Costs and benefits then take on the following appearance:

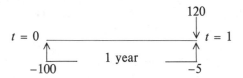

The net (undiscounted) return from this investment is $120 - 5 = 115$ dollars. If this is discounted back to the beginning of the period we have $115/(1 + 0.10) = 104.55$. Our profit is then the sum of discounted costs and benefits, or $104.55 - 100 = 4.55$. Similarly, let us take a situation where the machine is purchased with borrowed money, the rate of interest is 10 percent, labor costs are 5 dollars, and the cost of the machine is 100 dollars. We produce and sell goods for 120 dollars. In this situation the loan must be amortized, and this requires 100 dollars. Our net revenue upon sale of the goods that were produced is $120 - 10 - 5 - 100 = 5$ dollars. Discounted to the beginning of the first period, which is the only period of interest for this one-period machine, gives a profit of $5/(1 + 0.10) = 4.55$.

Something that should be brought out here is that the idea of discounting profits, costs, benefits, and such is not only of interest to the economist but also to the project analyst. The accountant, on the other hand, has only a limited interest in discounting techniques. For instance, in the above example, he would examine the profit at the end of the first period, *at* the end of the first period. On his balance sheet this profit would go down as 5 dollars.

The results for the one-period physical asset will be generalized using some simple algebra, but first a multiperiod numerical example will be examined. The case chosen will be for North Sea oil, with an extraction and investment program analogous, but not identical, to that shown in Figure 2-1. The extra information that the reader needs in order to be able to understand this example concerns what is known as "depreciation accounting." In very simple terms, it involves the following:

A firm borrows money, or uses its own funds, to buy a physical asset. In the case of North Sea oil this would mean, first and foremost, drilling equipment and accessories (such as platforms), as well as the expenses necessary to get this matériel into place. To permit the firm to recover the cost of these assets, the tax laws specify that a certain percentage of this cost can be deducted from revenue each period, and as a result the amount upon which the firm will be taxed is smaller. The reason for this sort of arrangement, of course, is to encourage investment in physical assets. A typical method of making these deductions involves what is known as *straight line depreciation*. If, for instance, the total cost of the investment was $1,000 dollars, and the firm was allowed to depreciate the equipment over five years, this would mean that $200 dollars would be deducted from revenue each year as a cost. Notice the term "allowed." This is used because depreciation is a legal as well as a physical concept. The equipment might have a physical lifetime of 20 years, but the tax laws would permit its depreciation, or "writing off," in five years. Obviously this sort of practice is an advantage for the owner of a physical asset, since it permits him to get his money back sooner.

To continue this example, suppose that the $1000 machine, which can be depreciated over five years, produces $350 worth of goods per year, and there are operating or variable costs of $50 per year. Profits, as defined by the accountant, are taxed at a rate of 50 percent. As stated above, the firm can deduct 200 dollars per year from revenue as its depreciation cost until it has recovered the cost of the machine. This means that during any of the first five years of operation an accountant could show the following calculation for profit: Profit = 350 (Revenue) − 200 (Depreciation) − 50 (Operating Cost) = 100. The tax on this would be 50 percent, and so profit after tax would be $50.

Before continuing, we might ask where does our discounting come in? What we must remember here is that the above calculation was made by an accountant, at the end of a given year, on the basis of revenue and expenses realized during that year. On the other hand an economist or project analyst, working with *estimated* revenues and expenses, and trying to decide whether to buy this machine or not, would discount both this figure and analogous figures from other periods.

Now, with North Sea oil, the British government has decided that depreciation is to work as follows: A firm exploiting a North Sea oil field is allowed to recover 150 percent of its investment costs before having to pay either a petroleum revenue tax (PRT) or the corporation income tax. The only payment to the government before this is a 12½ percent royalty on each dollar of gross revenue. (A royalty is a kind of fee paid by, among others, a mineral-producing company to the owner of the land on which the mineral is found. In the case of North Sea oil the property owner is the British government, acting for the people of Great Britain.) This type of depreciation has been termed "instantaneous writeoff." In the years after 150 percent of the investment cost has been recovered, the oil companies will continue to pay the royalty, and will also pay a PRT of 45 percent, and the corporation income tax of 52 percent. This arrangement functions as follows, assuming that oil sells for $11 a barrel, and the operating or variable cost is $0.625 per barrel.

Price of Oil (dollars/barrel)   11.000
 − Royalty (12½ percent) = 11 × 0.125 = 1.375   9.625
 − Operating Cost (0.625 dollars/barrel)   9.000
 − PRT (45 percent) = 0.45 × 9.00 = 4.05   4.950
 − Corporation Tax (52 percent) = 0.52 × 4.95 = 2.57   2.380

The return per barrel of oil thus falls from $9 per barrel before the equipment of the oil company is depreciated (= Price − Royalty − Operating Cost) to $2.38 per barrel once the PRT and corporation tax come into effect. But remember the theory under which the tax experts of the British government are operating: after 150 percent of investment costs are recovered, the oil companies should have amortized all loans and paid off all interest charges. Thus the $2.38 net profit per barrel goes straight into the company treasury, or to shareholders, or it can be used to finance other investments. In the circumstances, the tax authorities maintain, adequate incentive is being provided to ensure the exploitation of the North Sea reserves at a socially optimal rate. Let us now look at a benefit-cost scheme of the type we would expect to find in connection with an actual oil field. The price, royalty, and operating cost are the same as those used in the above calculation.

The flows represented in Table 2-8 are hypothetical, but in order of

Table 2-8. Some Hypothetical Costs and Benefits (Revenues) for a North Sea Oil Field

(1) Year	(2) Investment	(3) Cumulative investment	(4) Cumulative discounted investment	(5) Production and value	(6) Company revenue	(7) Cumulative company revenue	(8) Cumulative discounted company revenue
1	50	50	50				
2	200	250	181				
3	500	750	644				
4	500	1,250	1,020				
5	500	1,750	1,363				
6	0	—	—	10 (110)	90	90	61
7	0	—	—	50 (550)	450	540	341
8	0	—	—	100 (1,100)	900	1,440	851
9	0	—	—	150 (1,650)	1,350	2,790	1,537
10	?	?	?	150 (1,650)	358	—	—
11	?	?	?	150 (1,650)	358	—	—
12	?	?	?	125 (1,370)	298	—	—
13	?	?	?	110 —	—	—	—
14	?	?	?	100 —	—	—	—
15	?	?	?	50 —	—	—	—
				10 —	—		

Notes: (1) Production in millions of barrels. (2) Investment and revenues in millions of dollars. (3) Interest rate used for discounting: 10 percent. (4) In column (5), the value of production is shown in parentheses in millions of dollars.

magnitude they are not too far away from those that might be expected from an actual North Sea oil field. The reader should also take the following points into careful consideration. The investment program shown is a planned program: it is the program necessary to obtain the production flows shown in column (5). Notice that after the ninth year, the investment column, column (2), contains question marks. This means that it is uncertain as to whether the secondary investment that was shown in Figure 2-1 as beginning at t_e will actually take place. If it were to take place, however, it would mean that the production flows shown in column (5) would have to be changed, beginning with the tenth or eleventh year. It is also possible that if this secondary investment were to take place, there would be production flows after the fifteenth year.

The value of production is based on an oil price of $11/barrel. The cumulative undiscounted value of investment at the end of the fifth year is $1,750 million, and 150 percent of this investment has be "recovered" by the end of the eighth year. As a result, in the following year, the PRT and the corporation income tax come into effect. As shown in the calculation above, this means that the net return to the oil company falls from $9 per barrel to $2.38 per barrel. This is the reason why, with the same production in the ninth year as in the eighth, the revenue of the company falls from $1350 million to $358 million. Again it should be remembered, however, that this $358 million is the net profit for the relevant period. Discounted at an interest rate of 10 percent this gives a present value of $138 million, which is approximately the increase in wealth of the company from the operations of that one year if they do in fact make the investments shown and realize the revenue given in the table up to the end of that year.

Investment has been discounted back to the beginning of the first period, as have some values of company revenue. It can be seen from columns (4) and (8), where these values have been cumulated, the cumulative discounted benefits, or company revenues, become larger than cumulative discounted costs sometime in the eighth year. This is also an indication of an increase in wealth, or a worthwhile project. It should also be noticed that a number of values are not entered in the table. These are either values that are uninteresting, such as cumulative investment after the fifth year; or values for which there are no estimates, such as the value of production and company revenues after the eleventh year. The latter problem turns on an increasing uncertainty about the price of oil, and operating costs, in the distant future. One possible way of handling this problem is simply to assume that prices fell to 7 or 8 dollars a barrel for oil, while operating costs doubled. The reader who is especially interested in this type of analysis should make this calculation, and at the same time make some assumptions concerning secondary investment, to include the effect of this investment on production.[5]

Finally, the results given earlier in this section for the one-period asset will be generalized, using some simple algebra. We shall call the purchase price of the machine, or the cost of the investment, B. The rate of interest is r, and thus the discount factor is $1/(1 + r)$. The revenue or income is R_1; the operating, or variable, cost (such as labor cost, fuel, electricity, etc.) is E_1; and V is the profit, the increase in wealth, or, as it is sometimes called, the present worth of the return on investment. To begin with, let us take a situation where we borrow some money to buy a physical asset such as a machine. Remembering that we invest—that is, purchase the asset—at the beginning of the first period, or at time $t = 0$; and we get our revenue and pay our expenses at the end of the first period—or, what is the same thing, the beginning of the second period—at which time the asset depreciates completely (e.g., falls apart), we have the expression

$$V_{01} = \frac{R_1 - B - rB - E_1}{1 + r}$$

The reader should make sure that he understands this equation. V_{01} means that we have the profit obtained at the end of the first period, $t = 1$, discounted back to the beginning of the initial period, or $t = 0$. B is the amortization of the debt, or repaying the principle as it is sometimes called; while rB is the interest charge on B. The "undiscounted profit," which is what an accountant might be interested in, is $R_1 - B - rB - E_1$. The next step is to rewrite the above equation. We then have

$$\frac{R_1 - E_1}{1 + r} - B = V_{01}$$

Thus, if $(R_1 - E_1)/(1 + r)$ is greater than B, V_{01} is positive. This is the project analyst's approach to the problem of selecting profitable investments. In each period, $t = 1$, $t = 2$, $t = 3$, and so on, a *quasi rent* is calculated that consists of the difference between the revenue from an investment, and operating costs such as taxes, labor charges, energy costs, etc.—but *not*

---

[5]It should also be mentioned in connection with North Sea oil that there has been some discussion as to the possibility of allowing companies to recover 175 percent of capital expenditures before becoming liable to the PRT. Moreover, it has been decided that all fields are to have an allowance that will be free of PRT for ten years; marginal fields will qualify for extra relief; and the PRT will be waived for any year in which it reduces the return on a field, before corporation tax, to less than 30 percent on capital expenditure.

including interest charges or amortization. However, as will be made clear later, interest charges and amortization must be taken into consideration when computing taxes. Each of these quasi rents is then discounted back to $t = 0$, where the discounted values are added together, and this sum is compared to the cost of the investment. Thus, in our one-period case, the quasi rent is $R_1 - E_1$, and discounted this is $(R_1 - E_1)/(1 + r)$. If this is larger than B, as pointed out above, V_{01} is positive, and at the existing rate of interest the investment is viable.

The important thing with this restatement of the equation is that we have gone from an expression in which interest charges and amortization were explicitly denoted, to one in which they are absent. What this means is that the above expression is also valid for a situation in which, instead of borrowing money, the firm uses its own funds to finance an investment. What the reader should keep in mind is that even if a firm uses its own funds, there is still a cost: the opportunity cost of giving up the return from investing these funds in a safe asset, such as a bond.

PROJECT INDEPENDENCE

The previous discussion of North Sea oil had, at bottom, to do with a kind of British "Project Independence," to use the term coined by the former president of the United States, Richard M. Nixon. Without the North Sea oil, and assuming that the price of Middle East and African oil continues on its present course, Britain will be well on the way to becoming the Sick Man of Europe, if not of the entire industrial world.

Other countries face a similar dilemma. France, unlike Britain, has extremely limited energy resources to draw on, and she also lacks the financial resources of the Germans or Japanese. The French plans for meeting the new crisis call for a drastic increase in the production of coal and a colossal expansion in the output of nuclear power. From 2 percent in 1975, the share of nuclear power in the French energy output is scheduled to rise to 23 percent by 1985, and to 45 percent by the year 2000. According to the French Minister of Industry, nuclear power is the only real answer to the energy problem.

In the medium run—before the ultimate solution of fusion and/or solar energy—this contention may indeed be true. But in the short run, given the widely advertised shortcomings of nuclear equipment and output, another approach is warranted. This is for a huge augmentation in the world supply of traditional or near-traditional sources of energy to take place, together with a mammoth effort to restrict the growth of the energy supply. At the center of this program is the most rapid possible building out of the North

Sea oil fields, so that at least Britain and a large part of Scandinavia become independent of other sources of oil. But even more important, the American Project Independence must become a reality, and as close as possible to the original target date of 1980.

At the present time the American program is based on an expanded production in Alaska, as well as a more intensive exploitation of resources off the North American continental shelf. For various reasons, such things as synthetic gas from coal, shale oil, and oil from tar sands, are scheduled to play only a modest role in the U.S. energy equation up to 1985, and possibly beyond. The interesting thing is that given the present and expected price of oil, the huge amount of coal and shale that is found in the United States, as well as the cost of extracting oil and gas from these materials, it might be surmised that in a rational world efforts would be under way to make coal and shale the keystones of U.S. energy supply (and in addition exploiting such things as wind, geothermal, and tidal power up to the limit of their economic availability). It can also be argued that countries like the United States, England, and Norway should exploit their fossil fuel and synthetic oil resources to a point where a sizable export surplus is possible. After all, once the technical and environmental problems associated with nuclear power have been completely solved, the remaining reserves of petroleum will almost certainly decline in value.

Estimates of the amount of oil that can be taken from the continental shelf of the United States are so contradictory that they will be ignored here. But, where Alaska is concerned, it seems that present oilfields in that state may be capable of supplying up to 5 million barrels of the 25 or so million barrels per day of crude oil that the United States will probably be using in 1985 if the rate of growth of oil consumption is not checked. Moreover, according to many experts, it is far from unthinkable that there are still several fields the size of that now being exploited on Alaska's north slope waiting to be discovered. If by some remarkable stroke of luck this is true, and these fields are located, then we have every right to expect that the declining economic health of the United States and much of the rest of the industrial world will stage a definitive recovery. The reader should note the implication in the previous sentence: if the price of energy purchased from the OPEC countries continues to increase at its present rate, then a resumption of the economic and social progress experienced in the nonsocialist industrial countries since the end of World War II should not be expected—at least not at its previous speed.

The problem with Alaskan oil has mainly turned on the possibility of large-scale damage to the environment being caused by such things as pipeline breakages. The opinion here is that with the arrival of the energy crisis such considerations cease to be valid. The dependence of the indus-

Table 2-9. Crude Oil Production at Various Prices in the United States, in Thousands of Barrels per Day[a]

Price, dollars/barrel	1974	1977	1980	1985	1988
"Normal" development					
4	10,544	8,410	8,405	6,914	6,072
7	10,554	8,483	8,505	7,123	6,299
11	10,554	9,607	11,131	11,507	11,060
15	10,554	9,754	11,956	14,302	15,212
20	10,554	9,939	12,172	14,936	16,231
"Accelerated" development					
7	10,554	8,734	8,949	7,504	6,602
11	10,554	9,920	12,004	15,217	15,142
15	10,554	10,225	13,277	19,529	22,000
20	10,554	10,333	13,445	20,182	23,072

[a] Source: U.S. Government, Project Independence Oil Resources Task Force.

trial countries at the present time on low- to moderately priced energy is so complete that obtaining this energy should take precedence over all environmental considerations except those that involve a direct, or indirect, physical danger—which *might* be the case with nuclear energy. It is, of course, possible that there is a positive side to the sudden unavailability of energy in the amount that we have been used to obtaining it. Some people say that an energy shortage lasting a long time will stimulate cooperation between nations or groups of nations; however a more likely conjecture might be a drastic increase in the already high level of international tension. The same thing can apply domestically: in a country like the United States the "best possible" scenario connected to an extensive energy shortage would be a further eroding of the economic power of the weaker elements in the community, such as the aged, handicapped, socially disadvantaged, etc. The "worst possible" scenario, which seems to the author to be much more likely than the former, would involve an incarnation of some of the more colorful nightmares of the Reverend Dr. Malthus.

It is estimated that by 1985 the United States will be using about 25 million barrels per day of crude oil, with the total energy consumption in oil, gas, coal, and so on equal to about 45 million barrels per day of crude oil equivalent. All sorts of guesses are available as to how much of this crude oil will have to be imported and how much can be produced locally. The so-called Project Independence Oil Resources Task Force has made some estimates of the amount of crude oil that would be forthcoming given both a normal and an accelerated program for the development of energy resources. Their calculations are shown in Table 2-9.

It should be noted here that in the short run output is largely independent of both price and the type of program: today's output is determined by the actions of yesterday. This is a lesson that will be stressed in later chapters. It is in the long run that fundamental changes can be made. There are, however, several things that are misleading about this table. Obviously the price of crude does not have to go to $20/barrel right away for 23 million barrels/day to be produced in 1988. On this point there is something else that the reader should grasp that is often overlooked when such matters are broached: the $20/barrel price is not important in itself—it is the return on investment that it helps bring about that we should really be interested in. Given a different structure of capital costs, variable costs, taxes, and allowances, or for that matter a different economic policy in the United States, the price could be appreciably lower; but still the necessary financing of the equipment needed to produce this oil would be made available through normal channels.[6]

The capital requirements for the U.S. Project Independence have been placed by the Secretary of the Treasury at $850 billion, assuming that the present rate of inflation is halved. It would be spent over the 10-year period between 1975 and 1985. By way of comparison, the energy industry invested $20 billion a year in the United States between 1960 and 1970, with this sum representing, on the average, 20 percent of business capital investment during this period.

[6]As an example we can cite the investment behavior of a group of 30 petroleum companies surveyed by the Chase National Bank of New York during 1974. The profits of these companies came to $16 billion, while their investment amounted to $22 billion. Of this investment, 59 percent was for the purpose of increasing the output of petroleum, while the rest was for the expansion and modernization of processing facilities. The basis for the optimism leading to this kind of investment behavior was the increase in profitability of these firms between 1973 and 1974, which was no less than 39 percent. What happened was simply that the increase in oil prices resulted in such large increases in the return on fixed assets, measured in terms of the quasi rent on the output of these assets compared to their cost, that firms found it expedient to go into debt to obtain more of these assets. Obviously, if price increases are expected to be sufficiently high, it makes sense to borrow money in order to expand capacity, even if at the same time various costs are also on the increase.

MICROECONOMIC THEORY

3

Approximately 25 percent of this book involves the exposition of some elementary microeconomic theory, with the present chapter containing about one-half of that 25 percent. For the reader who has a background in academic economics this chapter serves as a review. Still, it may be a necessary review for many, since topics such as the stock-flow model and the price of capital services are not found in every textbook even though they are important tools for the economist.

The first section below, on long-run prices, contains no technical material and should be examined by all readers. The first part of the following section is also fairly easy reading, but after that the plot thickens as we get into some of the intricacies of the stock-flow model and short-run prices. The next section deals with the price of capital services, and the one after that takes up some elementary investment theory—much of which should cause no problem for the nontechnical reader. The final section treats some elementary production theory.

Many of the problems introduced in this chapter are treated in the next chapter, where such things as the world tin market and the smelting of lead are used to bring out important aspects of long-run pricing and increasing returns to scale. At the same time it should be emphasized that the next chapter, as well as most of the rest of this book, can be read independently of the present chapter.

LONG-RUN PRICE, DEMAND, AND SUPPLY

When studying the prices of raw materials, there are at least two prices that must be considered. The one underlying the discussion in this section is the long-run price, which under certain circumstances might be considered a trend or normal price, and is formed by the interaction of long-run supply and demand. The other price is a short-run price that is usually explained by speculation, lack of information, flights of fancy, panic, and so on. It will be discussed in the next section.

The method recommended here for predicting the long-run (or medium-run) price of a raw material involves no more than looking at the movement of trend supply and demand. For example, if demand for a mineral is increasing at an average rate of 4 percent a year, and the capacity of the particular industry is expanding at 6 or 7 percent a year, then it can be surmised that a surplus of the commodity will eventually come about and its price will fall. This is to be expected regardless of the existing direction of the price and regardless of what we find on the printouts of this or that econometric model, even if it happens to be the case that the econometrician or his sponsor actually understand the model or, more important, the mechanics of the market it is supposed to represent.

Where the determination of demand is concerned, the most interesting explanatory variable is probably industrial production, or an analogous index. This is so since materials such as iron ore (and steel), copper, zinc, etc., are important inputs for almost all capital and durable goods: machinery, structures, automobiles, and so on. At the time this book was in its initial stages, the high-trend growth rate of industrial production in the leading raw-material-consuming countries began to fall, orders for capital goods were being rapidly cut back, and undesired inventories of durable goods commenced increasing on a worldwide basis. Since then the price of raw materials has plunged at an exceptionally fast pace.

Where the supply of raw materials is concerned, the story is unfortunately more complicated. It might be interesting to begin from a point where the director of some raw-material-producing firm, and his colleagues, has come to believe that there will be a dramatic increase in the demand for his product. Take a situation where the international business cycle is rising at a fast rate, his installations are operating at close to full capacity, profits are good, and his salesmen tell him that orders are coming in at such a pace that, given the existing stock of orders, it is difficult to promise even old customers delivery dates that they regard as satisfactory, and this is so even if they offer higher prices.

In these circumstances the producer would normally attempt to increase production.[1] First, he would increase his variable inputs, of which labor is the most important. This would probably call for a considerable increase in overtime, which is usually more expensive than "normal" time; but even if there was no overtime and the work force simply expanded, we are likely to have a departure, or further departure, from the *optimal*

---

[1] Note the word "normally." In the U.S. copper industry, with this situation existing, there were many occasions in which producers did not increase production but simply resorted to rationing their output.

capital/labor arrangement, and a rise in unit costs. By this it is meant that for a given stock of capital equipment and structures, there is a quantity of labor that will produce the product with a minimum unit cost; and a sizable deviation of the labor employed from this amount will usually mean an increase in the unit cost of the product. Of course, if we stick to our example, it is probably the case that the increased demand causes the price of the product to rise in such a way that incremental or marginal revenue will increase faster than incremental cost, in which case an increase in the amount of the variable factor, and thereby production, is quite justifiable from an economic point of view. But even so, we may be away from, or farther away from, the minimum cost point, and elementary economic theory tells us that in the interest of profit maximization the producer should begin thinking about returning to this position. The way this usually happens is by increasing the amount of equipment, which often also means increasing the amount of equipment per worker. Much of the world mining industry has been extremely responsive on this point, and, as a result, capacity has often expanded at a rate unwarranted by the long-term demand.[2]

In the case of a mining operation, moreover, it is not just a case of mining within the same boundaries with a better and larger stock of equipment, but also locating and mining new sites, and/or expanding existing sites. This adds a new dimension to the resource-allocation problem of the firm, one that could be handled by concentrating attention on existing installations, but at the same time having a low-pressure exploratory, design, or pilot program in process as a matter of routine. Then, with the intensification of demand, these programs are stepped up, sometimes with the effect that new capacity comes into operation with a fairly short time.

If we can assume that our upswing in the business cycle lasts long enough, the above behavior will probably be duplicated by almost all the firms in a particular industry, and thus the industry supply curve should reveal a net shift to the right (or an increase).[3] (For example, in an industry of two firms the given supply curves would resemble those shown in Figure 3-1.) This will have a certain tendency to dampen price increases in the industry in question, but in only a few cases in the various raw materials industries have I been able to detect a situation in which this type of

[2]This situation has often been noticed in manpower-rich, but capital-poor, LDCs. For instance, in both Chile and Zambia the capital/labor ratio in the copper industry has shown a steady increase.

[3]The industry supply curve is the horizontal summation of the supply curves of the various firms that comprise the industry.

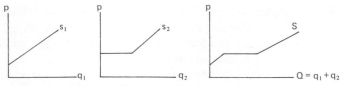

Figure 3-1. The aggregation of supply curves.

movement (or shift) has outrun price rises during a major upswing and managed to hold prices at a near-constant level. Instead, even after all signs indicate the upswing is reaching its culmination, prices still often show a pronounced vigor, which in turn encourages installing and bringing on stream the new capacity that has been ordered. It should be made clear, however, that this vigor can often be traced to the incompetence of speculators who prolong a certain trend in their own minds long after objective considerations show it to have changed directions.

The analysis now shifts to what happens when the business cycle downturn is certified by a rapid falling in demand. For one thing, producers most likely will not immediately cancel all orders for the equipment they have made plans to buy, but which may not have arrived—just as they did not initiate orders for machinery and buildings immediately upon the first sign of an upturn. Instead they wait to see whether the change in the economic climate is going to be a short- or long-run affair. More important, there may be an excellent economic reason for not only continuing, but rushing through new investment. New investment can mean better machinery that is often capable of producing at lower costs. It is sometimes reasoned that the firm with the latest technology stands the best chance of maintaining its competitive position, even though industry demand is definitely faltering, and even though acquisition costs for this new equipment are not inconsiderable. It is usually possible to cite a situation in the previous downturn where, although average profitability was low and declining, some of the newer plants in an industry were not only profitable, but highly profitable.

The upshot of all this is that many raw material industries show a marked lack of symmetry in their investment behavior. Business cycle upswings cause a rapid accumulation of new capital; but downswings do not bring about a corresponding disinvestment, and quite often no great underutilization of capacity. Moreover, this characteristic is reinforced by the fact that much of the world mining industry, to include a respectable proportion of processing facilities, is located in the LDCs. Many of these countries have shown a tendency to build up capacity as fast as resources allow. Such things as profitability and expectation of profitability are important, but the key factor would seem to be the lack of alternative investments.[4]

Two new factors will probably intrude upon the international raw materials scene in the not-too-distant future. The first will be the attention paid to the supply of natural resources by the governments of the major industrial countries. For this development the oil crisis following the October War is to be thanked, or cursed—depending upon how the reader feels about governments becoming involved in these matters.

The other is that many producers of raw materials in LDCs will show a tendency to expand their processing capacity (smelting, refining, etc.). What this will probably do is to increase the dependency of these countries on raw materials, and reinforce the secular aspects of raw material supply that have been discussed just above. This is so since not only will employment at the mining level be affected by the production of primary commodities, but so will employment in the installations for processing these commodities.

These last two factors, together with some of the mechanics of investment taken up earlier in this section, should manage to hold down any price explosions in the raw materials field in the near future. Of course, in the long run, the only thing that will keep these prices down will be an even more accelerated technical progress, as well as some basic changes in the utilization patterns of raw materials in the main industrial countries. Needless to say these changes eventually must be emulated by all countries.

---

[4]That is to say, the key economic factor. The political and social situation in most underdeveloped countries is such that employment must be kept up. Countries with only one or two export industries have no choice but to maintain production—regardless of the price they obtain for their exports. Thus these exports often appear to be independent of price. Some simple econometric analysis helps to reveal the strength of trend elements in the case of the supply of raw copper from Zambia and Zaire. Calling S_z and S_c the supply from these two countries, with t representing time, and annual data for 1950–70, the following two equations are obtained (t ratios are in parentheses):

$$S_z = 182 + 24.52t \qquad R^2 = 0.971$$
$$(19.0)$$
$$S_c = 138.2 + 10t - 40.9D \qquad R^2 = 0.973$$
$$(6.9) \quad (4.0) \qquad D = 1 \ (1961\text{-}63)$$
$$ D = 0 \ (\text{otherwise})$$

These equations do not prove anything, of course—for the simple reason that econometrics *cannot* prove anything. What they do is to suggest that trend elements are unusually strong in the production of these two countries. They are evidence, but they are far from being decisive evidence; however they are certainly better than no evidence at all.

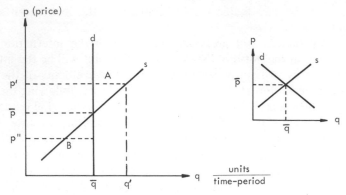

Figure 3-2. Elementary flow supply-demand model.

SHORT-RUN PRICES (1)

The issue here is a deviation from the long-run or normal price. These deviations are often quite pronounced, and if looked at in isolation can give a great deal of wrong information. For instance, during the darkest period of the great depression (1929–37), prices on the metal exchanges occasionally came close to regaining the levels they had enjoyed during the bull period just preceding the depression. Even more significant, when demand had fallen far under supply at the beginning of the recession, speculative forces on the market not only held up the prices, but on some days sent them climbing to levels that were above the average for that period. A similar situation existed immediately after the October War in the Middle East (1973) on the markets for primary metals. With demand faltering, and the actual supply–demand situation warranting a sharp fall in prices, speculation drove the prices of some of these metals so high that many observers came to the conclusion that the world was entering an era of permanent raw material scarcity.

The first thing we will do here is to review an elementary flow model, or what we called in Chapter 1 a "pure" flow model. This model has as its components $s = f(p)$, $d = g(p)$, and the equilibrium relation $s = d$, where s = *current* supply, d = *current* demand, and p = price. Supply and demand are given in units/time period; and it is because of the time element that this model is called a flow model. If we call the point of equilibrium (where $s = d$) a point where current supply is equal to current consumption, then it is also possible to identify situations where current supply is greater than current demand, and inventories (= stocks) are increasing, as at A in Figure 3-2; or where current supply (= flow supply) is less than current demand, and inventories are decreasing. This latter arrangement can be seen at *B* in Figure 3-2.

As shown in the larger diagram on the left, *d* is taken to be independent of price, indicating that it is a function of some variable or parameter exogenous to the model, such as industrial production. But take special note of the fact that in the event someone was so rash as to try to construct an actual demand curve for various raw materials, he would have to deal with statistics of sales or deliveries where it is almost impossible to say which portion was for current consumption and which for inventories. Because of this situation it is easy to justify employment of a "simple" flow model with a conventional demand curve of the type shown in the smaller diagram in Figure 3-2, where *d* covers the demand for stocks as well as current use: even if the demand for current consumption is independent of price, the amount demanded for inventories, with *given* expectations for future prices, would most likely increase if the current price decreased.[5] For pedagogical reasons, however, some attempt will be made to separate these two components in the ensuing discussion.

The simple flow model, powerful though it is, is not completely adequate for our purposes, since it is essential that inventories be singled out for special attention. We know that inventories are important in most raw materials markets, and in fact are central to short-run price formation. The most useful technique for determining which way the price is going to move involves studying the actual size of inventories in relation to some benchmark, such as "desired" or "normal" inventories. If actual inventories are larger than desired inventories, then price should fall. Another device is to observe the movements of the ratio I/d, where I indicates inventories: as inventories increase relative to flow demand, there should be a downward pressure on price. Deviations from this scenario can exist in the short run if for some reason inventory holders (producers, consumers, and/or speculators) decide that it will be advantageous at some point in the future to have more stocks on hand than they are customarily used to holding. But even so, if flow demand does not eventually move in such a way as to justify the accumulation of extra inventories, these additional units will be judged unprofitable, and in the course of readjusting inventories downward, a price decline should take place.

The next step involves introducing a demand curve for stocks that is analogous to our flow demand curve. To begin, we might postulate that the demand for stocks is a function of such things as (1) expected price, since if the price of the material is expected to rise, and you have the material available and have bought cheaply, then you can sell at a profit. Similarly, if

---

[5] For more on this topic the reader can refer to Desai (1972) and Banks (1974).

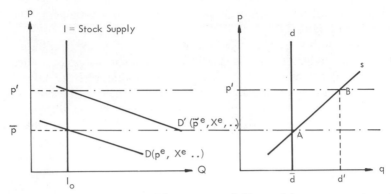

Figure 3-3. Elementary stock-flow model.

you use the material and you have it in stock, then you can avoid having to buy it at a higher price; (2) expected production, because if you expect that demand is going to increase, and thus it will be profitable to increase production, but you are uncertain as to the availability of your inputs, then it may be advisable to hold stocks of inputs for either precautionary or speculative reasons; (3) the rate of interest, since, if the rate of interest falls and everything else remains the same, the cost of financing a given level of inventories decreases. And so on.

The kind of demand curve that we are working up to is called a stock demand curve, and will be designated $D = m(p^e, X^e, r, \ldots)$, where the argument of this expression contains the variables mentioned above as well as any others that the reader might consider relevant. Similar formulations that are interesting and realistic are easily postulated—for example, we might try $D = w(p^e - p, X^e - X, r, \ldots)$, or something along this line. The unit for demand in the case of the stock demand curve would be pounds, tons, metric tons, etc. Note that the stock demand curve is quite a different thing from the flow demand curve, in that the unit for demand says nothing about time. As for the stock supply curve, this is simply a matter of the amount of the material in existence at any particular moment. It is not a function of time or anything else, but simply a datum. The stock-flow model thus takes on the appearance shown in Figure 3-3.

We can now commence our examination of how this model functions in regard to forming the short-run price. As we have said, this price is strongly influenced by speculation, and one way to discuss speculation is in terms of the desire to alter the size of inventories in response to changes in expectations. As is usually the case in economics when we want to discuss changes, we start our analysis from an equilibrium or a stationary point. An equilibrium in this model is a situation where stocks are constant, with stock supply equal to stock demand, and at the same time a flow equilibrium prevailing in which the amount being produced every period is equal to the amount being demanded (and consumed) in that period. In Figure 3-3 this equilibrium is shown at $(\bar{d},\bar{p})$, with stocks equal to I_0.

Now assume an increase in stock demand to D', due for instance to a change in price expectations (from p^e to $\tilde{p}^e$): with the present price $\bar{p}$, and the expected future price increasing from p^e to $\tilde{p}^e$, there is a desire by consumers and/or producers and/or speculators to hold larger stocks. (Producers might want to hold rather than sell more of their production in anticipation of being able to sell it for a higher price later.) What this does is to cause a pressure on the fixed amount of stocks in existence, I_0, in the sense that their price is bid up; and this increase in price is transmitted to the flow market where production increases to a point where it is in excess of current demand. This results in an increase in inventories.[6]

This phenomenon is shown in Figure 3-3, which indicates a movement along the flow supply curve from point A to point B, and a consequent gap between flow supply and flow demand of $d'-\bar{d}$, with this excess supply going into inventories. This in turn causes the stock "supply" curve to move from I_0 to I_1, where this new situation is shown in Figure 3-4.

When the price reaches p' there is no *further* demand for stocks. In other words, at price p' orders have been placed for just the amount of stocks that producers are prepared to deliver at that price. These orders are delivered at some time during the current period (which might be a month, six months, one year, etc.). As will be made clear later in this section when the concept "investment demand" is introduced, the reason the system settles at a particular price p' can be traced not only to the fact that individuals and firms want more stocks, but also to the *rate* at which they want these stocks.

The preceding material in this section is rather important, and a fairly extensive—but simple—example will now be presented to help bring its implications home to the reader. Suppose that we have a speculator who is a pure stockholder (and not, at the same time, a producer or consumer) and who forms the opinion that the price of a good will rise to 50, when its

---

[6]The demand for such increased inventories could manifest itself as follows: some people want more inventories right away, and show this impatience by offering a high enough price to place themselves first in line for new production, or even for the purchase of existing stocks—even though the holders of these existing stocks also expect some increases in price. Those who sold stocks then replenish their stocks from new production, either in the present or at a later period, with the exact time depending upon their desire to have new stocks, and the willingness to back this desire with money. The same situation holds for other categories of buyers who wanted more stocks immediately, but whose purchasing power did not allow them to buy existing stocks.

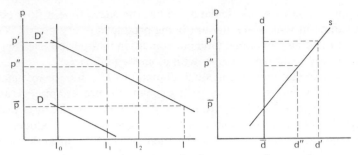

Figure 3-4. Increase in stocks due to excess flow supply.

present price is 10. ($\bar{p} = 10, \tilde{p}^e = 50$). Observe, however, that this is his opinion—he is not absolutely certain; and so he orders only 100 new units instead of 10,000 or 100,000. Now it should be carefully noted, since this point is crucial for all that follows, that he orders 100 units under the assumption that he will be able to get them at the prevailing market price of 10. There are, moreover, a number of speculators, and let us postulate that a majority of these expect a rise in price, although they have varying expectations as to just what the new price might be. Some expect 50, some 40, a few 12, and a few others 100.

Now when our speculator places his order, so do the other speculators. The industry producing the item, however, cannot cover the cost of producing more of the item unless they raise its price. As the reader probably remembers from his first course in economics, this is what a rising supply curve is all about.[7] But when the price starts increasing, many— though perhaps not all—of those speculators who had thought that they would be able to buy additional units at a price of 10 withdraw or modify their orders. Let us say, for instance, that at some point in time after these orders have been placed, the price quoted by suppliers has risen to 30, and indications are that it will go higher. This will almost certainly mean that those with price expectations under 30 will cancel or try to cancel their orders, since if they bought at 30 and sold at less, they would realize a loss.

And what about the speculator who thought that the price would go to 50. Should the price increase to 50 he would still make a profit if he could buy at 30, even though it is less than the profit he would have made had he been able to buy at 10, and so he is still interested in increasing his

---

[7]As indicated in the previous footnote, speculators might buy a certain amount from each other. For instance, someone who expects the price to rise to 45 will probably be able to buy from someone who expects it to go to 14. This type of buying should eventually reflect on flow production, just as bidding up the rents and prices of existing housing will stimulate new production.

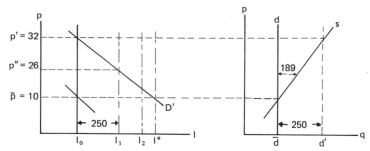

Figure 3-5. Stock increase in first period following a price rise.

inventory; however now he has some doubts as to whether he should increase it by 100. The price of 50 is still the expected price, but with the quoted price at 30 instead of 10 he is more aware than ever that his expectations might prove to be incorrect. In the circumstances, he decides that if the final quoted price is 30 he will not increase his stock by 100, but by 52, and he communicates these intentions to his supplier.[8] By reducing his order, if things go wrong, he will not lose so much.

Eventually, with all speculators following this behavior, the price will stop rising (since demand is being adjusted downward). For the purposes of the model it is only now, after all adjustments and so on have been completed, that we can specify the new price p'. We will take this to be 32 ($p' = 32$), and also take the resulting increase in production $d' - \bar{d}$ to be 250. Of this a certain amount belongs to our speculator. Let us assume that with the price at 32, and this price final, he decides to order 47 units.

What happens now? First we will make an assumption as to when these units are delivered. The assumption will be that the new orders will be delivered to all buyers at the end of the period (whose length we have not specified). This means that at the end of the period aggregate inventories will increase in a single jump by 250 units. Diagrammatically Figure 3-5 shows that this arrangement has the following significance for our stock-flow model.

With the arrival of these 250 units, some pressure is taken off the market. The system, however, has not reached an equilibrium. Our speculator, who had originally intended to order 100 units when he thought the

---

[8]Note that we have a lag here between the placing of orders and production. Thus the price quoted by the supplier is a provisional price until all orders are in, to include modifications of earlier orders, and indications are that there will not be further orders or modifications. At this stage the provisional price becomes the final price. To simplify the analysis we can postulate that orders come in, and prices are changed until we get p', during a very small time span at the beginning of the period.

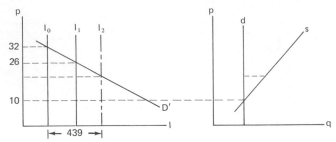

Figure 3-6. Stock increase in second period following a price rise.

price was going to be 10, but changed his order to 47 because of the large price rise, still expects the price to go to 50. He therefore decides to order the remainder of the 100 units (or 53 units). His colleagues, finding themselves in the same situation, make similar decisions. Thus we are once more at the beginning of a sequence such as that described above. This time our speculator wants 53 units, assuming that the price is 10. However, as before, if flow supply is to exceed flow demand, and thus permit an increase in stocks, the price will have to exceed 10. But should this happen, both our speculator and many of his colleagues will once again reduce their orders. This time they are reduced not only because of the element of uncertainty as to what the future price might be in relation to the price at which inventories must be bought, but because the original stock of I_0 has been increased by 250 units, and additional units are not so important.

The reduction in demand, together with the fact that orders this time were not so heavy as at the beginning of the previous period, causes the price at the beginning of the second period to be 26 ($p'' = 26$). At this price 189 units are ordered and produced, with 32 of them belonging to our speculator. As before, total stocks rise by 189 units at the end of the period. Thus, in two periods, stocks have risen by 250 + 189 = 439 units. This is shown in Figures 3-5 and 3-6.

Using Figure 3-6 the reader should carry this process through one more period to make sure that he understands it. What will be done below, however, is to examine several of the assumptions employed above, and in particular to sharpen the concept of "investment" that is being employed in this analysis. First of all the assumption that all the new units are delivered at the end of a period must be questioned. Economics, like the physical sciences, derives a large part of its power from approximations, and, as far as I can tell, very little is lost by assuming that deliveries to stocks take place at the end of the period rather than continuously during the period.

However, this was a pedagogic device; and once the reader has grasped the basic mechanics of the model, he can consider the possibility of a stream of deliveries during a given period. As it happens, the model that we have been considering above would have to be complicated somewhat to handle this matter, and so we treat this problem verbally. The big modification of the above model involves breaking up our period (of, for example, one year) into a number of subperiods, and then stating just when during the period any particular speculator would have his order filled. A not very precise answer, of course, might be after those who are prepared to pay a higher price for the item.

Again let us assume that at the beginning of the period the price is 32, and thus suppliers are prepared to increase production by 250 during the year. (That is, one period = one year, and for a subperiod we shall take one month.) This means that during the first month, January, 250/12 = 20.9 units will be added to the stocks of those individuals who paid 32. Now, at the beginning of the next subperiod, February, the price falls to 31.5. At this price producers are no longer prepared to increase production at a yearly rate of 250 but, let us say, they will increase it by 247. Thus, during February, the stock increase is 247/12 = 20.7, and is on the part of buyers paying 31.5. Continuing, at the beginning of the next subperiod (March) the price falls to 31. At this price producers are prepared to increase production only by a yearly rate of 243, and so during March the stock increase (= excess flow supply) is 20.3. If, for instance, at the beginning of the year a buyer had stated that he was only prepared to pay 31, then his order would have been filled in March.

If we take someone like our speculator in the example above, and still assume that he plans to add 47 units to his stocks during the year, but the price performs as in the preceding paragraph, then he receives his order over several subperiods, and at several prices. For instance, of the 20.7 units produced during the second subperiod (February) he might have obtained 15, taking the rest later in the year. And who increased his inventories in January? Just as our speculator expects the price to rise to 50, there are others expecting it to increase to 100. It is not inconceivable that these are the people who want their orders filled immediately, and are prepared to pay for this privilege. A similar behavior might be observed on the part of speculators who not only think the price is going to rise, but that it is going to rise in the very near future. Depending upon how much they think the increase is going to be, these individuals are also prepared to pay for the right to stand at the head of the line.

Some attention should also be paid to the manner in which the price fell in the present example. As postulated, the price fell by a half-unit a month, which is supposed to reflect the interaction of supply and demand. For instance, buyers wanted 20.9 units added to stocks during January, and this meant that during January producers would have to realize an excess supply of 250 units reckoned at a yearly rate—or 250/12 = 20.9 units at a monthly rate—something they were prepared to do if they received a unit price of 32. The fall in price can then be attributed to a lower rate of building up stocks. But by the same token it is possible to postulate a situation where buyers want to increase their stocks by 250 units, or less, during a year, but the price to some buyers would be more than 32. This could happen, for example, if they wanted the majority of these stocks in the first part of the year, thus causing the monthly rate of production to exceed greatly that used in the present example. In other words, price might depend upon whether production is at an even or uneven pace over a given period.

Another point of interest is that the stock increase in this example is no longer 250, as it was in the earlier example. In order for it to be 250 during the period, 20.9 would have to be added to stocks every month; but this could only take place if the price stayed at 32. With the price falling every month in the manner postulated above, the excess flow supply per month decreases also, and so the total stock increase during the year is approximately 229 units (= 20.9 + 20.7 + 20.3 + · · · + 17.2). Also, observe that with the above pattern of price changes only those willing to pay more than 26.5 obtain stocks during the first period.

The important thing here is how time has entered the analysis. If he is willing to pay a high enough price, a stockholder can increase his inventories during the present period; but, as considered here, this period is extended in time. Thus he must choose not only how much he wants, but when during the period he wants it. A given sum of money might buy only a small amount of the item at the beginning of the period, but a great deal more at the end of the period—or, for that matter, in a later period. It should also be pointed out that it does not make a great deal of difference in the verbal analysis if all the individuals buying during a given period are paying the same price and deliveries are taking place continuously in the course of the period. Determining who gets his delivery first might then be a question of who placed his order first, and so on.

The next question is: how do we know from the diagrams being used that stockholders continue to increase their inventories after the first period? The answer is that this information is to be found in the position of the stock demand curve: this curve retains the same position after the first *and* subsequent periods. Of course it would be easy to construct an argument justifying a change in plans for our speculator and his colleagues—for instance, they could not increase their stocks at the rate they had planned to increase them, the price was not reacting in a satisfactory manner, etc.; but any change in plans leading to a change in behavior would have to be shown by a shift in the stock demand curve. As long as this curve does not move again, and the price stays high enough to maintain flow supply higher than flow demand, then stocks are increasing. Moreover, as long as p^e remains higher than p for speculators as a whole, this would seem to be a logical state of affairs.

We can now concern ourselves with when this increase in stock would be terminated. In Figure 3-5 it would stop when stocks have attained the level I^*, at which point the price has fallen to the original price $\bar{p}^+$ (= 10 in the figure), and once more only enough is being produced to satisfy current demand or, what is the same thing, we are back at our stock and flow equilibrium.

The description of this sequence, from equilibrium $(\bar{p}, I_0)$ to equilibrium $(\bar{p}, I^*)$, is an example of economic dynamics. Of course it represents an idealization in that just as we had a change in expectations to initiate the sequence, it seems unlikely that a new change in expectations—or some other exogenous disturbance—would not take place before the new equilibrium is reached. (And which, depending upon the nature of the change, would be shown by a change in the stock demand curve or the flow demand or supply curve.) This, however, is not the point. Essentially what we want to do is to postulate changes in exogenous variables or in behavior, and to study the movement of endogenous variables as we move from one equilibrium toward another. If we have the right kind of model, this technique might lead to the raising of questions that will allow us some important insights into real-world phenomena.

SHORT-RUN PRICES (2)

We can now turn to the investment demand function. The issue here is not the amount by which inventories are to be increased, but the rate at which this is to take place.[9] To illustrate this matter we shall again take a

---

[9]If we are only interested in what happens to the endogenous variables at positions of equilibrium, then we have a problem in comparative statics. We might, for instance, have a system that can be represented by

$$f_i(x_1, x_2, \ldots, x_n; y_1, y_2, \ldots, y_m) = 0 \qquad i = 1, \ldots, n$$

The x's are endogenous variables, or variables to be determined within the system; and the y's are exogenous variables or "shift" parameters that are external to the system in one sense or another. Comparative statics presumes that $x_i = x_i(y_1, y_2, \ldots, y_m)$, or the equilibrium values of the x's can be determined as a function of the exogenous variables, and that the new equilibrium actually exists. One of the crucial points of this analysis involves the

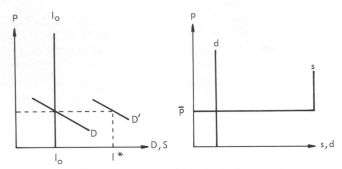

Figure 3-7. Stock-flow model with inelastic flow supply curve.

case where an increase in stocks is desired, but, in contrast to the previous example, the industry supplying these stocks can supply the entire increased demand without raising the price.[10] We therefore have the stock-flow model as depicted in Figure 3-7.

The excess stock demand is $I^* - I_0$, which, as postulated, the supplying industry can provide during the present period at no increase in price.[11] It may be so, however, that all these stocks are not desired during the present period. Remember that stockholders in the previous example demanded more stocks because they "thought" that prices were going to rise—they were not absolutely certain. Similarly, in the present example,

---

"Jacobian" of the system being nonsingular, or

$$J = \begin{vmatrix} \dfrac{\partial f_1}{\partial x_1} & \cdots & \dfrac{\partial f_1}{\partial x_n} \\ \vdots & & \vdots \\ \dfrac{\partial f_n}{\partial x_1} & \cdots & \dfrac{\partial f_n}{\partial x_n} \end{vmatrix} \neq 0$$

Comparative statics involves getting the values $\partial x_i/\partial y_1, \ldots, \partial x_i/\partial y_m$. For example, we can differentiate the above n equations with respect to y_1, keeping $y_2, \ldots, y_m$ constant. In matrix terms this gives the system

$$J\bar{x}_1 = -a_1 \text{ or } x_1 = -J^{-1}a_1$$

In this expression a_1 and x_1 are column vectors, where $a_1 = (\partial f_1/\partial y_1, \ldots, \partial f_n/\partial y_1)$ and $\bar{x}_1 = (\partial x_1/\partial y_1, \ldots, \partial x_n/\partial y_1)$. We might then differentiate with respect to y_2, holding the other y's constant. Our system is now $\bar{x}_2 = -J^{-1}a_2$, with $a_2 = (\partial f_1/\partial y_2, \ldots, \partial f_n/\partial y_2)$ and $\bar{x}_2 = (\partial x_1/\partial y_2, \ldots, \partial x_n/\partial y_2)$; and so on.

[10]Either because it is a "constant cost" industry or because it has excess capacity.

[11]The new stock demand curve D' is not extended up to an intersection with I_0 since this intersection would have no meaning in the present situation.

stockholders may—because of uncertainty—prefer to take only a part of the planned or desired increase in stocks during the present period, preferring to take the rest when they have more information or, with the passing of time, they have no reason to change their opinion of what the future will bring. The *investment demand* function, or the relationship giving the desired *rate* of change of stocks, might then be some fraction of the excess stock demand. For instance, we might have investment demand $= k(I^* - I_o)$.

If, as an example, we have $I^* - I_0 = 1000$ and $k = \frac{1}{2}$, then investment demand for the present period would be 500 units/period. At the beginning of the next period the planned excess stock demand is 500 units, and, if k has not changed, investment demand is 250 units/period; and so on. Bushaw and Clower (1957) have diagramed the investment demand function, but the fact is that almost 20 years have passed without their construction receiving any special recognition in the literature. The trouble is that although the concept is essential for understanding this type of problem, its diagrammatic form is difficult to combine with the other components of the model. In a sense, however, this is irrelevant, since Bushaw and Clower have provided an extensive mathematical analysis that permits a meaningful discussion of investment demand.[12]

If we take the first example presented above, where an increase in the demand for stocks meant an increase in price, it should be recognized that the desire to spread out the acquisition of these stocks over a number of periods (instead of just one period) moderates the rise in price. Obviously it makes a difference in so far as the pressure of demand on the industry supplying the stocks if, instead of trying to get these stocks in one or two periods, the buyer spreads out their acquisition over five or ten. Note, however, that even though the intention may be to reach the new level of stocks in, say, two periods, it will probably take more than two periods. This is so since the intention is to reach the new level in two periods *if* the price stays at the initial price—say $\bar{p}$ in Figure 3-3. When, however, the price increases, this makes the initial planned rate of acquisition unwise—or

---

[12]This model looks about as follows:

(a) $x(p) = d(p) - s(p)$

(b) $x(p) + \phi[D(p) - S] = d(p) - s(p) + \phi[D(p) - S] = 0$

(c) $\dfrac{dp}{dt} = f[x + \phi(x)]$

(d) $S(t) = S(t_0) + \displaystyle\int_t^{t_0} x[p(t)]\,dt = S(t_0) - \int_{t_0}^t x[p(t)]\,dt$

Here S is the size of the stock, and $\phi[D(p) - S]$ is the investment demand function.

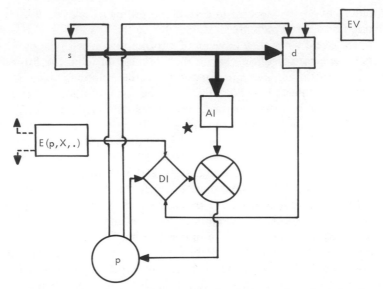

Figure 3-8. Supply-demand system showing the interaction of actual and desired inventories.

unprofitable—in the eyes of the stockholder, and so he reduces the rate at which he desires to accumulate stocks.

The place of inventories in price formation should probably be gone into in a little more depth. To begin with the reader can examine Figure 3-8.

In the figure s is flow supply; d, flow demand; p, price; AI, actual inventories; DI, desired inventories; Ep, expected price; and EV, various exogenous variables. As before, if $d \neq s$, then AI increases. At the junction ⓧ AI is compared with desired inventories, and if $AI > DI$ there is a downward pressure on the price. Where desired inventories are concerned, these are taken as a function of the expected value of variables such as price, sales, etc., in line with the discussion above. The reader should also note the arrow going from d to DI. What this indicates is a possible relationship between flow consumption and desired inventories of the type $DI = f(d)$. At the level of the individual firm such a relationship is known to exist, since inventories of both finished goods and raw materials are needed as insurance against interruptions of production.

The law of price movement implied by the discussion in the above paragraph has $p_t - p_{t-1} = \lambda(DI - AI)$, where $\lambda > 0$. A variant on this might be $p_t - p_{t-1} = \lambda[\Delta(DI) - \Delta(AI)]$, where $\Delta(DI) = k\Delta d$. In reality, of course, desired inventories are determined by a number of things; but in empirical and econometric work it is often difficult, if not impossible, to separate them out.[13]

In dealing with the present topic, it might be useful to introduce some expressions from macroeconomic theory. There are clearly both "speculative" and "transaction-precautionary" motives for holding inventories. The speculative motive has to do with the possible appreciation in value of inventories (and the chance to sell them at a profit); while the transaction-precautionary motive involves inventories to meet requirements of one type or another whose extent is not known in advance.

In the discussion above, the impression may have been gained that price movements are in general initiated in the stock market rather than the flow market. This is not necessarily true—the first step in a price adjustment can just as easily begin in the flow market. For instance, take a situation in which there is a sharp increase in industrial production (which is also a flow) leading to an increase in the flow demand for a raw material. This is represented by the flow demand curve shifting to the right, and the price increasing. We do not, however, talk of an equilibrium—as we would in the course in elementary economic theory—since we do not have an equilibrium in the stock market: stock demand is now less than stock supply. This situation is shown in (a), Figure 3-9, where the new flow demand curve is d'', and the new price p''.

---

[13] In the case of refined zinc, a price equation can be estimated employing the relationship

$$\Delta p = p_t - p_{t-1} = \lambda(k\Delta d_{t-1} - \Delta I_{t-1})$$

In this relationship d represents the demand for refined zinc to be used in current consumption or to add to inventories. The problem here is that the data dealt only with consumption, or "disappearance," and thus it was impossible to say just where it was going. The estimating equation then takes the form $p = \alpha_0 + \alpha_1 \Delta d_{-1} + \alpha_2 \Delta I_{-1}$, from which we have $\lambda = -\alpha_2, \alpha_1 = \lambda k$, and so $k = \alpha_2/\alpha_1$, with $\alpha_2 < 0, \alpha_1 > 0$. Using yearly data for the period 1953–68, and with t ratios in parentheses, we have

$$\Delta p = -0.885 + 0.0403 \, \Delta d_{t-1} - 0.195 \, \Delta I_{t-1} \quad \bar{R}^2 = 0.5339$$
$$(1.476) \qquad\qquad (3.13) \qquad\quad D.W. = 1.74$$

This equation is not particularly "strong." Somewhat more satisfactory was the following:

$$p' = 74.46 + 4.55\frac{d_{t-1}}{I_{t-1}} + 0.348\frac{\Delta d_t}{\Delta I_t} + 5.254D \quad \bar{R}^2 = 0.754$$
$$(4.70) \qquad (1.95) \qquad\quad (1.00) \quad D.W. = 1.89$$

The dummy variable D is unity for 1967 and 1968 (during and after the severe strikes in the United States) and zero at other times.

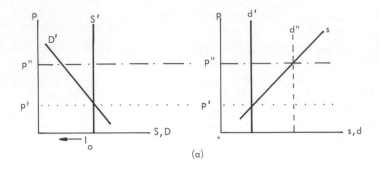

(a)

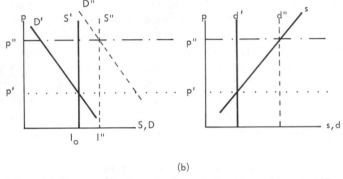

(b)

Figure 3-9. Some implications of a change in flow demand in a stock-flow model.

Some conjecture on what is taking place behind the scenes of the above figure is now in order. *If* expectations are constant, the increase in price has decreased the expected profitability of holding stocks. For example, if yesterday's price was 25, and speculative stocks were being held because it was thought that the price would increase to 50 or so in a few months, and today the price increases to 35, it might be reasoned that it is sensible to sell some of these stocks at 35. The argument here might be that the price of 35 is a fact, while the price of 50 is hypothetical and, in truth, may never be realized. The result would be some selling from inventories to meet at least a part of the new demand. The effect of the ensuing decrease in inventories would show up in the stock market by a shifting of the stock supply curve *(SI)* to the left. (This movement is not shown.)

At the same time, *if* there is a transaction-type motive operating in the system, an increase in flow consumption from d' to d'' would call for an increase in inventories from kd' to kd'', assuming a relationship of the type $DI = kd$. This would call for a shift in the stock demand curve—for instance, to D''. A situation of this type is shown in (b), Figure 3-9. What happens with this shift is that the price must increase until flow supply is greater than flow demand, and thus inventories can increase. This price increase must move the level of the price to greater than p'', since among other things this would arrest the decline in stocks. In (b), Figure 3-9, the new equilibrium is shown, with the final level of stocks greater than the initial. What the reader should notice here is that the stock demand is a function of flow demand, as well as a number of other variables.

The above scenario is only one of a number that are possible; but regardless of what the actual chain of events turned out to be, some of the elements in the above analysis would probably be present. At this point the reader is invited to introduce some new assumptions into the analyses offered in this section. For those desiring more background material on the stock-flow model, the work of Clower (1954) and the already mentioned textbook of Clower and Due (1973) and Bushaw and Clower (1957) should be examined.

THE PRICE OF CAPITAL SERVICES

In the latter part of the previous chapter the reader was introduced to the elementary theory of capital values. This material has, of course, a considerable amount of interest in its own right; but the reason it is presented in this book is because it is essential to the reader desiring more than a superficial knowledge of the raw material industries.

The price of capital services can also be called the rental price of a unit of capital, and is the amount that a firm would have to pay per period if it hired or rented a machine from someone, or if it borrowed money to buy a machine. It could also be called the implicit rental price, or opportunity cost, if the firm uses its own money to buy a machine, since this is what the firm would get in a perfect market if it loaned out its money.[14]

[14]The reader will also remember that in a *perfect market* there should be no difference between the return or yield obtainable from buying a machine or buying a financial asset. If, for example, a sum of money P_m is loaned out at an interest rate r, it gives after z periods $P = (1 + r)^z P_m$. If it is used to buy a machine which at arbitrary timepoints $t_1, t_2, t_3,$ and t_4 gives net yields $d_1, d_2, d_3,$ and d_4—where net yields are gross yields minus operating costs—then we must have in a perfect market

$$d_1(1 + r)^{z-t_1} + d_2(1 + r)^{z-t_2} + d_3(1 + r)^{z-t_3} + d_4(1 + r)^{z-t_4} = (1 + r)^z P_m$$

It can easily be seen that if both sides of this expression are divided by $(1 + r)^z$ we get the so called "present value rule." The value of an asset (in this case P_m) is equal to the discounted value of its net yields.

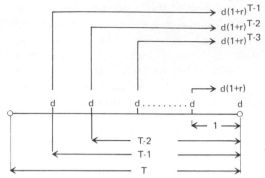

Figure 3-10. The growth of d by the end of the last period.

This price can be divided into two parts. The first is termed a depreciation or amortization cost; and the second an interest cost. For the purposes of this part of the analysis, the amortization cost can be viewed as a sum of money d that is set aside every period so that, after T years, it will suffice to pay for the machine. One way of getting this is as follows: if an amount d is put into a bank account at the end of the first year in which the machine was purchased, and the rate of interest was r, it grows to $d(1 + r)^{T-1}$ by the end of the T'th, or last, period. Similarly, d put into a bank at the end of the second period grows to $d(1 + r)^{T-2}$ by the end of the T'th period, and so on. Figure 3-10 presents this operation diagrammatically.

At the end of the last period, at time T, the amount set aside must equal the price of the equipment P_m, or

$$d(1 + r)^{T-1} + d(1 + r)^{T-2} + \cdots + d(1 + r) + d = P_m$$

If we now multiply both sides of this expression by $(1 + r)$ we get

$$d(1 + r)^T + d(1 + r)^{T-1} + \cdots + d(1 + r)^2 + d(1 + r) = P_m(1 + r)$$

We can now subtract the first expression from the second to get

$$d(1 + r)^T - d = P_m(1 + r) - 1$$

Solving this for d, or the depreciation cost, gives

$$d = \frac{rP_m}{(1 + r)^T - 1}$$

Now if we still use the assumption that we borrow a sum of money P_m, part of which is paid back by setting aside an amount d every year in a kind of "sinking fund," and at the end of the T'th year giving the lender these d's together with the interest they have accumulated, we see that we also have an interest cost of rP_m that must be paid the lender each year. This is so since we borrowed this P_m at the beginning of the first year and, according to the assumptions of the derivation above, it remains in our posession over T years. Before continuing, it should be pointed out again that nothing is changed in the present analysis if the sum P_m is borrowed or not. If we own a sum P_m and invest it in a machine, the depreciation and interest costs given above remain as opportunity costs. We now write as the price of capital services

$$P_s = \frac{rP_m}{(1 + r)^T - 1} + \frac{rP_m}{1} = \frac{P_m\, r\, (1 + r)^T}{(1 + r)^T - 1}$$

Readers familiar with financial mathematics have probably seen this expression before. If we use P_m to buy a T-year annuity, then we obtain P_s every year. This P_s can be obtained without difficulty from standard annuity tables.

It is possible that some readers will not find the assumptions on which the above derivation was based completely to their liking. If so, then they might be interested in the alternative derivation that will be presented now, and which uses the concept given in footnote 14: the return on a physical investment should be equal to the return on a financial asset in a perfect market. If we have P_m to lend out, and we take the return on the financial asset over T periods as $P_m(1 + r)^T$, and if we assume that we get a value P_s from the physical asset every period as a kind of net return, then we must have as above

$$P_s(1 + r)^{T-1} + P_s(1 + r)^{T-2} + \cdots + P_s(1 + r) + P_s = P_m(1 + r)^T$$

As was done earlier, this expression can be multiplied by $(1 + r)$, and from the result the above expression can be subtracted. After simplifying, we once again get $P_s = P_m r(1 + r)^T/[(1 + r)^T - 1]$. Thus we have obtained P_s without having to consider explicitly the amortization and interest costs d and rP_m. This is not necessarily a good thing, however, since an investor in a machine or industrial structure is often able to deduct d—either calculated as above or using some other method—from gross income for tax purposes. The logic is that investors must be allowed to recover the cost of their investment. But, algebraically, this poses no problems. Instead of P_s in the expression just above use $d + rP_m$ ($= P_s$). This gives

$$d(1 + r)^{T-1} + \cdots + d + rP_m(1 + r)^{T-1} + \cdots + rP_m = P_m(1 + r)^T$$

Table 3-1. Costs for a 60,000 Ton Smelter-Refinery, 1967

Cost item	Cost per ton of refined lead (in dollars)
Labor	33.00
Limestone	2.04
Coke	10.35
Electricity	1.65
Natural gas	3.20
Amortization and interest	17.16
Maintenance and repair	10.00
Insurance and taxes	5.01

Once again this expression can be multiplied by $(1 + r)$, and from the result the original expression can be subtracted. When simplified we obtain as before $d = rP_m/[(1+r)^T - 1]$. Moreover, this derivation brings out the simple but key fact that the borrower must pay P_s every period for a loan of P_m taken for T periods. Thus the scenario employed in the first part of this section need not be given any institutional significance.

The question that might be posed at the present time is whether this method is ever used in the "real world" to compute the price of capital services. The U.S. Bureau of Mines has made some cost investigations of various installations in the lead industry. In Table 3-1 costs have been given for a 60,000 ton smelter-refinery in 1967.

Amortization here is based on a plant capital cost of $10 million, amortized over a 15-year period at 6 percent. Since amortization plus interest charges are equal to P_s, we get:

$$P_s = \frac{rP_m (1 + r)^T}{(1 + r)^T - 1} = \frac{10,000,000 \times (0.06) (1 + 0.06)^{15}}{(1 + 0.06)^{15} - 1} = 1,030,000 \text{ (dollars)}$$

This is for the entire plant of 60,000 tons, and so dividing by 60,000 tons gives

$$P_s = \frac{1,030,000}{60,000} = 17.1 \text{ dollars/ton}$$

Although the U.S. Bureau of Mines is using the method derived earlier in this section to compute capital charges, it should be recognized that there are other methods—in fact, there are an infinity of them. Take another two-period situation in which P_m is borrowed to buy a machine. This time, however, at the end of the first period the lender receives d_1 as amortization, and rP_m as an interest charge. At the end of the second period an amortization payment of d_2 is made. The interest charge in this case will be on $P_m - d_1$, and thus is equal to $r(P_m - d_1)$. Obviously, many possibilities exist for d_1 and d_2. Take a situation in which $d_1 = d_2 = d'$. We then have in our habitual perfect market

$$d'(1 + r) + rP_m(1 + r) + d' + r(P_m - d') = P_m(1 + r)^2$$

If P_m is lent out for two years—e.g., used to buy a bond—at an interest rate r, then we have $P_m(1 + r)^2$ at the end of two years. If, on the other hand, P_m is invested in a machine which gives d' *plus* rP_m after the first year, and d' *plus* $r(P_m - d')$ after the second year, then d' must be such as to make these yields the same. To get the value of d' we once again multiply the above expression by $(1 + r)$, and subtract the result from the original expression. Simplifying gives $d' = P_m/2$. In other words, we have a straight line depreciation rule.

The reader interested in exercising his algebra can work with the three-year case. Here he would get $d' = P_m/3$, with interest charges rP_m at the end of the first period; $r(P_m - d'')$ at the end of the second; and $r(P_m - 2d')$ at the end of the third.

A great deal has been made in this section of the "perfect" market with its underlying assumption of certainty. This concept is more than a pedagogic convenience. As in the last part of Chapter 2, the point is that, at the prevailing rate of interest, an amount P_m can always be lent out to obtain, in T periods, $P_m(1 + r)^T$. If, however, another type of investment can be found that at timepoints $t_a, t_b, t_c, \ldots$ etc., gives yields of d_a, d_b, d_c, and so on, and if the sum

$$d_a(1 + r)^{T-t_a} + d_b(1 + r)^{T-t_b} + d_c(1 + r)^{T-t_c} + \cdots$$

is larger than $P_m(1 + r)^T$, then this investment should be made.

Uncertainty modifies some of the above discussion. With uncertainty lenders prefer money "sooner" rather than later, and thus they are not indifferent between different payback schemes having the same yield. This topic will not be taken up in the present book, but the reader interested in these matters will be pleased to learn that a growing and very complicated literature is at his service.

SOME ASPECTS OF ELEMENTARY INVESTMENT THEORY

The expression "investment" has already been used in this chapter in connection with the simple stock-flow model, and, to a certain extent, the first part of this section is a restatement of a part of that discussion, employing a different conceptual apparatus. As indicated earlier, stocks are considered an investment good; and changes in their level per time period is called investment. The most common investment goods, however, are real durable producers' goods held by firms, such as machines or structures.

To begin, it is necessary to distinguish between gross and net investment. Gross investment is a concept of investment, or addition to the stock of capital, that does not make any allowance for the using up of the stock of capital. Net investment then is gross investment *minus* depreciation. It is net investment that is the actual increase in the capital stock over a given time period. Disinvestment, on the other hand, is negative investment. Roughly speaking it is the running down of the capital stock.[15]

Although as yet there is no consensus within the world of academic economics as to what comprises a satisfactory theory of investment, it is clear that certain approaches are considered better than others. The idea of an optimal capital stock seems to be a necessary ingredient in discussions of this topic, where the optimal capital stock can be considered that capital stock which, when considering a certain output, will permit production at minimum cost. This, by itself, is undoubtedly a familiar problem to anybody who has taken a course or two in economics; however the matter is complicated by having to consider, at the same time, the *movement* to the optimal capital stock: do we want all our new equipment now; or some now and some later; or none now and all later? In other words, we have to face up to the same kind of problems that we introduced with the investment demand function in an earlier section. As the reader will soon notice, these are not difficult problems to treat as long as we do not require comprehensive answers that are capable of being summarized in a few equations or diagrams. Investment theory is, and will probably continue to be for some time, a part of economics where many of the key underlying issues effectively elude the pretensions of the model builder.

If we continue along this line we can imagine a situation in which we have a so-called optimal capital stock, and then our judgment of what the economic climate is to be changes. To be specific, we come to believe that the demand for the product we are producing will increase, and we will require additional production capacity. Put another way, for the production level that we are interested in attaining at some time in the future, our present capital stock is not optimal.

We then proceed to order new equipment. It may, of course, have

---

[15]A common definition of depreciation is the deterioration and obsolescence of plant and equipment, generally during a specified time period. (It is also a flow.) But consider the word "obsolescence." This implies that a piece of equipment could be in perfect working order, but still regarded as depreciated. In other words, depreciation is an economic as well as a technical or physical concept.

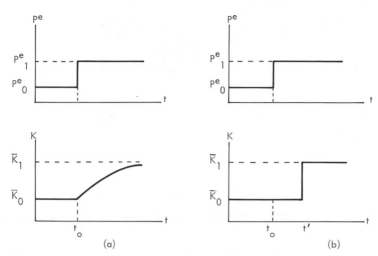

Figure 3-11. Movement to the new optimal capital stock given a change in price expectations.

taken some time for us to decide just how much we were going to order, and—at least—the rate at which the initial deliveries should take place. That is, we experience a so called "decision lag." Similarly, other lags may be important in the investment process: administrative lags of one type or another, delivery lags, etc.

A simple graphical device can be used to illustrate some of this. At time t_0 let us assume that the expected price of the product we are producing increases from P_0^e to P_1^e. With the cost of investment goods given, we come to the conclusion that our stock of capital should be increased from $\overline{K}_0$ (its present equilibrium level) to $\overline{K}_1$. We might then get one of the situations shown in Figure 3-11:

Note that in (b) of this figure there was a lag of $t' - t_0$ before the capital stock increased toward its new equilibrium value; however, as shown here, the movement to the new equilibrium—or optimal capital stock—takes place in one jump. On the other hand, in (a), there was no lag, but the capital stock moved up to the new equilibrium or optimal level in an asymptotic manner. At this point it should be emphasized that we are dealing with a demand, but it is not a demand for investment. It is the demand for a stock of capital.

We can now postulate an adjustment rule for the capital stock that goes as follows. The capital at the end of period t is equal to that at the end of period $t-1$ *plus* some percentage of the difference between the optimal capital stock and the capital stock at the end of period $t-1$. In symbols this amounts to, with optimal capital stock K^*

$$K_t = K_{t-1} + (1 - \lambda)(K^* - K_{t-1}) \qquad 0 < \lambda < 1$$

$(1 - \lambda)$ is the proportion achieved of the adjustment in any given period. A few computations with this relationship show that we get the same movement to the new equilibrium as illustrated in (a), Figure 3-9. Take the initial capital stock as 1000; the optimal or desired capital stock (K^*) as 2000; and $\lambda = \frac{1}{2}$. Then $K_1 = K_0 + \frac{1}{2}(K^* - K_0) = 1000 + \frac{1}{2}(2000 - 1000) = 1500$. Next $K_2 = K_1 + \frac{1}{2}(K^* - K_1) = 1500 + \frac{1}{2}(2000 - 1500) = 1700$; $K_3 = 1850$, and so on. What happens is that after some periods we get very close to 2000.[16]

[16] As in the discussion above, the optimal capital stock can be made a function of the expected price, or $K^* = f(P_t^e)$. Then we have

$$K_t = K_{t-1} + (1 - \lambda)[f(P_t^e) - K_{t-1}]$$

This can be written

$$K_t - K_{t-1} = \text{Investment } (i) = (1 - \lambda) [f(P_t^e) - K_{t-1}]$$

Instead of making the optimal capital stock a function of expected price, it could be made a function of output Y. For instance, $K^* = vY_t$. Thus

$$K_t - K_{t-1} = i = (1 - \lambda) [vY_t - K_{t-1}]$$

Investment depends positively upon output, and negatively upon the existing capital stock. This result should be familiar to those who have studied the simple acceleration principle. It should also be emphasized that not only is Y_t the real output in period t, but also the output that was expected for period t. The above equation is clearly a difference equation of the type $x_t - ax_{t-1} = b$, with the solution $b/1 - a + Aa^t$, for we have

$$K_t - K_{t-1} = (1 - \lambda)f(P_t^e) - (1 - \lambda)K_{t-1}$$

i.e.,

$$K_t - \lambda K_{t-1} = (1 - \lambda)f(P_t^e)$$

Thus we have $a = \lambda$ and $b = (1 - \lambda)f(P_t^e)$. To find A we set $t = 0$, and with $K_t = K_0$ at $t = 0$ we get

$$K_0 = \frac{(1 - \lambda)f(P_0^e)}{(1 - \lambda)} + A\lambda^0$$

This gives $A = K_0 - f(P_0^e)$. Thus the solution is

$$K_t = [K_0 - f(P_0^e)]\lambda^t + f(P_t^e)$$

This could have also been written $K_t = (K_0 - K^*) (\lambda)^t + K^*$, which gives the asymptotic movement shown in the lower diagram in (a), Figure 3-11.

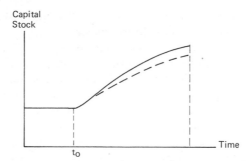

Figure 3-12. Capital stock adjustment: actual and desired.

This part of the discussion can be concluded by pointing out that our adjustment rule can be taken ex-ante or ex-post—that is, as desired or actual adjustment. If it is ex-ante then λ could be regarded as a parameter of "intent" for a firm. Otherwise it is a kind of descriptive parameter; and *if* it could be estimated from actual data then it would show how adjustment actually takes place. Graphically we might have the following situation shown in Figure 3-12.

The adjustment begins at time t_0. The solid line after that point in time could be the desired path of adjustment, while the dotted line is the actual adjustment.

One of the reasons for the mostly unsatisfactory handling of investment theory in the empirical and the theoretical literature is that the behavioral basis of the desired adjustment path has been difficult to pin down in other than highly general terms. At the beginning of 1975, for example, world planned investment expenditure in the copper industry came to $9.8 billion, according to an Engineering and Mining Journal survey. (Observe that this is not investment for 1975, but the total amount of money that firms in this industry have programmed for the purchase and installation of plant and equipment during 1975 *and* a number of years in the future.) In financial terms this is a great deal, and given the fact that, in 1975, the price of copper was much weaker than the price of many other metals, the feeling was that while expenditure plans would not be scaled down, construction schedules would be lengthened. No definite statement could be made, however, as to just how long these schedules would be lengthened.

ELEMENTARY PRODUCTION THEORY

The production process, as it will be treated in what follows, involves producing a single output by the use of several inputs, as inexpensively as possible. This process can be described employing a production function, which for the purpose of this section will be written $x = f(v_1, v_2, \ldots, v_n)$, where x is the output, and the v's are inputs.

In order to keep the exposition on as elementary a plane as possible, some graphical devices will be used to describe the production relationship; but first we will say something about the inputs. Instead of the above general form, we could write $q = f(K,L,M)$, where K is the input capital; L, labor; and M, raw materials. K consists of both machines and structures, but structures are usually assumed away by treating them as given and constant—as with land. Thus we have, in essence, a structure or structures containing some machines, and if we decide to increase the number of machines the assumption is that there is a place for them within the buildings and land that we have at our disposal.[17]

The input L is called the current input. It is also, at various times, called the variable input, although it may be just one among several variable inputs. Given a certain amount of capital that, for better or worse, has been purchased, is in place, and in many instances cannot be sold or used for anything else, production can often be varied by increasing or decreasing the amount of labor used with this capital. Economics textbooks generally regard this as a short-run measure; and in the event substantial changes in output are desired, additional capital is also used. This additional capital can involve a small addition to existing capacity; a facility that will be operated parallel to the existing one, and that could be identical to the existing facility; or a brand new plant, incorporating all the latest technology, that completely replaces the existing production unit.

This leaves M, or raw materials, and here we have a small problem. If the reader examines the literature, it is only rarely that we would see the production function written $q = f(K,L,M)$. Instead he would almost always find $q = f(K,L)$. The reason for this is the fundamental difference made in the input account between capital and labor, and raw materials. Capital and labor are called primary inputs, while raw materials are an intermediate input. When given in value terms, the production function $q = f(K,L)$ registers what we call *value added*. To see this, consider the following simple example.

A superman, employing his bare hands, digs out 100 bauxite rocks a day on a plot of land that he was given free of charge. These he sells to an aluminum company on an adjoining plot of land for one dollar a rock. The

---

[17]There are several reasons for putting a question mark next to this assumption. One of these reasons turns on investment, and how investment is categorized. It is often necessary to distinguish between "efficiency increasing" and "capacity augmenting" investment. The first of these mostly involves the substitution of capital for labor, with unchanged output. The second, which has to do with increasing the output, very often involves extra construction.

Table 3-2. Input Combinations for $q = 100, 200$; $q = K^{1/2}, L^{1/2}$

	$q = 100$				$q = 200$		
K	$K^{1/2}$	L	$L^{1/2}$	K	$K^{1/2}$	L	$L^{1/2}$
100	10	100	10	100	10	400	20
200	14.1	50	7.1	144	12	278	16.7
50	7.1	200	14.1	200	14.1	200	14.1
150	12.2	67	8.2	400	20	100	10

aluminum company, employing only some machines and labor, turns the bauxite rocks into aluminum. (By specifying that only machines and labor are used, it is meant that no electricity, coke, natural gas, oil, etc., are employed in the production process.) For the superman the production function is $q_b = g(K_b, L_b) = g(0, L_b) = 100$. Here there is no intermediate input; since the land is free there is no rent; and since he uses his bare hands we do not have to concern ourselves with a capital cost. His revenue is 100 dollars; and his value added is 100 dollars.[18]

As for the aluminum firm, let us say that with the 100 dollars worth of bauxite they buy, together with a certain amount of capital and labor, they produce 25 units of aluminum. It will also be assumed that this aluminum sells for 1100 dollars. What we should observe here is that only 1000 dollars of this 1100 is value added; the rest went for payment for the intermediate good bauxite. (Note that bauxite is an intermediate good in the production of aluminum, while aluminum is an intermediate good in the production of tennis rackets.) This 1000 dollars of value added is also the return to the primary factors (K and L) used by the firm to produce aluminum.[19]

---

[18]The first thing that should be noticed here is that the production function is written $q_b = g(K_b, L_b)$ instead of $q_b = g(L_b)$. The reason for this is that it might be so that our superman could use a pick, shovel, electric drill, and the like if he had them. For instance, we might have $q_b = aK_b + bL_b$ as the explicit form of the production function.

There is also the matter of the units for the production function. K_b would be in physical units (machines or machine hours) or monetary units; L would most likely be man-hours, although it could also happen that L was expressed in value terms—or for that matter simply as "men." q_b would also be in physical or value units per time period. In the example above we have 100 units of physical output (per day) selling for 1 dollar each, and therefore a monetary value for this output of 100 dollars/day. Value added has mostly monetary connotations, although in certain situations it is possible to put it in physical terms. For example, our 100 monetary units has already been shown to be equivalent to 100 bauxite units, and as will be shown below they also have an aluminum equivalent.

[19]22.73 units of capital together with 22.73 units of labor and 100 units of bauxite produce 25 units of aluminum that sell for 1100 dollars. This means a price of 44 dollars per unit of aluminum. 100 dollars goes to the producer of bauxite, and with an aluminum price of 44 dollars/unit this is the equivalent of 2.27 units of aluminum. The 1000 dollars value added is

The next step is to examine a typical production function of a type in which substitution between inputs is possible. Take one where we have $q = f(K,L) = K^\alpha L^{1-\alpha} = K^{1/2} L^{1/2}$. Here we will not concern ourselves with the units for K and L, but concentrate on the computational aspects of the relationship. In Table 3-2 if we begin by arbitrarily choosing outputs of 100 and 200, it is possible to calculate various combinations of inputs that will give us this output.

The reader is advised at this point to extend Table 3-2 by a few values, and to construct another table—say, for a value of $q = 144$. We can now take the above figures and use them to construct a production map or isoquant system as shown in Figure 3-13.

Next we want to look at a situation where we have a given amount of capital, and output is varied by varying the current input. (Of course, any

---

divided up between—or *imputed* to—the two primary factors K and L. To keep things simple let us say that each gets 500 dollars.

Now let us look at this situation in input–output form. Consider a case in which we have only bauxite and aluminum in our economy, with bauxite the intermediate good and aluminum the final good. Using the above figures we have the following, where F is final demand; T, total demand; and B and A signify bauxite and aluminum.

	B	A	F	T			B	A	F	T
B	a_{BB}	a_{BA}	F_B	T_B		B	0	100	0	100
A	a_{AB}	a_{AA}	F_A	T_A	=	A	0	0	1100	1100
K	K_b	K_a				K	0	500		
L	L_b	L_a				L	100	500		

We can now consider the production function for aluminum:

$$q_a' = h(K_a, L_a; M) = 25 \text{ units of aluminum} = \text{gross output}$$

$$q_a = z(K_a, L_a) = 25 - \text{payment for bauxite} = 25 - 2.27 = 22.73 = \text{value added}$$

We can also consider the outputs in value terms:

$$q_a' = h(K_a, L_a; M) = 1100 \text{ dollars of gross output}$$

$$q_a = z(K_a, L_a) = 1100 - \text{payment for bauxite} = 1000 = \text{value added}$$

It can be seen that $q_a' = q_a$ + Payment for Intermediate Product. The student of macroeconomics can also learn something here. The GNP of this "economy" is 500 + 500 + 100 = the Total Payment to Primary Factors. Also, if we were interested in a macroeconomic production function it would have $F(K_a + K_b, L_a + L_b) = 1100 = $ Value added in the entire economy. The entries in the input–output table are all in money values, which means that we show the payments to the primary factors, and not their physical amounts.

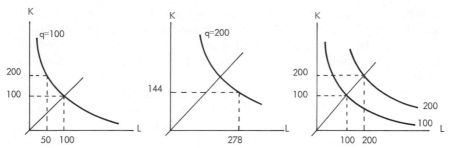

Figure 3-13. Representative isoquants for the production function $q = K^{1/2} L^{1/2}$.

time there is an increase in output it should also be understood that the input of raw materials and other variable inputs is also increasing.) Begin, for simplicity's sake, with a completely empty factory, and increase the input of labor. At first there is hardly any increase in output, which might be explained by the fact that the efficient operation of a factory requires many functions to be performed at the same time, and not just a few people working directly with machines—although this is the most important function. But then, as we put in more personnel, the machines or work stations find themselves with crews of optimal size, lights go on and off when necessary, repairs are made without delay, the payroll goes in on time, etc.

If we continue to increase the labor and other variable inputs we can probably continue to raise output. Small low-productivity jobs such as helping to move output away from the machines can be found, but, given the design of the factory, as well as the composition of the machinery, there

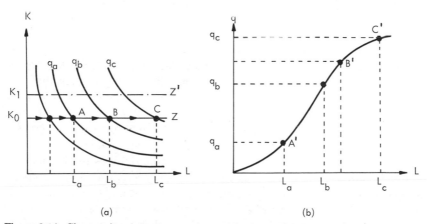

Figure 3-14. Changes in production as the variable factor L (and some other variable factors, such as raw materials) is increased.

is little room for sizable increases in output just by increasing some of the variable inputs. This situation is expressed in Figure 3-14, where K_0 represents the amount of capital (or size of the factory), while labor is increased along the line K_0Z. Corresponding points are noted by A and A', B and B', and so on.

Next we will examine the concepts average product and marginal product. These can be taken from (b), Figure 3-14. The average product of labor is defined as $AP_L = q/L$. This is shown in (a), Figure 3-15. As we go from x to y we have an increase in AP_L. The reason for this is that q_y/L_y is greater than q_x/L_x. The reader should now explain why AP_z is less than AP_y.

The marginal product of labor is defined $MP_L = \partial q/\partial L \approx \Delta q/\Delta L$. This is the slope of the TP curve. In (b), Figure 3-15, the marginal product is shown to reach a maximum at x, which means that the slope of the TP curve is steepest at x. The reader should now elaborate on the situation at z, in particular comparing the size of the MP and the AP. A point of interest in (b), Figure 3-15, is the situation at y. Here the marginal product and average product are equal. If the reader draws a straight line from the origin out to y he will notice that q_y/L_y is equal to the slope of this line $\Delta q/\Delta L$ at the point y.

The next topic involves going from curves showing a physical product to cost curves. In doing this we can continue the discussion of cost curves that was begun in Chapter 2. The total product curve that was shown in Figures 3-14 and 3-15 was generated by increasing labor (and perhaps some other variable inputs) in the presence of a fixed amount of capital. Corresponding to this fixed amount of capital—which, for example, might be shown by K_0 in Figure 3-14—we have a fixed cost. This is shown by FC_1 in (a), Figure 3-16.

The variable cost is somewhat more complicated. This consists of the cost of labor as we move out along the line K_0Z in (a), Figure 3-14 *plus* the cost of the other variable inputs (raw materials, electricity, etc.). If we take these other inputs to be directly proportional to the output, then the *shape* of the variable cost curve is determined by the labor input. As an example let us say in (a), Figure 3-14, that $q_a = 100$, $K_0 = 100$, $L_a = 100$, and the input of raw materials is also 100. Now let us move to an output of $q_b = 200$. K_0 is still 100, raw materials 200 (since the input of raw materials is taken as directly proportional to output, and when output doubles the input of raw materials doubles), and $L_b = 250$. In other words, with capital constant, labor had to be more than doubled to double output. Continuing in this vein, as we move out along K_0Z it becomes more and more difficult to raise output just by increasing the variable inputs. For instance, to get another

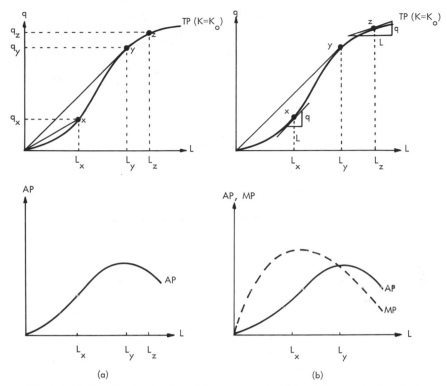

Figure 3-15. Graphical derivation of the average product and the marginal product.

increase in output of 100 it might be necessary to increase the input of labor to $L = 535$, which is an increase of 285. Thus the variable cost curve, which assumes a fixed price for the variable factors, turns up in the manner shown in (b), Figure 3-16. At this juncture the reader should compare (b), Figure 3-16, with the top diagram in (a), Figure 3-15. This latter diagram shows the difficulty in raising *physical* output with no change in the capital input. Figure 3-16 (b) translates this situation into monetary terms. Initially, when the machines were largely unmanned, increases in production were expensive; but as optimal-size crews for machines—together with the necessary supporting personnel—became available (in the stretch $s-t$) it was possible to get large increases in output with relatively small increases in VC.

The next curve, shown in (c), Figure 3-16, is the total cost curve. This is just the vertical sum of the two previous curves. A more interesting concept is the *Average Total Cost Curve,* which is obtained by dividing the total cost by the physical quantity. When $q = q_t$ in (c), Figure 3-16, $ATC_t =$

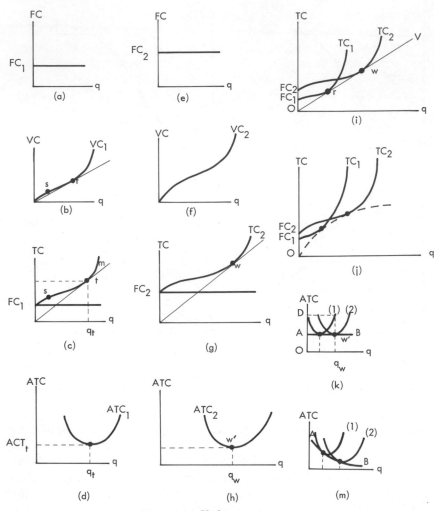

Figure 3-16. Various cost curves.

TC_t/q_t. What the reader should do now is verify the shape of the ATC curve. For instance, if he takes points s and m, he should verify that at both these points the ATC is greater than ATC_t.

In Figures 3-16 (e) to 3-16 (h) we have the same thing as in the first four diagrams. The difference is that we have a larger input of capital (e.g., a larger plant) and corresponding to this a larger fixed cost—FC_2 as compared to FC_1. What should be noticed now is the average total cost curve ATC_2, and the fact that its minimum point is further to the right than the minimum point of the ATC curve for a smaller installation.

The next, and most important, thing for the purpose of this section is to plot all the total cost curves on the same diagram, and to look at the *envelope* of these curves, where the envelope is the curve that touches each and intersects none.[20] In the present example we have only two cost curves, but we could easily have had a large number of curves, and as the discussion proceeds the reader might like to draw in another curve, in particular one with a value of FC between FC_1 and FC_2.

We now can examine OV, which is the envelope of the total cost curves. If, in (i), Figure 3-16, we take a point such as w, which is on OV, and where the total cost and production is TC_w and q_w, and if we perform the operation TC_w/q_w, we get a point that is a minimum cost point on some average total cost curve. (As the reader already knows, it is the average total cost curve derived from TC_2.) For example, a corresponding point would be w' in (k), Figure 3-16. In (k), Figure 3-16, we have reproduced the curves in (d) and (b), Figure 3-16, but our principal interest in these curves is their minimum points. These minimum points, such as w', can be calculated from the envelope OV, and lie on the *long run cost curve AB*.

The line AB in (k), Figure 3-16, is also an envelope. It is the envelope of the average total cost curves, and it shows the minimum point on all of these curves. To be more precise, it shows the minimum cost at which any output can be produced. For instance, q_w can be produced at cost OA. In fact, given the situation in (i) and (k), Figure 3-16, any output can be produced for a unit cost of OA: it is simply a matter of building the right size plant. If we want to produce q_w, for example, then we should build a plant corresponding to FC_2—that is to say, whose fixed cost is FC_2. What we have here is the *constant cost case*. In connection with this case the reader should observe that if the desire is to produce q_w, and the plant available is not the one corresponding to FC_2, but instead the smaller plant FC_1, then the average total cost per unit of q_w is OD.

[20]Let $f(x_1,x_2,y) = 0$ be an implicit function of x_1 and x_2, with the form of the function depending on y. For instance x_1 could be output, and x_2 cost; while y is an "index" of capital employed, or plant size. x_1 and x_2 describe a curve in the x_1,x_2 plane, with a different curve for each y. For example, in (i) and (j), Figure 3-16, we have $f(TC,Q,FC,) = 0$, with FC taking on the values FC_1 and FC_2, and our being able to draw a curve for each of these values. The envelope of this family of curves is itself a curve with the property that it is tangent to each member of the family. The equation of the envelope is obtained by taking the partial derivative of $f(x,y,k)$ with respect to k, and eliminating k from the two equations:

$$f(x,y,k) = 0$$
$$f_k(x,y,k) = 0$$

From the implicit function theorem we know that for a solution to be possible we must have $f_{kk} = 0$ and $f_x f_{yk} - f_u f_{xy} = 0$.

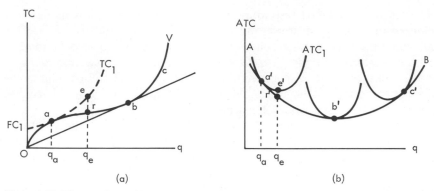

Figure 3-17. The envelopes of total cost (*OV*) and average total cost (*AB*) curves when there are first decreasing and then increasing costs.

One item remains before we go to some applications. This concerns the shape of the envelope *OV,* and, by extension, the envelope *AB:* must these be straight lines? The answer, of course, is that, *a priori,* it is impossible to say just how *OV*—and therefore *AB*—will appear. As already pointed out in Chapter 2, many manufacturers seem to feel that their long-run cost curve is nearly flat—that is, they can build a larger plant that will enable them to produce a larger output at the same unit cost as the existing plant. It is clear, however, that in many industries larger plants mean lower unit costs.[21] In this case we would have a situation of the kind shown in (j) and (m), Figure 3-16. Here we have the *decreasing cost case.* Once again *AB* can be labeled a long-run cost curve.

Another possibility, and one that many readers are undoubtedly familiar with, is the long-run cost curve that first decreases and then increases. This is shown in (b), Figure 3-17, while the envelope of total cost curves from which it is derived is shown in (a), Figure 3-17.

[21] Hufbauer (1966) has looked at the relation of plant size to unit cost for some plants manufacturing synthetic materials. His findings are roughly as follows: when the plant size doubled, the capital cost for styrene decreased by about 29.3 percent, polypropylene and butadiene by 21.6 percent, ethylene by 20.5 percent, and so on. In fact, on the basis of the material presented in Hufbauer's book, it is easy to come to the conclusion that in this industry there are indefinite economies of scale. Similarly, when comparing so-called "Mini Steel Plant Technology" with the technology of integrated steel plants, the miniplants seem to give constant returns to scale, while the integrated plants exhibit for the most part increasing returns to scale. The steel industry will be taken up in Chapter 7. In the text, the discussion, for the most part, has been carried on without using the expression "economies of scale." For the purpose of this book, economies of scale signify decreasing unit costs as the amount of capital being used increases. Likewise, constant unit costs as the amount of capital increases would mean constant returns to scale, if the assumption is also that the input of labor increased in the same proportion.

In this figure only one total cost curve, TC_1, has been shown. What the reader should note, and if possible verify, is that ATC_1 can be derived from TC_1; that point a' corresponds to point a; and point e' to point e; and that it is at e' and not a' that we have the minimum cost for operating the plant whose costs are represented by FC_1. Virtually the same situation prevails in the decreasing cost case, and is shown in (m), Figure 3-16. Thus if the desire is to produce q_a in (b), Figure 3-17, a plant with a fixed cost of FC_1 is built that is operated at a point where the unit cost of production is higher than the minimum unit cost for that size of plant, which is at e'. Furthermore, if the desire is to produce q_e, this can be done at a lower cost than that realizable by building a plant corresponding to FC_1 (or ATC_1). In particular the plant that should be built is the one tangent to the AB curve at r', or whose TC curve is tangent to the envelope OV at r. The reader interested in demonstrating his fluency with the concepts treated in this section can draw in the relevant TC and ATC curves.

AN INTRODUCTION TO SOME INDUSTRIAL
RAW MATERIALS

4

Many of the theoretical points taken up in the previous chapter are also treated below, though in a much simplified form. In addition, a number of topics that will be discussed more intensively in later chapters are examined here.

Questions involving long-run pricing, investment, returns to scale, inventories, substitution, the terms of trade of LDCs, etc., are reviewed in the context of specific natural resources, and the industries for obtaining and processing these resources. It should be stressed that the reader need not have digested the technical material in the previous chapter in order to come to grips with the information presented in this chapter. In fact, after a reading or two he should have a reasonable intuitive grasp of the kind of problems that the technical material in this book is attempting to investigate; and, even more important, should understand that there is a certain range of issues that automatically crops up when the subject of natural resources or primary commodities is raised. Contrary to much published opinion, these issues are not very difficult to comprehend.

The resources treated below are tin, zinc, nickel, manganese, lead, aluminum, and copper. The discussion of each of these is, of necessity, brief; but, as mentioned above, we find that, regardless of the resource, the economic problems are similar, and for the most part so are the solutions to these problems. The final section in this chapter consists of a largely nontechnical discussion of optimal resource extraction. The exposition employs a simple numerical example that is generalized in Appendix C of this book.

THE WORLD TIN MARKET

The world tin market offers some interesting insights into the manner in which simple supply–demand interaction determines the price of an important industrial input. The main producers of tin are Malaya, Bolivia, Thailand, and Indonesia. Important deposits are also located in Nigeria,

Australia, and what at one time was called the Sino-Soviet Bloc. The processing of tin is also limited to a small community. There are large smelters in Malaya and Singapore, the United Kingdom, Belgium, Holland, and the United States, and a few smaller ones in such places as Thailand and Nigeria. The United Kingdom is the principal smelter of Bolivian ores, while Indonesian tin is smelted in Malaysia. On the consumption side, the United States is the big factor, taking, on the average, about one-third of the tin metal produced in the non-centrally-planned countries. Where use is concerned, tin is always found in alloy form, with its main use being tinplate. It is from tinplate that such things as tin cans are made.

The history of the tin price has been largely the history of trying to keep this price above a certain level, or "stabilized," to use the prevailing euphemism; but a number of problems have been encountered by various practitioners of the stabilizing arts. There has been a considerable weakening in the amount of vertical integration in this market over the past 10 or 15 years, and, in addition, the primary producing countries now display widely varying scales of production and costs. Malaya, for instance, has very low costs, while those of Bolivia and Nigeria are relatively high. This kind of situation works against producers attempting to design a common price policy. The demand side of the market, together with technological progress, has also created some difficulties for suppliers. To begin, the natural rate of growth of demand for tin has been quite slow relative to that of most other minerals. Then, too, although very large increases in the price of tin metal results in only minute increases in the price of tin cans, the producers of tin cans have worked diligently to substitute plastics and aluminum for tin, or even to employ "tin-less" tin cans made of steel. On this point it can be recorded that the demand for tin from the British tinplate industry fell between 1948 and 1961, even though the consumption of preserved foods doubled over this period.

We can now examine some price movements in this market. After World War I there was an oversupply of tin, with the price of tin dropping to £ 170/ton. The main producers at that time, in Malaya and the then Dutch East Indies, therefore decided to practice some sales restriction and, as a result, 20,000 tons were purchased in 1921 and stored by the representatives of these producers. This metal was not returned to the market until 1923, and even then it was reinjected at a rate of only 1000 tons per month, thus permitting maintenance of the £240/ton price that had been reached toward the end of 1923.

With the strong upswing in the international business cycle that took place in 1925 and 1926, tin prices climbed rapidly and a great deal of new capacity came into existence. The industry as a whole became much more capital intensive, particularly as new installations employing the most advanced techniques entered into full production, and the potential supply of tin increased to a level regarded as unsatisfactory by many producers. It was while producers were discussing this situation that the great depression began gathering momentum, and tin prices zoomed downward. In February 1930 the Tin Producers' Association elected to resort to a compulsory output-limiting scheme.

The International Tin Control Scheme of 1931 involved a simple cartel formed of Bolivian, Malayan, Nigerian, and Dutch East Indies producers, and British producing and financial interests. Their mode of operation was simply to restrict output until they brought about the price they wanted. Whether such a scheme would work today is a moot question, since the employment-restricting effects of such an action might possibly provide some traumatic experiences for many modern governments. At that time, however, it was the custom for officialdom to regard such things as unemployment with a certain amount of detachment, and they were generally sympathetic to the need to prevent producers from undercutting each other: not only would this cause consumers to accumulate large inventories of tin that would hold down prices once the upswing came, but it could create a tradition of low prices that conceivably might reflect on share prices.

As was *not* the case with most of the postwar price-regulating shemes, output restriction enabled the price to be held up almost to the desired level even during some of the darkest days of the great depression. Moreover, given the worldwide shortage of venture capital during this period, there was no building up of production capacity. With the onset of the armament programs that began in Europe in the late 1930s, it was possible to phase out the output restriction program. Between August and September 1938 the price of tin rose by £113 to £398/ton, and, although it could not maintain this level, it was clear to one and all that the days of low-price tin were over for a while. In the circumstances, previously stated intentions to stabilize the price between £200 and £230/ton were conveniently forgotten.

The price of tin was mostly fixed during World War II, but discussions were already under way as to what the postwar price should be and what measures should be taken to correct deviations from this price. The proposal of both the producers and the U.S. government was a buffer stock whose management would buy tin when the price became too low and sell when the price was too high. Difficulty arose, however, when it came time to fix the minimum price: the U.S. government wanted a price of £520/ton, while producers were thinking in terms of £880/ton. Initially a certain amount of haggling took place, but, in the end, the Cold War and the Korean War solved the problems of both sides: when the postwar recession came in 1948 the U.S. strategic stockpile absorbed the excess production of the industry, while the Korean War (and the so-called Korean Boom) created a situation of excess demand on the market, and drove the price to new highs.

Somewhere during this period a buffer stock of 15,000 tons was agreed upon, and a floor price of £730/ton established. The level of the floor price, as well as the rules of operation of the buffer stock management, were formalized in a new Tin Agreement. It was specified, among other things, that there was a lower range of prices in which the buffer stock manager must enter the market as a buyer; a middle range where he was to remain inert; and a higher range where he must sell. If prices fell too low, output restriction was allowed. Interestingly enough, no great wrangle was made over what action to take against excessively high prices. To begin, the producers had nothing against high prices; and the main consumers figured that during a major business cycle upturn they could afford high prices. Besides, high profits and prices paved the way for a high level of investment, which in turn tended to increase supply in such a manner as to force down prices in the future.

Recession came to the industrial world in 1958, and tin prices responded by falling. The buffer stock management, as should have been expected, eventually had to stop buying due to a shortage of funds, and output restrictions came into play. These were employed during 1958–60, being discontinued only after the business cycle turned up. It was now time for the German "miracle" to move into high gear, and the Japanese "miracle" to start picking up speed, and on the tin market both prices and production lunged upward. In line with this situation there was considerable investment in new capacity, and a great deal of existing capacity was modernized. In addition, in 1964, the General Services Administration management agreed not to make large sales of tin without entering into consultation with the Tin Council.

Prices began to slip again in 1966, with the decline being given an additional impetus by a slight recession in the United States and Europe in 1967. This small downturn was quickly reversed, but now production capacity whose construction had been initiated in the previous upturn was coming into operation, and the industry definitely was capable of producing more than was required for current consumption. As a result, the recovery lasted only a few months before prices turned down again. This time export controls were applied without delay, and removed only when industrial output in Europe and the United States was accelerating rapidly enough to cause a slight rise in price.

In 1969–70 production moved up to exceed all previous levels, but by 1971–72 it was clear that the growth in production was of sufficient magnitude to dampen the large increases in price that had been expected. Toward the end of 1972 prices began drifting downward, and in early 1973 export controls were once again called upon to restore the situation; but this time—under the influence of the large production capacity that had been built up during previous booms, as well as the high level of tin inventories that were being held around the world—prices were unable to stage a full recovery. It was only under the spell of the 1973 war in the Middle East that the market was resuscitated and prices soared to new all-time highs. This situation did not last for long, however, since much of the increased buying this time was prompted by fears about future supplies that were founded on hallucinations rather than facts. When this situation was finally understood by the major consumers, the price of tin began to fall.

The price has not gone down at the rate experienced by most of the other metals, but producers are not optimistic. In 1974 the production of primary tin fell to 179,400 tons compared to a production level of 184,900 tons in 1973 and 190,000 tons in 1972. Consumption, on the other hand, fell from 212,400 tons in 1973 to 200,300 tons in 1974, with the difference between consumption and production accounted for by releases from inventory. The matter of the *real* price of tin is also of interest to us at this point, where the real price is the market price deflated in such a way as to give an indication of the purchasing power of the commodity. The deflator most commonly used is a price index constructed from the price of industrial and/or consumer goods in the countries with which the tin producing countries trade, and the market price is simply divided by this index. The index should be adjusted to take into account changes in the exchange rate.

According to Barkman (1974) the real price of tin during the period 1954–61 was less than it was during the middle 1930s. The real price then hit a new high in 1965, but began to decline soon after. This decline was reversed after a short time, but has since continued. If we want to compare the change in the monetary price with the change in the real price between 1966 and 1973, we see that the increase in the monetary price was 58 percent, while the increase in the real price was about 3 percent. For a deeper insight into these and other matters the reader is referred to Barkman (1974) and Desai (1966).

ZINC

The next two sections in this chapter will take a brief look at what was happening on the world markets for zinc and nickel up to the early 1970s.

Zinc is, in most respects, a typical industrial raw material, and in both its production and marketing resembles most of the other metals that have been talked about in this book or that will be taken up later. More than a million tons of zinc, or slightly less than a third of total world consumption, is used for protective coatings on steel. These coatings are applied by hot-dip galvanizing (which is the most widely used process), spraying, shepardizing, and also in the form of zinc-rich paints containing more than 90 percent metallic zinc dust. A comparison of the growth of zinc with some other metals is shown in Table 4-1.

The use of zinc has been expanding rapidly of late because of the attention being given to corrosion prevention and protecting of steel. At the same time, the zinc industry has recognized that it will have to face increasing competition from alternative methods of protecting steel, as well as from the development of rust-resisting steels, the use of aluminum (which does not rust) and of nonmetallic materials.

The cost of zinc in a coated article would seem to range from 5 to 20 percent of the material cost of the article, and thus changes in the price of zinc have only a small effect on the cost of the final product. However, the cost of zinc can be an important component in the total finishing cost, and in the medium run can influence whether zinc is chosen as a finishing material. Very high zinc prices would undoubtedly cause a reversion to inexpensive protective systems such as painting. However, here it must be remembered that the cost of labor and materials used in the maintenance of painted steelwork has shown a tendency to increase much faster than the price of zinc.

In the United States, die casting has replaced galvanizing as the principal market for slab zinc. In this use, zinc is found mostly in the form of various alloys—in particular die-cast alloys containing approximately 4 percent aluminum. Because of its mechanical strength, corrosion resistance, acceptance of chromium plating and enameling, etc., zinc allows these alloys to be cast in various complex shapes that are particularly useful in automobiles, household appliances, and business equipment. The principal rival to zinc in this area is probably plastics. The reader should take particular note of this point, since zinc is one of those metals whose known reserves seem rather limited, and the newer high-quality engineering plastics are capable of replacing a great deal of zinc. For instance, of 400,000 tons of die-cast zinc used by the U.S. automobile industry in 1965, about half could be replaced by existing plastics or plastic-plated materials. Presently available nylon or acetal plastics are about ⅙ the weight of zinc, cost less per unit of volume, and also have better paintability—which is especially important where a consumer durable like automobiles is concerned. The big problem for plastics just now, however, is their large use of oil. Not only has the price of oil increased very rapidly, but future price increases could be equally as steep.

Table 4-1. World Consumption and Growth Rates of Some Typical Metals

Material	Consumption (thousands of metric tons)					Compound growth rates		
	1900	1938	1950	1960	1965	1900 –1938	1950 –1960	1960 –1965
Zinc	455	1,276	1,828	2,454	3,333	2.8	3.0	6.3
Lead	851	1,423	1,683	2,212	2,725	1.4	2.8	4.3
Copper	483	1,631	2,619	3,828	4,853	3.3	3.9	6.1
Steel[a]	29	113	191	345	456	3.7	6.0	5.8
Aluminum	7	437	1,339	3,248	4,777	11.5	9.2	10.1

[a] Million tons.
Source: International Lead and Zinc Study Group.

Determining the effect of price on the demand for zinc to be used in die castings presents some interesting problems in economic theory. To begin, it is clear that from time to time high prices have reduced the demand for zinc by die casters, but not immediately. There is usually a lag of several years between deciding to change a die and its appearance on the production line, depending upon the complexity of the equipment, the amount of new tooling required, and whether other components of the particular system are influenced by the change. The key thing here would seem to be the trend price. If manufacturers were to become convinced that the long-run price of substitutes such as plastics and aluminum were to increase at a much lower rate than zinc, then there is undoubtedly room for a great deal of substitution, and provision for this substitution will be noticeable in the designs for forthcoming plant and equipment.

It is also true that the metal cost of the zinc in a finished die casting represented, until fairly recently, about one-third of the manufacturing cost. In most industrial countries, however, labor and other relevant costs have been rising at least as fast as the price of zinc, and so, from this point of view, zinc retains its attractiveness. In addition, recent technical advances are making it possible to reduce the thickness of various parts, which means a decrease in the percentage of manufacturing cost attributable to zinc. The principal exception to this situation is to be found in the United States where the extensive use of automation and labor-saving equipment has tended to keep the cost of zinc a higher proportion of variable costs.

The zinc market is, of course, highly oligopolistic. Two type of prices—which will be taken up in detail in the next chapter—are of interest here. The first are so called *producers' prices,* and these are determined as follows: in Europe the major producers simply meet and fix a price; while in the United States the producers—or their representatives—apply to the Federal Price Commission for permission to charge a certain price. (In both cases here we are talking about the price of the metal, and not the ore. There is a fixed relationship, via costs, between the price of ore and the price of metal.) On the other hand there is a kind of free market price quoted on both the London Metal Exchange and the New York Commodity Exchange. Again, this is a quote dealing with zinc metal and not ore. Price movements are highly correlated between these latter two markets, at least as far as the direction of movement is concerned; but during a considerable part of the postwar years the price has tended to be somewhat lower in London than in New York.

This is an important point and deserves a few clarifying remarks, since there is almost a balance between production and consumption of metal in North America (as well as a surplus of ore), while Western Europe is a net importer of both zinc metal and ore. A partial explanation for the lower price is to be found in the substantial movement of zinc from East to Western Europe, in particular since the 1960s. This movement was apparently a response to the high zinc prices that began to appear after the arrival of American forces in Vietnam; and once these supplies began arriving, they undoubtedly had a dampening effect on prices. It should also be mentioned that statistical material covering these movements seems to contain certain deficiencies: a year that shows a deficit of 100- or 150,000 tons was probably a year in which there was close to a balance on the market.

There is also the matter of the U.S. strategic stockpile. Beginning in 1946, a situation began in the United States in which there was an excess supply of both raw and processed zinc; but, at the same time, the U.S. government began extensive stockpiling of these and other materials. Among other things, it absorbed sufficient zinc to hold up the price, and perhaps helped set the pattern for the generally higher prices noted in the United States as compared to Europe in that it conditioned zinc consumers to higher prices.

NICKEL

Like zinc, nickel is an extremely important raw material. Its main use is in stainless steels, and it has major applications in the superalloys that are found in jet engines, nuclear reactors, and electronic equipment. Substitutes for nickel include chromium, manganese, molybdenum, cobalt, vanadium, and plastics; but, in fact, in many of its uses nickel is almost irreplaceable.

There are two principal types of nickel ore: sulphides and oxides. The largest concentration of sulphide ores is found deep underground in Canada. These ores contain up to 3 percent nickel, plus copper and small quantities of other metals. Oxide ores are formed by weathering or "lateralization," are created near the surface, and can be worked by open-pit methods. They are mostly to be found in tropical and subtropical areas such as New Caledonia, Cuba, the Philippines, and Indonesia. Approximately 70 percent of the world's current nickel output comes from sulphide ores, but about three-fourths of the world's known reserves are oxides. At the present growth rate of consumption of 6 percent a year, known reserves are considered sufficient to last for between 75 and 100 years.

Somewhat more than 50 percent of the world's supply of primary nickel is produced in the developed countries; 28–30 percent in the centrally planned countries; and the remainder in less developed countries.

About two-thirds of the world nickel supply comes from Canada, and almost another quarter from New Caledonia. Minor producers of some importance are the United States, Australia, and South Africa; and the centrally planned economies are, on the whole, self-sufficient. Smelting is less concentrated than mining, with about 45 percent of the world smelter capacity in Canada, 25 percent in Western Europe (using mostly Canadian and New Caledonian ores), 15 percent in Japan (with all ore imported), and about 10 percent in the United States (where about 50 percent of all ores smelted come from Canada).

As to be expected, most nickel consumption is by the major industrial countries. The major consumers are the United States, Japan, the Federal Republic of Germany, the United Kingdom, France, Italy, and Sweden in that order. On the producing side, a few large companies play a major role. Predominant among these are the International Nickel Company of Canada (INCO), which handles approximately 50 percent of production; Falconbridge Nickel Mines Ltd., which has about 10 percent; the French-owned Société Le Nickel, which controls almost all of New Caledonian production; and the Hanna Mining Co., which controls all U.S. nickel production and is also a major iron ore producer. Some figures on the world mine production of nickel, and nickel reserves, are given in Table 4-2.

The pricing of nickel shows a marked similarity to the pricing of zinc. Primary nickel is sold by producers or their agents at prices established by the producers and only infrequently changed. As with zinc, they are called producers, or posted, prices, and they refer to certain standard grades sold by the major companies. What might be called the "nickel content prices" of the various categories of the metal differ somewhat. For instance, the price of nickel contained in ferronickel is about 5 percent below that of pure nickel (or nickel cathodes). There is, in addition, a small open or "free" market for the sale of secondary nickel, as well as primary nickel. The primary nickel found on the free market often originates in the Soviet Union and the other centrally planned countries, and is mostly bought by merchants or dealers who resell at prices that depend on the basic pattern of supply and demand. In 1969–70 the supply of nickel from the main producers was often far less than current demand and, as a result, there was considerable recourse to the "free" market. On this market prices commanded a large premium over the producer price. In 1969, during the big strike in the Canadian mines, the British Steel Corporation doubled its purchases from the free market, paying prices that were six or seven times the producer price.

Nickel consumption in the principal market economies rose at a rate of 6.2 percent/year from 1947 to 1969; while consumption in the centrally planned countries increased by about 9.5 percent a year during this period.

Table 4-2. World Land-Based Nickel Reserves; and World Mine Production of Nickel

| Area | Estimated reserves 1970 | Mine production[a] | | |
		1959–1961 (annual average)	1969–1971 (annual average)	1973
Developed market economies	11,200	205	308	335
Australia	1,000	—	25	40
Canada	9,000	191	246	241
United States	200	10	14	15
Others	1,000	4	23	39
Less developed countries	45,000	63	194	208
Cuba	16,000	16	37	32
New Caledonia	15,000	47	135	116
Dominican Republic	800	—	—	30
Indonesia	7,000	—	10	14
Philippines	4,000	—	—	—
Others	2,000	—	12	16
Centrally planned economies of Eastern Europe and Asia	9,000	66	119	123
World Total	65,200	334	621	666

[a]In thousands of metric tons of metal content.
Source: *Metallgesellschaft;* United States Bureau of Mines, Minerals Facts and Problems; World Metal Statistics, 1974, London; various UNCTAD Documents.

The fastest rates of expansion were in Japan (17.9 percent), Italy (11.4 percent), and Sweden (10.2). Consumption in the United States and United Kingdom grew by about 3 percent/year.

On the production side, all major producers except the United States expanded their mine production in the 1960s. On a worldwide basis, however, these expansions were uneven. Major increases took place in New Caledonia (whose share of world production rose from 20 to 23 percent in 10 years), South Africa, Cuba, and the U.S.S.R. The share of Australia rose to 4 percent in 1970, although there had been almost no production at all in that country five years earlier. Australia has not lived up to expectations, but it is anticipated that Australia has an increasingly important role to play in world nickel production.

Supplies of nickel have tended to be fairly tight during the postwar years and this has reflected on the price of the metal. The producer price of nickel was almost constant at U.S. $0.35/pound from 1929 to 1948, and then rose steeply to more than $1.40 in 1972. In constant money, this involved a price rise of considerable extent; some costs also rose rapidly during this period. This was particularly true in Canada, where there was a progressive decline in the nickel content of sulphide ores, rising wages, and the need to mine at increasing depths.

Similarly, the expansion of capacity was hindered by the high costs of investment. The investment cost of a ton of new production came to about $7500 in 1971 (as compared to approximately $3000 for a ton of copper). Of course, the investment decision depends upon the price of the product as well as the cost of investment, and given the fact that the current price has expanded at a rate of 5.8 percent per year over the period 1947–70 (and the constant or "real" price at a rate of 4.4 percent) it might be thought that price increases have been, and probably will be, sufficient to cover increasing investment and operating costs. This may or may not be so. In particular, the profitability of today's investments may be threatened by technical change that lowers costs to tomorrow's investors, and thus encourages them to finance drastic increases in capacity. In addition, new mines may be opened by certain suppliers in the LDCs that do not require the high profit rates that many firms in the developed countries have come to think of as essential.

The final point here concerns production from the sea bed, or ocean floor. According to UNCTAD and the International Bank for Reconstruction and Development, possibilities exist for obtaining important quantities of nickel (and other minerals) from "nodules" that cover various parts of the oceans' floors. The technology for mining these nodules is being rapidly perfected, and a good chance exists that large-scale mining might be able to begin by the early 1980s. The effect of such operations on the world supply of nickel is uncertain at the present time, but it is not unthinkable that there will be a major downward pressure on the price of this commodity.

MANGANESE ORE

The demand for manganese ore is almost entirely a function of the production of iron and steel, since between 90 and 95 percent of manganese supplies are used in the iron and steel industry. The chief function of manganese is to counteract the brittleness that results from the presence of sulphur in the steelmaking process; to harden and toughen steel; and to serve as an alloy in other metallurgical industries—in particular those manufacturing brass, bronze, and aluminum. A small percentage of total manganese production is used in the manufacture of dry-battery cells, and an even smaller percentage in the preparation of chemicals such as potassium permanganate and manganese chloride.

Manganese ore is normally given a ferroalloy form before it is used for steelmaking. The most commonly used ferroalloy is ferromanganese, which contains 80 percent manganese. Other forms are silicomanganese and spiegeleisen. It is also the case that since the demand for manganese originates in three different industries (metallurgical, battery, and chemical), and that the ores required in each industry are not good substitutes for each other, it is not entirely correct to speak of a single market for manganese.

As is often the case with this type of commodity, a small number of very large mines accounts for the bulk of supplies to the world market. These large mines, most of which are highly mechanized, are characterized by extensive economies of scale. Moreover, the production at these mines does not show any marked tendency to change as the price of the ore changes. Among other things, this tends to accentuate price movements that result from sharp changes in demand.

The less developed countries supply a major part of the manganese ore entering into international trade; however, the trend, since 1960, has been for the developed market economies to increase their share of production. Reference was made in the previous paragraph to the supply side of the market for manganese, but it can be added that close ties exist between a number of steel companies, mineral trading firms, banking interests, and manganese mines. These links have contributed to the noticeable increase in "tied" sales and the use of long-term contracts that have characterized this industry over the last decade. Some data on production and exports are given in Table 4-3.

Although no claim will be made here that the manganese ore industry is one of the more important of the industrial raw materials industries, it does permit us to introduce a number of important economic problems. One of these has to do with the U.S. government's stockpile of metallurgical manganese. The purpose of this stockpile was, and perhaps still is, to accumulate a supply of raw materials that could be used as inputs to essential industries in the event of war, boycotts, and so on.

Almost from the beginning, this stockpile has been used for other than "strategic" purposes. As a result, the mere presence of this stockpile has had an important influence on the price of a number of raw materials, where the "price" here means both the North American price and the world price. Lately, the fairly large releases of manganese from this stockpile have tended to depress its world price.[1] Furthermore, the opposite situation is not unknown. The stopping of Soviet supplies to the United States in 1948, the Korean War, and the Suez crisis of 1956 created a near panic on the markets for manganese ore; and the resulting increases in both private and governmental stockpiling caused a very sharp rise in the price.

At the present time, with stocks at a higher level consumptionwise

---

[1]Some work of Joseph Shaw (1973) at UNCTAD has provided a weak confirmation of this effect. In his investigation Shaw has worked with an equation of the type $P = \alpha_0 + \alpha_1 \Delta I_g + \alpha_2 I_c$, where I_g are government inventories, and I_c private inventories.

Table 4-3. World Production, Exports, and Some (–) Imports of Manganese Ore (Estimated Manganese Content), 1950–70[a]

Area	1950 Production	1950 Export (Import)	1960 Production	1960 Export (Import)	1970 Production	1970 Export (Import)
World	3,035		5,524		7,900	
Developing countries						
Brazil	87	67	450	390	905	715
Gabon	0	0	0	0	741	822
Ghana	355	313	266	267	288	193
India	450	346	535	553	701	557
Morocco	141	119	224	178	66	75
Zaire	9	160	183	146	167	131
Others	137	256	356	246	187	115
Developed market economies						
Australia	9	15	30	23	363	300
Japan	54	–22	124	–103	89	–958
South Africa	323	278	467	353	1,194	829
United States	69	–815	53	–1,101	50	–768
Others	34		46		29	
ECE[b]		–250		–723		–1,107
Centrally planned economies						
U.S.S.R.	1,326	125	2,642	438	3,078	540
Others	41	12	148	23	131	13

[a] Figures in thousands of tons.
[b] Excluding intra-trade.
Source: UNCTAD documents.

Table 4-4. U.S. Stockpile of Metallurgical Manganese, in Thousands of Short Tons

(1)	(2)	(3)[a]	(4)	(5)[b]
			Disposals:	
	Stockpile	Total	previous 12	Uncommitted
End of	objective	inventory	months	excess
December, 1967	7,900	12,951	415	5,051
December, 1968	7,900	12,817	390	4,917
December, 1969	4,000	12,638	34	8,638
December, 1970	4,000	12,112	48	8,165
December, 1971	4,000	11,190	922	7,244
December, 1972	4,000	9,932	1,244	5,985
June, 1973	982[c]	7,675	1,001[d]	6,692
November, 1973	982	—	2,997[e]	—

[a] Total inventory consists of stockpile and nonstockpile grades.
[b] The uncommitted excess excludes unshipped sales.
[c] This entry consists of metallurgical manganese ore (750,500 short tons); ferro-manganese, high carbon (200,000 short tons); ferro-manganese, medium carbon (10,500 short tons); silico-manganese (15,-900 short tons); manganese metal, electrolytic (4,750 short tons).
[d] Preceding 6 months.
[e] Preceding 11 months.
Source: U.S. Government Stockpile Reports and U.S. Department of the Interior, Bureau of Mines, Mineral Industry Surveys.

than is considered necessary, and with considerable optimism being shown in regard to the availability of future supplies, the prediction is for a considerable amount of destocking. The recent behavior of the U.S. strategic (GSA) stockpile has followed the pattern shown in Table 4-4.[2]

The next topic has to do with the access to world markets enjoyed by the LDCs. On this point it should be made clear that although there are hardly any significant trade barriers facing the export of unprocessed manganese to the industrial countries, important barriers do exist where such things as manganese alloys are concerned. This is not to say that extensive further processing would take place immediately in the LDCs if these barriers were removed; however, there is little question but that some

---

[2] Some figures for the U.S. government's strategic stockpile of copper are also available. These are as follows, where units are metric tons:

1956	884,300	1963	1,122,800
1957	931,800	1964	1,095,500
1958	1,011,400	1965	910,200
1959	1,136,100	1966	459,600
1960	1,140,600	1967	282,200
1961	1,146,600	1968	268,500
1962	1,134,200		

The above, and other information on the U.S. stockpile, can be obtained from the U.S. Government's Stockpile Reports.

of the producers of manganese ore also have the capability to establish an important transforming capacity, and an improved access to world markets might well provide an incentive for the development of this capacity.

Needless to say, this is a matter of the greatest importance for those countries in this category; and to understand this we have only to compare the value added from processing raw materials to that involved in simply removing these materials from the earth. In 1974 the price of a unit of ferromanganese was about four times the value of the manganese ore it contained, and this ratio may be increasing as the trend unit price of manganese ore declines. It is also the case, as is to be expected, that the price of the manufactured goods for which the ore is exchanged is increasing rapidly; in 1970 manganese-exporting countries had to export 1.8 tons of ore to realize the same purchasing power as was obtainable by 1 ton of ore in 1950; and today they are up to more than 2.5 tons. Figure 4-1 gives some idea of the deterioration in the purchasing power of manganese ore exports.

In the circumstances, it might be claimed that there is hardly a bright future awaiting the producers of this ore. If the expression "international equity" has any meaning, then it is obviously the case that all artificial barriers to trade in manganese ore and alloys should be removed immediately, and perhaps—where possible—a system of preferences introduced that would favor the expansion of further processing in the less developed of the producing countries. Although a number of minor theoretical arguments could undoubtedly be introduced that would cast some shadow on the validity of Figure 4-1 as a precise measure of the declining terms of trade of manganese producers, it certainly is a useful device in the hands of anyone wishing to argue that trade impediments of one kind (tariffs and quotas) should be answered by trade impediments of another (such as producers' cartels).[3]

Tariffs on raw manganese ore hardly amount to anything. Most industrial countries have a zero tariff; only Japan and the United States have a duty on this commodity, and these are trivial. Japan's import regulations call for a duty free entry of manganese ore in such quantities as are necessary to meet domestic demand. Imports exceeding this are subject to a 10 percent ad valorem duty in respect to ores containing more than 39 percent magnesium; and to a temporary duty of 2400 yen per ton for other qualities of ores. (This is equivalent to 40 percent ad valorem. By ad valorem it is meant that the tariff is a percentage of the *value* of the product.)

In the United States a duty has existed that, under the so-called Kennedy Round, has been reduced to 0.12 cents/pound—or about 3 per-

---

[3]One of the "arguments" that I have heard here is that the low price of ores such as manganese has stimulated an increase in demand that, in one way or another, has led to an increase in "welfare" for the exporting countries. It so happens that this argument applies for a number of products, but manganese is not one of them.

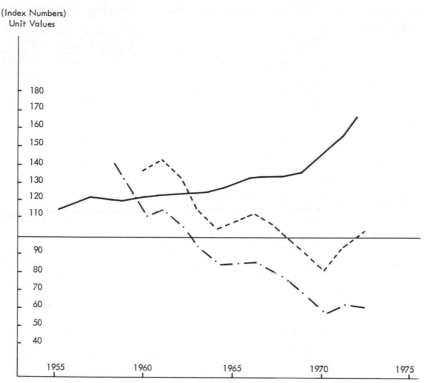

Figure 4-1. The unit value of manganese ore exports from the LDCs and the unit value of manufactured goods exported from the most important of the industrial market economy countries (1950 = 100). Solid line indicates average unit value of manufactured goods; dashed line indicates average unit value of manganese ore (current prices); and the dot-dash line indicates the average unit value of manganese ore (deflated). Source: United Nations statistics and documents.

cent ad valorem. This duty, however, has been suspended since 1964, and it has recently been decided that the suspension will remain until 1976. For countries not enjoying the most-favored-nation status, the duty is one cent per pound, or about 25 percent ad valorem.

On the other hand, imports of manganese products (such as alloys) are subject both to tariffs and to nontariff barriers. These obstructions, which ostensibly are designed to protect local manufacturers, have generally served to make it impossible for LDCs to enter this market. In fact, among the LDCs only India is an important exporter of ferromanganese, and that country has had extensive difficulty in maintaining its competitive position. Table 4-5 provides a summary of the world tariff schedule for manganese alloys.

Table 4-5. Import Tariffs on Manganese Ferroalloys in Some Important Industrial Countries and Areas

Area	Product	Type and rate of tariff		
		General	MFN	GSP
EEC[a]	Ferromanganese			
	containing more than 2%	2%	4%	4%
	by weight of carbon	6%		
	Other	8%	8%	8%
	Ferrosilicon manganese	6%	5.5%	5.5%
United Kingdom[b]	Ferromanganese			
	1. containing less than 3% by weight of carbon	Free	Free	Free
	Other: 2. containing less than 65% by weight of manganese	3.149/ton or 8%	Free	Free
	3. Other	6.8890/ton or 8%	Free	Free
United States[c]	Ferromanganese (not containing over 1% by weight of carbon) and ferrosilicon manganese	1.875¢/lb. valorum	0.3¢/lb. + 2% ad valorum
			0.46¢/lb. +3.5 ad valorum	
	Ferromanganese (containing over 1% but not over 4% by weight of carbon)	1.875¢/lb.	0.46¢/lb.	
	Ferromanganese (containing over 4% by weight of carbon)	1.875¢/lb.	0.30¢/lb.	
Japan[d]	Ferromanganese	10%	12%	Free

[a] EEC: Discretionary licensing for ferromanganese, other than carbonized, and for silicomanganese. For the general tariff, Benelux 2%; other EEC countries 6%. For MFN, ferrosilicon manganese free within 50,000 tons/year.
[b] United Kingdon: The general tariff is the amount in pounds *or* 8%, whichever is greater. Free to Commonwealth and Ireland.
[c] United States: Tariffs in ¢/lb. (cents/pound) on manganese content.
[d] Japan: General and MFN tariffs not applicable at present; for GSP, free within annual quota of 2,983 tons.

The last matter to be gone into in this section concerns the effects of production from the seabed. As things stand, the price of manganese is on a declining trend and, under the pressure of a high and increasing level of productive capacity, U.S. government stockpile releases, and imports from the centrally planned economies, this trend is expected to prevail for some time. A medium to high level of production from the seabed could only make this trend more pronounced, but whether it would be prolonged by large supplies from this new source is unclear and depends to a considerable extent on the long-run reaction of land-based producers.

A number of international organizations have already begun to forecast production from the seabed and its effect on the price of manganese and other resources. The feeling here is that these exercises are, for the most part, of little practical value, since not enough is presently known of the costs associated with large-scale mining of the seabed. One thing, however, would seem to be certain. If it is feasible to mine the seabed, and in the long or very long run this will almost certainly be the case, the price of manganese will probably come under a very strong downward pressure.

THE SMELTING OF COPPER AND ALUMINUM

At this point, in keeping with the overall aim of this book, some issues connected with the smelting (and refining) of copper and the smelting of aluminum, will be taken up. Many copper companies process their own ore, and a great deal of information is being provided in the trade literature these days about *integrated operations* where mining and further processing are being brought closer and closer together by revolutionary new systems for transporting ore and concentrates, and by highly automated and computerized facilities for receiving, storing, and transforming these inputs into metal. At the same time many other firms employ independent or "custom" smelters. At present, the amount of concentrates going into custom smelters is approaching the two-million mark, which is somewhere in the neighborhood of 20 percent of the world's smelting capacity.

Questions are constantly being raised as to the availability of smelter capacity for the future. The problem, of course, is simply one of expected prices and costs, which determine expected profitability, and thus reflect on investment. Builders—or potential builders—of smelters maintain that, at present costs, the price that they will probably obtain for processing copper does not justify new capacity.

Where these costs are concerned, Perlman (1974) has given the cost of a medium-sized smelter (plus refinery) as about $1300 per ton to construct. If we take the required rate of return at 15 percent, and the depreciation period at 15 years, the capital costs come to approximately 11 cents per pound. If direct operating costs of between five and nine cents per pound are added to this, a potential builder would require a treatment charge of at least 16 cents per pound before commencing construction.[4]

[4]At the time Perlman published his paper (1974), this type of smelter could, depending upon where it was being built, be considered a high-cost installation. Since that time the high inflation rate has given a certain validity to his conclusions—though not all of them. For example, he seems to think that the price of smelting copper is logically determined by the costs of high-cost installations. This idea is also to be found emanating from the executive suites of several copper producing companies. It is, however, quite wrong. The world copper market may resemble many things, but one thing it does not resemble is the perfect competition model of the elementary textbooks.

Any discussion of costs and their influence on investment must also consider processing equipment that is already amortized; and at present the world smelter and refinery population contains a substantial amount of matériel falling in this category. These facilities, whose capital costs can be regarded as paid, can often offer to process copper at charges that are two-thirds of those desired by new smelters, and still realize a profit. Thus, at a time like the present, when the industry as a whole is experiencing excess capacity, brand-new smelters occasionally are put in a position where they must bid down their processing charges to levels that are considerably below their total unit costs. This type of behavior, if it occurs often enough, has a dampening effect on the spirits of potential investors in this industry.

One of the new problems facing the management and owners of smelters is pollution control. This has resulted in increased capital costs for installations under construction; and the enforcement of pollution control legislation has at times caused some smelters to close down, since apparently they could not afford the extensive alterations and addition of "cleansing" equipment necessary to meet pollution standards. At the present time, in the United States, it is estimated that the cost of copper will be raised by about three to five cents per pound by the additional investment required to bring pollution down to the level stipulated by antipollution legislation; while in Japan pollution control measures may add as much as $100/ton to the capital cost of new installations. The matter of pollution and suppression will be commented on more extensively in Chapter 8; however, it can be pointed out now that those firms and industries in Sweden that have made a serious effort to meet the new environmental standards have often been able to do so at costs that were not at all as high as originally estimated. Moreover, it must never be forgotten that pollution is a community problem rather than the problem of a single firm or industry. Obviously it doesn't make sense to pass and enforce pollution legislation that will make a distinguished contribution to the number of unemployed. Instead, a part of the financing of pollution control or suppression must fall on the community as a whole.

There is also a bright side to the cost problem for this industry. Recent development work indicates that real possibilities exist for increasing the technical efficiency of processing facilities, and for coming to grips with the environmental deterioration that this has often introduced. For instance, Duval Mining has developed a process called CLEAR (Copper Leaching Electrolysis and Regeneration) that ostensibly generates no gaseous, liquid, or solid waste—thus enabling it to satisfy all existing antipollution legislation; and which features the continuous discharge of electrolytically produced copper. Duval is building an installation whose capital costs, they say, are well under the existing average for the industry; and given that operating costs may also be lower for this process, it is possible that the next generation of processing capacity may halt the inexorable rise in various costs that we have witnessed over the last few years. Of course, no amount of technical progress can cancel out the rise in costs brought about by an inflation rate between 15 and 25 percent.

While the Duval process and other so-called hydrometallurgical techniques have a definite place in the future scheme of things, it will be some years before they dominate the processing field. In the meantime there will be a more intensive use of such things as flash smelting, which reportedly reduces the energy requirements per ton of smelted metal by 50 percent; and continuous oxygen smelting, which also features greatly reduced capital and operating costs, together with the possibility of almost total recovery of noxious gases. For more on the technical side of these developments, the reader is referred to Hobson (1974).

The smelter situation in the world aluminum industry allows further insights into some of the topics considered above, and in addition permits the introduction of several new issues.

Capital requirements in the aluminum industry, together with the presence of risks of various types and magnitudes, have encouraged the formation of international joint ventures or consortia for investing in aluminum smelters, as well as mines, alumina producing factories, and semifabricating facilities. These consortia represent international groups of companies and, if present trends continue, it is possible that they will control a significant part of this industry some day. One of the reasons for this is that these consortia are building plants of a very large size that produce at lower costs than many other plants in the industry—to include new factories with a smaller capacity.

Management in the aluminum industry is under the same pressure to produce an acceptable rate of return on investment as management in general. For the most part their efforts have been directed toward reducing costs, over which they have more control than prices. It is worth noting that they have often been helped in this task by the tendency of governments in various LDCs to subsidize, in one way or another, the building of port facilities and workers' housing; and to provide free plant sites, give loans at a low rate of interest, reduce taxes or grant tax holidays, and even to subsidize the consumption of electric power.

Although a cry goes up from time to time that investment in smelter capacity is becoming impossible due to tightening profit margins, it remains a fact that up to now capacity has expanded at a smooth and impressive rate. From 1969 to 1974 world smelter capacity increased from 10,900 thousand short tons to 17,848 thousand short tons. Some explanation for so rapid a rate of expansion must exist, and perhaps the answer is in the historical profitability of the industry.

If we consider the United States, we see that although profitability on either total invested capital or the investment of common stockholders (i.e., shareholders) fell by almost 50 percent between 1955 and 1960, recovery almost to the earlier level had been registered by 1969. In that year, profits before taxes were almost 22 percent of stockholders' investment; while the largest aluminum company, Alcoa Aluminum, had an after-tax profit of 10.3 percent in the same year.[5] These results are only slightly inferior to the median return, after taxes, on share capital for the 500 largest nonfinancial corporations in the United States: Half of these earned more than 11.3 percent; and half, less. If return on total capital, which includes long-term debt, is examined, both Alcoa and Alcan Aluminum did better than half the corporations in the United States.

As is true of copper, the money cost of producing primary aluminum has been rising in tandem with the general price level over the post-World War II period. In certain cases, however, the real cost may have been declining, at least up to the early 1970s. This is mostly due to technological improvements that have reduced the input of labor per unit of output, and have brought about similar reductions in the input of electric power and carbon. Also, the trend toward larger smelters has reduced the average real investment cost per unit of output; and at least one organization (Alcan Aluminum Ltd. of Canada) has reported a reduction in both real *and* dollar costs due to technical advances. In general, expectations seem to favor the possibility of holding costs in line via rationalizations, reorganizations, and the like; but whether this, together with present price expectations, will promote an expansion in capacity consistent with past trends remains to be seen.

THE SMELTING OF LEAD

We can now look at some processes for smelting lead. The basic raw material here is galena and, chemically, the reaction involves the oxidation of galena to metallic lead. Table 4-6 gives some of the main costs for smelting a ton of galena, while ignoring some incidental expenses such as license fees, assaying charges, the cost of certain types of overhead, etc. The figures under S refer to a small plant with a throughput of 10,000 tons/year, while L is a larger plant with a throughput of 50,000 tons/year.

As Table 4-6 indicates, there are considerable returns to scale to be won from several of these processes. In addition, some fundamental eco-

---

[5] Lanzilotti (1958) has reported that Alcoa's target rate of return on investment was 10 percent for the period 1947–55. This was, of course, after taxes, and represented the rate of return they believed they could earn.

Table 4-6. The Inputs for Various Processes Used to Smelt a Ton of Galena Concentrate Containing 72 Percent Lead (1968–69)

Per ton of concentrate	Blast furnace		ISF	Round hearth		Self-fluxing		Boliden	
	S[a]	L[b]	S	S	L	S	L	S	L
Direct labor (man-hours)	9.7	3.2	1.5	11.6	3.4	7.1	3.3	4.0	1.5
Fuel (kg)									
Oil	13.3	6.4	—	85.0	51.0	83.3	74.0	—	—
Coke	168.0	150.0	—	13.0	13.0	—	—	12.5	12.5
Coal	—	—	—	150.0	150.0	24.0	24.0	—	—
Electrical energy (kwh)	154	135	58	70	60	161	43	750	596
Materials									
Limestone	44.0	44.0	113.0	80.0	80.0	—	—	200.0	200.0
Soda ash	—	—	—	15.0	15.0	7.4	7.4	—	—
Maintenance (man-hours)	5.5	2.2	1.1	3.4	2.0	6.0	4.0	3.0	1.0
Capital costs (dollars)	16.1	3.2	4.5	12.1	8.9	16.9	14.0	15.0	7.5

[a] S = small plant.
[b] L = large plant.
Source: UNIDO documents.

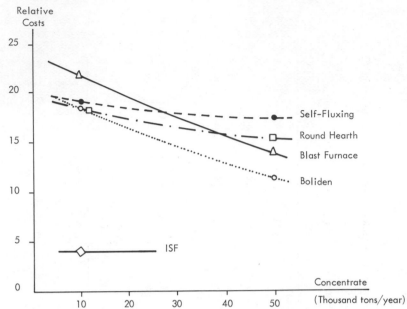

Figure 4-2. The relative cost of smelting lead in terms of capacity of smelter and type of process.

nomic differences exist between the processes. The round hearth or self-fluxing processes (which are termed roast reaction processes) are basically very simple and can extract lead at low production costs, but their main efficiencies are realizable at a relatively small scale of operation. It does not appear to be the case that the efficiency of this type of process can be carried over to large installations and, as a result, a larger production means increasing the number of smaller units. This unfortunately means a disproportionate increase in the cost of labor and equipment as compared to the other processes. Also, these processes are quite restrictive as to the chemical properties of the concentrates they treat.

Another process of considerable interest is the Boliden process. This process is relatively capital intensive, and requires a fairly highly skilled labor input to handle the complicated equipment that is involved, although maintenance costs are fairly low. If electric power and coke are fairly inexpensive, then this process is advantageous for almost any level of production. With energy costs rising, however, it may have lost some of its competitive strength.

Where large tonnages of both low- and average-grade concentrates are concerned, the blast furnace process remains a good alternative. It is true that it requires an expensive fuel (coke), and has relatively high labor and maintenance costs, but it has proved to be extremely flexible and reliable. Where these processes are concerned, Figure 4-2 shows the relation between costs and size somewhat better than Table 4-6. It should be kept in mind, however, that these costs are for 1969. Since that time there have been changes in the relative cost of inputs that could reflect on the position of these curves.

The curves in Figure 4-2 are analogous to long-run cost curves. For example, if we have a "small" plant, with a throughput or rated capacity of 10,000 tons/year, this does not mean that it cannot process more or less than 10,000 tons/year. The point is that it does so at a higher cost. In general, larger plants mean lower unit costs in this industry.

Two things remain in this section. The first has to do with the ISF, or Imperial Smelting, process. Some information about this process is given in Table 4-6. As the reader can see in the table, this process would seem to have a distinct advantage over the other processes where a plant of small size is concerned. However, in those situations where lead concentrates can be processed together with zinc concentrates, the Imperial Smelting process may well be—from the cost point of view—superior to any of the processes for smelting lead at any scale of operation.[6] Here it should be mentioned that lead and zinc are a joint product—in that they are found in the same ore—and thus it is normal to process them together. In 1969 it was

---

[6]The ISF process has also experienced the most dynamic expansion of any zinc smelting process. Only in the United States and the U.S.S.R. has there been an exception to this situation. On a worldwide basis, the following figures can be cited for the smelting of zinc:

Zinc smelting process	1959 (%)	1968 (%)
Electrolytic	51.0	59.2
Imperial smelting	0.6	10.5
Electrothermic	4.1	5.7
Vertical retorting	10.9	8.6
Horizontal retorting	33.4	16.0

In general the low energy input—both direct and indirect—of this process should cause it to gain ground rapidly at the present time.

The Imperial Smelting Furnace makes possible the clear cut separation of lead and zinc in a single unit, as well as making possible the recovery of other materials. For instance, in 1969 the capital cost of installing a complete Imperial Smelting Furnace capable of producing 70,000 tons of slab zinc (to include 35,000 tons of high-grade zinc) was $375/ton. The other materials that could be recovered were lead bullion (40,000 tons/year), cadmium (100–200 tons/year), copper in bullion (4000 tons/year), and a fairly large amount of sulphuric acid. This $375/year included the smelter and most auxiliary plant and installations, to include such things as offices, workshops, laboratories, transport, and general site development.

At the present time it may be that more than 20 percent of zinc and 15 percent of lead is smelted by this process.

considered that an ISF unit capable of processing about 40,000 tons of zinc and 25,000–30,000 tons of lead per year was the minimum size for optimal economies of scale.

AGGREGATE INVESTMENT BEHAVIOR IN THE UNITED STATES

Finally, for those readers intending to delve further into the empirical aspects of production and investment, the following may be of interest.

There has been an occasional tendency in recent years toward a stagnation in the increase in capacity in various raw materials industries. Zinc is one industry that slowed down for a time—in fact, no smelter was built in the United States between 1942 and 1970, although extensive capacity-increasing modernizations took place—and there have been all sorts of rumors about the possible inadequacy of capacity in the copper, aluminum, and iron and steel industries later in the 1970s or early in the 1980s. In looking at the bare figures it may, in fact, appear that there have been sizable additions to capacity in the nonferrous metals industries as a whole in the United States, just as total investment figures show a definite trend increase in U.S. manufacturing as a whole (though not in iron and steel). The problem here is that only a part of this investment went for new capacity; the rest was for modernization, safety measures, and pollution control, or represented cost increases.[7]

Where this last item is concerned, the U.S. Commerce Department's price index showed a 20 percent increase for 1969–73. For the same period, the current dollar value of fixed investment increased by about 20 percent. This means that in real terms there was no increase in investment. Moreover, as indicated above, the investment figures show both capacity-increasing investments *and* so-called nonproductive investments. For example, environmental control expenditures increased from about 4 percent of all manufacturing expenses in 1969 to about 11 percent in 1973; and, in addition, about $1.3 billion were spent as a result of the Occupational Safety and Health Act. What this adds up to is a situation where there was at least a stagnation, and most likely a decline, in the *rate* of increase of capacity in the United States over the period covered. This situation is reflected in Table 4-7 dealing with the nonferrous metals industry in the United States.

[7]For an extremely readable account of the problem being discussed here, the reader is referred to "Why Business Ran Out of Capacity," by Lewis Beman, *Fortune* magazine, May, 1974. What the reader should note here, however, is that the issue is actually *investment* and not *capacity*. Capacity *is* increasing, but at a slower pace.

Table 4-7. Total Investment in the U.S. Nonferrous Metals Industries in Billions of Current Dollars, with Breakdown by Category

	1969	1970	1971	1972	1973
New capacity	$17/30$	$15/34$	$21/46$	$17/44$	$17/44$
Modernization	$7/30$	$9/34$	$9/46$	$9/44$	$8.5/44$
Safety	—	—	—	$1/44$	$1.5/44$
Pollution	$1/30$	$3/34$	$5/46$	$4/44$	$5/44$
Inflation	$3/30$	$7/34$	$11/46$	$13/44$	$14/44$
Total investment (billions of current dollars)	$1^{2}/_{27}$	$1^{7}/_{27}$	$1^{18}/_{27}$	$1^{15}/_{27}$	$1^{18}/_{27}$

No comment will be made on Table 4-7 except to say that since 1973 there has probably been a fall in the aggregate standard of living in the United States due to inflation, to an extremely high unemployment, and, of course, to a growing uncertainty. Thus the trend shown in this table has undoubtedly continued. It should also be emphasized that where the author is concerned, many of these so-called unproductive investments—such as pollution control and modernization, especially the latter—are among the most productive investments that an economy can make, since they are concerned with the health and welfare of the most productive and important group in an industrial society: the individuals who are directly involved in the production of industrial goods.

THE BASIC ANALYTICS OF RESOURCE DEPLETION

The purpose of this section is to treat, at the elementary level, some fundamental concepts of resource depletion. In order to get at the basic issues, the exposition is framed so as to imply that we are dealing with a single firm operating one extractive facility (e.g., mine or well). This is the approach most often used in the technical literature; however, with a small amount of complication the analysis could be extended to a multiunit firm. In addition, most of the analysis applies to an entire economy concerned with the optimum rate of extraction of its natural resources.

One of the things that distinguishes much of the technical literature dealing with this subject is the way many simple and useful ideas have been buried beneath an avalanche of highly complex and, for the most part, unnecessary mathematical manipulations. What will be done in this chapter is to work with an elementary numerical example. This example will, hopefully, give the reader some insights into the problem of exhaustible resources and, at the same time, introduce some concepts that are useful in the study of intertemporal economic theory.

The first topic to be treated here concerns the extraction decision: how much, if any, of a mineral deposit should be taken out of the ground now; and how much should be left for a later extraction? To begin, let us construct a simple numerical example having a two-period horizon. What this means is that we must make a decision now in which we determine how much of the mineral should be removed in this period, and how much in the next, with the sum of the amounts to be removed in each period given. In certain conditions it might be useful to think of the sum of the amount to be removed as the total availability of the resource.

If we assume that we have a given capital structure, and further assume that within the range we are operating we have a constant unit cost of production that is equal to 2 dollars, the profit on any extracted unit is $p - 2$. If this price at the present time is, for example, 12 dollars, then the profit that we can realize by extracting the unit now is 10 dollars. Suppose also that the market rate of interest on "perfect" or "safe" financial assets, to include a bank deposit, is 10 percent. Thus, if the unit is removed now, sold, and, with the profit obtained, a financial asset is bought, the owner of the unit will have 11 dollars at the beginning of the next period [$10(1 + r) = 10(1 + 0.10) = 11$].

We now consider the profit that the unit would bring if it were extracted in the next period. Assuming that the cost of extraction is unchanged, and the price increases to 12.5 dollars, the profit realized through extracting the unit in the second period is 10.5 dollars. It should then be obvious that the correct decision is to extract the unit in the first period, since, under the force of interest, the 10 dollar profit from the first period grows to 11 dollars by the second period.

This argument can be put in another way. 10.5 dollars after one period's time is the same as $10.5/(1 + 0.10) = 9.9$ dollars now. Thus a commodity that can be extracted now at a profit of 10 dollars is to be preferred to one that will give a profit of 10.5 dollars one year from now. With this in mind we can determine, for any number of units that are to be extracted in any number of periods, the number that are to be extracted per period.

The first thing to do is to discount marginal profitability in all future periods back to the present period so that marginal profitabilities can be compared. Note the expression "marginal profitability." This is the profitability of the additional unit. For instance if, regardless of the amount extracted, the cost per extracted unit was 2 dollars, and the price it brought was 12 dollars, then the marginal revenue (MR) would be 12 dollars,

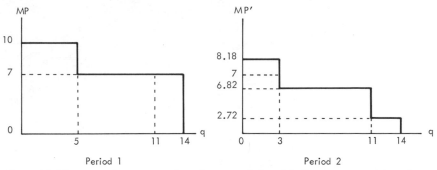

Figure 4-3. Diagrammatic representation of a two-period model of resource extraction, given a total availability of 14 units.

marginal cost (MC) 2 dollars, and marginal profit (MP) = MR − MC = 10 dollars.

Now suppose we have a situation where, in the first period, up to and including 5 units can be sold at a price of 12 dollars; and from 6 to 14 units at a price of 9 dollars. Similarly, in the second period, up to and including 3 units can be sold for 11 dollars; from 4 to 11 units for 9.5 dollars; and from 12 to 14 for 5 dollars. In both periods unit costs are constant at 2 dollars. We then have the situation as indicated in Table 4-8, where MP′ is discounted marginal profit.

The object here is to mine 14 units in two periods, where 14 could be taken as the capacity of the installation, or the availability of the resource. The optimal program for doing this is to extract 11 units in the first period, and 3 in the second. The 11 units extracted in the first period consist of 5 units with a marginal profit of 10 dollars, and 6 with marginal profits of 7 dollars; while those from the second period give discounted marginal profits of 8.18.

Put this another way. If we desire, it is possible to extract and sell 14 units in the first period. This would mean 5 units with a marginal profit of 10, and 9 with a marginal profit of 7. But since we only have 14 units, this means giving up the possibility of extracting 3 units in the next period, each of which has a marginal discounted profit of 8.18. Thus if we take 14 in the first period instead of 11 in the first period and 3 in the second, we decrease our profit by 3 × (8.18 − 7) = 3.54. The reader can now examine Figure 4-3.

Figure 4-3 helps to show how production should be allocated between periods. If, for example, there were only 4 units, they should all be extracted in the first period, since by doing so we get the highest marginal profit per unit, and thus the highest total profit. If there were 7 units, then 5

Table 4-8. Marginal Revenue, Cost, and Profit in a Two-Period Model

	Period 1				Period 2			
Units	Marginal revenue (MR)	Marginal cost (MC)	Marginal profit (MP)	Units	Marginal revenue (MR)	Marginal cost (MC)	Marginal profit (MP)	Discounted marginal profit (MP')
1	12	2	10	1	11	2	9.0	8.18
2	12	2	10	2	11	2	9.0	8.18
3	12	2	10	3	11	2	9.0	8.18
4	12	2	10	4	9.5	2	7.5	6.82
5	12	2	10	.	.	.	.	.
6	9	2	7	.	.	.	.	.
7	9	2	7	11	9.5	2	7.5	6.82
.	.	.	.	12	5	2	7.5	2.72
.	.	.	.	.	.	.	.	.
14	9	2	7	14	5	2	3	2.72

should be extracted in the first period and 2 in the second, and so on. Figure 4-3 also indicates that the value of the last extracted unit—or, what is almost the same thing, the value of the last unit left in the ground—is 7 dollars. What this means is that *if,* instead of 14 units, we had 15 units mine capacity, the marginal profit of this last unit (which would be removed in the first period) is 7.

The question that can now be asked is: if there is another unit in the ground, should it be added to the mine's capacity? This, of course, is a matter of comparing the cost of adding the unit to its value. If its cost is less than its value, then it should be added. What we are doing now is altering our problem from one dealing with nonaugmentable resources to one where resources are augmentable through investment. What we have arrived at, in fact, is a situation where we are comparing the cost of an investment, made at the beginning of the initial period, with the discounted returns from the investment.

Consider the following example. Suppose an investment of 25 dollars will add five units to capacity. Moreover, we continue to use a two-period "planning" horizon. We first must extend our "demand" curves. In other words, what do we have for the marginal profitability of the five new units. We might have the information as presented in Table 4-9.

It should be made clear that the 25 dollars of investment merely "uncovered" and made available the new resources. There is still the cost of removing them that, as assumed here, remain 2 dollars per unit. It should also be made clear that the information found in Table 4-9 for the second period consists of estimates—estimates that are made at the beginning of the first period when we design our extraction program. Remember that if the time horizon was longer than two periods then, at the beginning of the second period, we would update our estimates and redo our extraction program.[8]

With a total of 19 units to be extracted in two periods (14 plus the 5 new units) the optimal extraction program calls for taking out 16 units in the

---

[8]The reader may not recognize it now, but the problem being treated in this section involves the following Lagrangian:

$$W = \int_0^T [p(q) - c(q)]e^{-rt} dt + \lambda \left[\int_0^T q dt - \bar{K} \right]$$

The time horizon or planning period is T. In the numerical example above, this is 2 periods. $\bar{K}$ is the total amount of the resource; $p(q)$ and $c(q)$ are unit price and unit cost, with both taken as a function of output q. λ is a Lagrangian multiplier, which, by definition, is equal to the value of an additional unit of resources. In Appendix C this matter will be taken up again, employing some simple nonlinear programming.

Table 4-9. Marginal Revenue, Cost, and Profit in a Two-Period Model

	Period 1				Period 2			
Units	Marginal revenue (MR)	Marginal cost (MC)	Marginal profit (MP)	Units	Marginal revenue (MR)	Marginal cost (MC)	Marginal profit (MP)	Discounted marginal profit (MP')
1	12	2	10	1	11	2	9.0	8.18
·	·	·	·	·	·	·	·	·
·	·	·	·	3	11	2	9.0	8.18
5	12	2	10	4	9.5	2	7.5	6.82
6	9	2	7	·	·	·	·	·
·	·	·	·	11	9.5	2	7.5	6.82
·	·	·	·	12	5	2	3	2.72
14	9	2	7	·	·	·	·	·
—	—	—	—	—	—	—	—	—
15	9	2	7	15	5	2	3	2.72
16	9	2	7	·	·	·	·	·
17	9	2	7	·	·	·	·	·
18	5	2	3	·	·	·	·	·
19	0	2	-2	19	5	2	3	2.72

first period and 3 in the second. The reader should verify this arrangement. Note also that the added profit is 35 dollars, and thus, with a given cost of 25 dollars, the investment should be made. It should also be observed that there is no market for a 19th unit in the first period. This is signified by a value of zero for the marginal revenue of the 19th unit.

The next matter is the time horizon. The above example used two periods, but if we have a longer time horizon the technique is the same: the discounted marginal profit is calculated as above for all periods and extractions are distributed over periods in such a way as to maximize the sum of the MPs at each step. There is, however, a well-known problem with long time horizons—the problem of uncertainty. The farther away a certain date is, the more difficult it is to say anything meaningful about prices and costs at that time. Still, where major investments are concerned, some idea—no matter how rough—must be available as to prices and costs for the entire time horizon.

It is here that we can pay some attention to the difference between the situation facing a firm and a country. The usual arrangement is for a firm to schedule an output for a coming period more or less on the basis of what they think demand conditions will be in that period. What this would normally mean is that variations in production as great as those implied in the example above are very rare. If we look at the history of a large mining firm exploiting a given amount of reserves, we are most likely to see a slowly rising production, at least on a trend basis. (Of course, as the deposit nears exhaustion, we would expect production from it to taper off and fall.) Moreover, if profits are reasonable, it would be very surprising if an extractive firm elected to lower production in a given year because they thought that profits in four or five years time might be very much larger.

On the other hand, a country interested in preserving its natural resources might be very much interested in the "theoretical" rate of exploitation. It should be remembered that the governments of most civilized countries claim to have some responsibility for future generations, and in the name of future generations it might be best to leave certain resources in the ground that might otherwise be exploited at the present time.

We might now ask would anything be changed in the above numerical example if, when we added the 5 new units, we introduced some improvements in technique so that the marginal cost of getting out these new units was not 2, but 1. As far as the analysis is concerned, a great deal is changed. To begin with, if these 5 new units are just as accessible as the old, then the cost of *any* 5 of the 19 units can be taken as 1. In other words, it is not necessary that the cost of the 15th through the 19th units be taken as 1. It might be that it is desirable to remove these low-cost units first, and

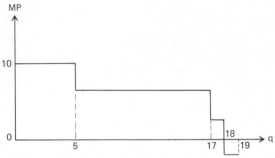

Figure 4-4. Marginal productivity in a single-period model.

given the technique that we are using to designate which units are to be removed, the left-hand section in Table 4-9 would have to be altered so that the *MC* for the first five units was 1 instead of 2 (while the *MC* for the 15th through the 19th remains as 2).

There is, of course, a logical reason for removing low-cost resources first. (For example, it is clear that if we are only going to remove five units, then we should remove the five with the lowest cost, thus maximizing our profit). Even so, it has been the case with many coal mines in Britain that for various reasons all the low-cost coal was not mined first. To see what this might mean we can look at the last set of tables above, and change them so that *MC* = 1 for the first three units in period 1, and *MC* = 1 for the first two units in the second period. What this does is to ensure that two of the low-cost units will be taken out in the second instead of the first period.

It should be remembered, however, that at the beginning of the first period the future (= second period) is to a considerable extent a question mark. It might then happen that we take out 16 units in the first period—as we should if we set out to maximize profit over a two-period time horizon—but then, at the beginning of the second period, all *MR's* fall to 1.

In the circumstances, we should not remove any units during the second period. Thus total extractions are 16 in the first period and zero in the second. But notice that had all the low-cost units been taken out during the first period, profit would have been increased by 2—even though only a total of 16 units were removed. At this point the astute reader will probably think, and be correct in thinking, that the rules of the game have been changed. In particular, uncertainty has entered the discussion in a meaningful way, since ordinarily the assumption would have been that the schedule of prices and costs postulated for the second period represented the actual prices and costs for that period. The economics of uncertainty will not be gone into in this book, but the reader will be warned that once uncertainty becomes a part of the intertemporal allocation process, in that it must be explicitly taken into consideration, we can forget about constructing so-called simple examples.

One final point. The reader may wonder what happened to the Marginal Revenue = Marginal Cost rule that we usually see so much of where questions of profit maximization are concerned. The answer is that if we were only dealing with a single period, then we would produce where $MR = MC$—assuming that we could extract enough units to bring this about. To see this, take Table 4-9 above and assume that we have only a single-period horizon. (This means that we are not interested in the right side of Table 4-9). Figure 4-4 then gives us an idea of what we have for a marginal profit curve.

As we move from zero up to and including 18 units, our MP is greater than zero. As a result each additional unit increases the total profit by the amount of its marginal profit. But as we move from 18 to 19 units, our marginal profit goes from positive to negative. We thus stop with the 18th unit. (Immediately after the 18th unit, $MP = 0$, and since $MP = MR - MC = 0$, we must have $MR = MC$.) If, on the other hand, more than one period is involved, then an extraction now must compensate for the profit lost if the unit stayed in the ground. What this means algebraically, as shown in Appendix C, is that the $MR = MC$ rule is changed to $MR = MC + \lambda$.

This λ can be interpreted as a royalty. Roughly speaking, if the resource is extremely scarce, then λ is fairly large. If, on the other hand, it is plentiful, then λ approaches zero. As Nordhaus (1973) has shown in a brilliant article, the value of λ for energy resources is—contrary to a great deal of opinion in the popular press—very small. For more on this topic the reader should refer to Nordhaus and to Solow (1974).

MARKET FORMS AND THE WORLD COPPER MARKET

5

Much of this chapter deals with the copper market. Where such things as pricing and price formation are concerned, most of what can be said about copper applies to any metal that can be traded on the major commodity exchanges.

The operation of the two largest commodity exchanges is also taken up, and the mechanics of hedging—or insuring against price risk—is gone into in some detail. In the section on market forms both producer pricing and exchange pricing are considered, and the relation between these two clarified. The chapter is concluded by a nontechnical survey of the world copper industry in which particular attention is paid to such things as the relationships between the various producing companies, substitution, and the price of copper. There is also a review of the various cartels and producers' associations that have been interested in fixing or manipulating the price of copper.

COMMODITY EXCHANGES

Many industrial raw materials have their prices quoted on exchanges such as the London Metal Exchange (LME) and the New York Commodity Exchange (COMEX). Of these two, the LME is generally considered to be the most important in terms of turnover, physical deliveries, and its influence on the pricing of metals in general. However, COMEX handles a wider variety of metals, and also provides facilities for trading hides and rubber.

It should be carefully observed that most buyers and sellers of raw materials do not come to the commodity exchanges to make their deals. For the most part, these are made through individual encounters in which so and so much of a commodity is traded at such and such a price. But it happens that in many cases the "formula" for pricing the commodity is related to the prices that are being quoted on a commodity exchange. For instance, buyer X might buy y tons of copper from producer Z for delivery to X's warehouse in two months time. The price that will be paid for the metal is specified on the contract as being the average of the "spot" price prevailing on the LME during a period extending two weeks before the delivery date.

The LME dates from 1882, although copper and other metals had been quoted in London much earlier. During World War II and the immediate postwar period, when the government controlled the price of raw materials, the exchange was closed; but it reopened in 1953, and since that time a steady increase in activity has been recorded. At the same time it should be noted that this activity has only a small physical component. In 1968, with the world consumption of refined copper at close to 7 million tons, approximately 2 million tons of copper "futures" were traded on the LME. Of these futures, however, there were only about 12,000 tons per month of physical deliveries. This matter will be taken up below, but the fact is that physical deliveries have never amounted to very much on either the LME or COMEX. It would hardly make sense, for example, for African or South American producers to deliver a commodity into an LME warehouse when the final customer was in Japan or Italy. (There are eight LME warehouses and delivery places in the United Kingdom, plus warehouses in Rotterdam, Hamburg, and Antwerp.)

As for the categories of buyers and sellers on the various exchanges that *are* concerned with physical deliveries, buyers are usually merchants buying for their own account, or acting on the part of consumers desiring to make marginal adjustments in their stocks; while sellers are also usually merchants representing large producers that are selling small quantities, small producers lacking a comprehensive sales organization and market contacts, and fabricators selling excess stock. Merchants also sell from their own inventories.

The principal function of the LME and COMEX, however, is to provide facilities for "hedging," or transferring price risk from buyers and sellers of physical commodities to "speculators," through the medium of buying and selling futures contracts. This is an important function, given the volatility of commodity prices, and later in this chapter the technique of hedging will be explained in detail. Just now we will occupy ourselves with distinguishing between the "futures," "forward," and "spot" or "cash" market, while at the same time remembering that, with the possible exception of a futures market, none of these markets need exist in the form of an organized exchange where all buyers and sellers or their representatives can congregate.

The spot market is the market that concerns itself with more-or-less immediate delivery. In some textbook situations it also implies immediate consumption. The forward market, on the other hand, involves "forward" sales, or sales having future delivery. In this case, a buyer and seller, or their representatives, can meet, and a commodity can be sold with delivery arranged for one, two, or more months in the future at some mutually agreed upon fixed price, or perhaps a price related to the price on a metal exchange about the time of delivery. The thing to note here is not the time aspect that necessitates distinguishing between the spot and forward market, but the matter of physical delivery. In particular, in comparing the forward and futures market, it should be appreciated that a forward market involves a forward contract that, in the majority of cases, implies physical delivery.

A futures market, on the other hand, features physical delivery in only a minority of cases. Strictly speaking, a futures contract *is* a forward contract in that the delivery of such and such an amount is specified on the contract. However, this market is so organized that sales or purchases of these contracts can be "offset" in such a way that deliveries are unnecessary. The key element here is the presence of speculators who buy or sell futures contracts in hope of making a profit on the difference between sales and purchase price of the contract. A full clarification of this will be provided with the help of some numerical examples later in this chapter, but, in brief, such an arrangement functions as follows: A producer sells a physical commodity for forward delivery at a price related to the price of the commodity on a metal exchange at the time of delivery. At the same time he sells a futures contract. Then, at the time of delivery, he buys a futures contract, offsetting his previous sale. If the price of the commodity has fallen, he loses on the physical transaction; but if the price of futures contracts fall, as they should, then he will gain on the futures (or "paper") transaction. (The matter of how the price of futures contracts should move in relation to the price of the commodity will also be explained later.)

What has happened in this example is that the seller has turned most of his risk over to the buyer of the futures contract, the speculator, who in this case might have thought that the price of the commodity was going to increase, in which case the price of the futures contract would also normally increase, and he would be able to sell this contract for a higher price than he paid for it. The difference between the producer and the speculator in this example is that the producer is primarily concerned with insurance, and regards the selling and buying of the futures contract as being of secondary concern; in the long run, with extensive buying and/or selling of these contracts, he should break even. As for the speculator, his business is to make money on the difference between the price at which he buys the contract and that at which he sells it. Naturally, he can also sell contracts, hoping to make the offsetting purchase at a lower price. In both cases his profit per contract is Sales Price *minus* Purchase Price.

Speculation can also take place in physical items. If, for instance, the producer referred to in the above example had produced a certain amount of metal, and held it in inventory without hedging it, in hope of selling it at a high price later, then he could be labeled a speculator. The same thing is true of someone who bought a commodity in the spot market at a certain price, and hoped to sell it later at a higher price. This is called being *long* in the commodity. Another way of speculating is to sell a commodity *short*. What happens here is that the speculator agrees to sell a commodity in the future for a price above the price at which he thinks he can buy the commodity around the time of delivery. Put another way, when the (forward) contract comes due he buys on the spot market for a price that, if all goes as planned, is under the price on the contract. The designation "short," as used in the above context, means selling something that one does not own.

One of the principal speculators in the commodity markets—particularly in the United States—is the merchant or dealer, and it is instructive to consider his role vis-à-vis the producer and the consumer. As a start, it should be appreciated that an approximate balance on the raw materials market comes about through bilateral deals between major producers and consumers, or their agents. Given the perfect market of the textbooks, at least insofar as information is concerned, producers would produce just enough during a given period to satisfy consumers. As we have come to find out, however, the market is not perfect. Demand increases or decreases in an unpredictable way, while producers over- or underestimate the amount they will be able to sell. Because of these and many other things, a kind of third party is needed to play a residual or balancing role in the market. This is the function of merchants.

Merchants buy and sell commodities both within and without the main producer–consumer channels. As a rule they do not acquire production facilities, but are active in the financing and holding of stocks—both hedged and unhedged. They participate in arbitrage operations, buy scrap materials for refineries processing secondary materials, and act as agents for buyers and sellers on the various commodity exchanges. All in all they have made themselves indispensable to the smooth functioning of the world commodity markets—as they are usually the first to point out.

EXCHANGE CONTRACTS

The various contracts for copper on the LME and COMEX will be the principal subject of this section, the assumption being that copper is a typical industrial raw material, and the stipulations of an exchange contract for copper would be analogous to those of any other commodity traded on an exchange of this type. But first some general remarks concerning this subject will be made.

Contracts in the spot and forward markets are a matter having to do with judicial practice in the country or countries involved. An Austrian manufacturer buys for immediate or forward delivery some manganese from a producer in country B. His principal concern is that he gets his manganese when he wants it, at the agreed price, and that it is the right quality. All of this is specified in the contract entered into by the two parties. At the same time, this contract should be regarded as a unique instrument—that is, a Belgian manufacturer wanting to buy manganese would not necessarily be interested in this particular contract, since it may involve an unsuitable quality and delivery date, and in addition he may be skeptical of the integrity of the seller. On this latter point, the Belgian manufacturer may require stronger provisions in any contract that he might sign in order to insure that he receives compensation in the event delivery was not made on the date specified, or any other provisions of the contract were not fulfilled.

Futures contracts such as those found on the LME and COMEX, however, are standardized. These markets are organized by corporate bodies that determine the conditions under which individuals can trade, standardize contracts, and establish and enforce rules for trading. One of the features of these contracts is that they specify within rigorous limits the grades that are to be dealt in, and the places of delivery. Since many primary commodities do not favor this type of specification, commodity exchanges on which contracts for such commodities may be bought and sold may not exist. In the case of the LME and COMEX, remember that although the majority of the contracts being handled are futures contracts, these are also forward contracts in that delivery *is* specified for all commodities, and thus such things as quality and place of delivery must be rigidly specified in case the buyer decides to take delivery. However, as pointed out, the facilities for buying and selling these contracts without having to consider the matter of delivery—together with the use of these facilities on such a vast scale—makes the futures contract basically uninteresting as a forward contract.

Before looking more closely at some of these contracts, two points that were brought out by Rowe (1965) should be noted and commented on. According to Rowe, if speculation by means of futures contracts is to make sense for the speculator, there must not be a high degree of oligopoly, or monopoly, on the production or distribution side of the market; and the supply of the commodity must not react too quickly to a change in price.

Looking at the first of these, Rowe is saying that with monopoly or a high degree of oligopoly, the speculator is put in the position of trying to "guess" what the seller is going to do. If, however, the seller is involved in the futures market as well as controlling physical supplies of the commodity, he can make such guesswork extremely costly. The reader can consider the following situation.

Speculators who are not in physical possession of a commodity are convinced that the price of the commodity is too high, and so sell short in the forward market. By selling short they agree to deliver a commodity they do not posess, but which they will themselves buy on the spot market at the time of delivery. Other speculators, with the same conviction, *sell* futures contracts, reasoning that when the price of the physical commodity falls the price of futures contracts will also fall—since these two prices have a tendency to move together. Thus, when the futures contract *matures,* and they must *buy* a futures contract specifying the same quantity—in this way offsetting their original purchase of a futures contract—they will make a net profit. (The date of maturity is found on the contract, and the understanding is that either the seller has made an offsetting purchase of a futures contract by that date, or he is prepared to deliver the type and amount of commodity specified by the contract.)

The sale of futures contracts may force down the price of this type of contract; while the forward sales of the physical commodity may give the impression that the future price of the commodity will be lower. Under ideal conditions, individual producers without any extensive communication with each other, and using market prices as signals, would sell in the spot market before the price falls, thus reducing the present high price. But in the case of a monopolist, for example, this need not happen. The monopolist would not sell in the present, and by witholding supplies he would see to it that the commodity price did not fall in the future. Indeed, he might even buy the speculators' futures contracts, and sell them back later at a higher price. Similarly, the short seller on the forward market would find himself having to buy the commodity from the producer at a higher price.

As for the second arrangement cited by Rowe, where he says that futures markets cannot work if the supply of a commodity responds very quickly to a change in price, we can consider the following. If speculators were to predict a low future supply of a commodity, and thus a high price, and consequently *bought* a great many futures contracts, which would normally force up the price of these contracts; and if producers were to interpret the high price of these contracts as an indicator of what the actual price was going to be, and reacted by increasing supply so rapidly as to force down the price about the time the futures contracts were maturing—that is to say, about the time when speculators were making their offsetting sales—then speculators would take serious losses. What Rowe is saying is that, after this happened a number of times, speculators would leave the market. A point of interest here is that instead of speculation causing a high price instability, as is often believed, the presence of speculation may imply the absence of excessive instability.

As for the contract forms themselves, three standard forms for copper are available on the LME. These cover:

1. Electrolytic or fire refined high conductivity wirebars, in standard sizes and weights.
2. Electrolytic copper cathodes, with a copper content of not less than 99.90 percent, or first quality fire refined ingot bars, with a copper content not below 99.7 percent.
3. Fire refined ingot bars with a copper content not below 99.7 percent.

Anybody can buy or sell on the LME, and the only limitation is that the transaction must involve 25 long tons. The brand and place of delivery are chosen by the buyer; however, it must be remembered that by place of delivery we mean one of the LME warehouses. It is this provision that makes the LME of only limited interest as a physical market, although it does not affect its attractiveness for hedging purposes. Each of the three types of refined copper traded has its own daily quotation for both spot—or cash—and forward deals. The spot price is also occasionally called a settlement price, while the forward quotation—which, in terms of practice, is mostly a futures price—is a three-month price. What this means is that if this contract is to be used as a futures contract, the offsetting arrangement must be made within three months time; or if it is to be used as a forward contract, then delivery must be made within the same period.

As for COMEX, only one standard contract form is available. The basic commodity is electrolytic copper in wirebars, slabs, billets, ingots, and ingot bars, or standard weights and sizes, with a copper content of not less than 99.90 percent. The standard unit for trading purposes is 50,000 pounds. In addition to electrolytic copper, a number of other varieties of copper may be delivered at the option of the seller. These include fire refined high conductivity copper, lake copper, electrolytic copper cathodes, etc. According to the regulations of the exchange, copper may be delivered from any warehouse in the United States that is licensed or designated by COMEX, but other warehouses are excluded. Deliveries must be to designated delivery points, and the period of forward trading must be within 14 months. There are seven delivery months: January, March, May, July, September, October, and December.

With the above two sections as an introduction, we can go now to the use of the exchange by hedgers.

THE MECHANICS OF HEDGING

As an introduction to this topic, the reader should examine the following rule: "Those wishing to insure against a fall in price sell futures; while those wishing to insure against a rise in price buy futures." We can now go to some simple examples that should serve to fix this rule in the reader's mind.

A miner sells a commodity for delivery two months in the future at the spot price prevailing on a certain commodity exchange on that day. Let us take 50 as the spot price of the commodity on the day of the sale, and 53 as the price of a five-month futures contract. The miner then contacts his broker, and orders him to *sell* a futures contract for 53. Two months later he delivers his commodity, with the spot price on the exchange on that day being 45, and the price of a futures contract at 46. He thus gets 45 for his commodity, and pays 46 for a futures contract—which offsets his earlier sale. These deals can be summed up as follows:

$$
\begin{array}{rl}
+53 & \text{Sale of futures contract} \\
+45 & \text{Sale of commodity} \\
-46 & \text{Offsetting purchase of futures contract} \\
\hline
+52 & \text{Realized on the sale of the commodity}
\end{array}
$$

The broker's commission should be subtracted from the $+52$ to get the net value of the sale. There are some other technicalities concerning this operation that will be taken up below.

Right now, however, we can concern ourselves with some essentials. On the day that the sale was arranged, the spot price was 50 and the futures price 53. The difference between these is called the *basis*. In other words, Futures Price *minus* Spot Price = Basis, and, in the present example, this is equal to 3. Notice also that the futures price here is larger than the spot price, which is the normal situation, and this is called a *contango*. When the opposite situation prevails it is known as *backwardation*. The insurance aspect of the hedge should now be noted. Had the producer held the commodity unhedged he would have made 45. By hedging he gets 52, from which the broker's fee is subtracted.

It should also be appreciated that for the operation of hedging to work, the basis must experience more or less parallel changes over time, in that there should be no widespread moving from contango to backwardation, nor should there be excessive movements in the value of the basis. This is what we meant earlier when we talked about the way the futures price "should" move in regard to the spot price: when the spot price increases, the futures price should also increase or, as in the case of the example, when the spot price decreases the futures price should follow it down. The reader of the commercial literature might also be aware of the fact that the risk to hedgers is termed *basis risk*.

To see this a little better, we can take the above example and change it so that the futures price on the date of arranging the sale was 51, and the price of a futures contract at the time of delivery is 52. The other prices—the spot price on the date of arranging the sale, and the spot price at the time of delivery—will be left the same (50 and 45) as in the previous example. We then have a change in basis from 1 to 6, and the net value of the sale, not including broker's fee, is 51 + 45 − 52 = 44 (Sale of Futures Contract + Sale of Commodity − Offsetting Purchase of Futures Contract). The hedger has lost on this deal in the sense that, had he not hedged, he would have obtained 45 (= the spot price on the day of delivery). The reader should also be aware that while this loss may seem insignificant, it involves only one unit. Had the producer hedged 150,000 units then it would have been a serious matter. In practice, however, abnormal changes in the basis happen to be rare, and the regular hedger will generally experience a small over- or undercoverage on each deal that will, in the long run, give him neither profit nor loss.

As mentioned earlier in the chapter, commodities are bought on the exchanges employing standard contracts. If we consider copper, a standard contract on both the LME and COMEX is for 50,000 pounds; and so, if a deal involved 150,000 pounds, then 3 contracts would be bought or sold. There is also a time element connected to these contracts. In the first example above, it was mentioned that on the date of arranging the sale the price of a five-month contract was 53, and presumably this was the type of contract sold by the producer. He delivered his commodity in two months, at which time he bought an offsetting contract. Logically, the contract he bought was a three-month contract—logically, because the rule is that when one sells a futures contract it involves a certain month, and when the offsetting purchase is made it must be made for the same month. The same thing is true if we begin the process by buying a contract: we buy for a certain month, and the offsetting sale concerns contracts for the same month. It is also possible to think in terms of a certain date—the maturity date. If someone has sold or bought a contract with a certain date of maturity, then before that date he must make the offsetting purchase or sale of a contract referring to that date.

The next example takes a situation where a *buyer* of copper arranges for delivery of 150,000 pounds of copper two months in the future at the price prevailing on the exchange at that time. Assume the spot price on the day the copper is bought as 30 cents per pound and the futures price 32 (the basis, which is a contango, is thus 2), so the buyer then *buys* 3 futures contracts at 32 each. If we assume that the spot price rises to 40 cents on the day of delivery, with a futures price of 41, then the buyer makes the offsetting sale of 3 contracts (= 150,000 pounds) at 41 per pound, and buys his copper at 40 cents per pound. His book now appears as follows:

-32	Purchase of futures contracts
$+41$	Sale of Futures contracts (offsetting)
-40	Purchase of copper
-29	Net price paid for copper (per pound)

He pays 31 cents per pound (gross of brokerage) for 150,000 pounds of copper. Notice what would have happened had he not bought and sold these futures contracts: he would have paid 40 cents per pound for the copper.

It might be instructive to alter this example slightly. Take a situation where copper is bought for a *fixed* price of 40 for delivery several months in the future. On the same day the futures price of copper is 42, and so the buyer *sells* a contract for 42. On the day the copper is delivered its spot price is 30, and the price of a futures contract 31. The buyer then makes his offsetting purchase of a futures contract at 31. These transactions can be summarized as follows:

-40	Purchase of copper
$+42$	Sale of futures
-31	Purchase of futures (offsetting)
-29	Net price paid for copper (per pound)

Several things are important where this last example is concerned. Had the buyer not hedged, he would have bought copper at 40, while some of his fellow producers bought at 30 or 29, either by waiting to buy spot, or buying at 40 and hedging.

There is also the matter of what the situation would have been had the buyer expected the price to rise dramatically. In this case, had the basis remained constant, it could be reasoned that it might have been better to buy at 40 and not hedge. (Had the price risen to 65, and the basis stayed the same, then hedging would have meant selling a futures contract for 42 and making the offsetting purchase at 67. The cost of copper would then have been $40 + 67 - 42 = 65$.) This type of situation could, of course, happen; but normally we would expect that the large price rise would have been signaled by the price of the futures contract. Instead of selling a futures contract for 42, it might have been possible to sell one for 55 or 60.

Before concluding this section, something should be said about the people who are busy buying and selling the futures contracts that are so important to hedgers. Again an example might be instructive. Let us assume that through one channel or another a speculator comes to believe that there will be a strike in a country mining a very important raw material. What this would mean is a substantial shortfall in the global supply of the commodity, a running down of inventories, and, almost certainly, a considerable increase in the price of the commodity. The speculator thus contacts his broker and orders him to buy futures contracts equivalent to 500,000 pounds of the commodity. For the purposes of this example, let us assume that the contracts are three-month contracts, which are bought in May. Assuming that each contract involves 50,000 pounds, then 10 contracts are bought.

Let us suppose that the price rise does take place. In normal circumstances this would be accompanied by a rise in the price of futures. The speculator therefore contacts his broker and has him make the offsetting sale of 10 contracts. The broker does this, and after subtracting his fee notifies the speculator that he has a profit of $(p_{FS} - p_{FB})$ $(500,000) - f$, where p_{FS} is the selling price per pound, p_{FB} the buying price per pound, and f the broker's fee for the transaction. Had the buying and selling been reckoned by contract instead of by pound, the previous expression would have been altered to $(p'_{FS} - p'_{FB})$ $(10) - f$, where p'_{FS} and p'_{FB} are the selling and buying prices of contracts. All this can be summarized as follows:

Month		Amount	Price
May	Bought August futures	500,000 pounds 10 contracts	p_{FB}/pound
June	Sold August futures	500,000 pounds 10 contracts	p_{FS}/pound

It should not be forgotten that futures contracts for the most part have delivery conditions written into them and this makes them forward contracts. Thus, had the speculator not made the offsetting arrangement, he would actually have owned the commodity in the sense that either he or his broker would have been legally bound to pay for it.

MARKET FORMS

The market forms that are relevant to the sale of most industrial raw materials are oligopoly and something that is a blend of oligopoly and what the textbooks would call "perfectly competitive" or "free market" pricing.

This second type of pricing will be termed *exchange pricing,* and examined rather thoroughly later in this section.

In the case of iron ore, the pricing mechanism would appear to be strictly oligopolistic. The price is negotiated between large producers and large buyers, taking into consideration world supply and demand, and contracts are drawn up specifying dates of delivery, quality of ore, etc. These contracts are both short- and long-term affairs, where short-term means one year, and long-term can mean anything. There are also a great deal of "tied sales," in which buyers of ore own or have helped to develop a source, and therefore are able to buy at prices that may or may not be related to the price that other buyers are paying for the same quality of ore.

Given the above situation, it is impossible to speak of a representative world market price for iron ore. The closest the iron ore market has to this kind of price is the price of Swedish Kiruna D ore, c.i.f. Rotterdam, which is used by the sales company Malmexport on short-term contracts with European buyers. As the following figure shows, however, this price has only a limited value as a proxy or composite price, since the price of iron ore depends upon such things as the quality of ore, the duration of the contract, etc. Price movements are also influenced by transport costs, and the fall in ore prices since 1958 is to some extent the result of a decline in transport prices. Some representative prices are not shown in Figure 5-1.

The information presented in Figure 5-1 deserves a short comment. The price declines apparent during the 1960s had, in fact, begun in the previous decade. They are probably the result of an increasing availability of supplies rather than any extraordinary pressures from the demand side. It should also be pointed out that the Swedish price, beginning toward the end of the 1960s, was countercyclical to some extent to international business conditions and undoubtedly reflected the result of setting prices in advance through the medium of long-term contracts. Japan, on the other hand, has renegotiated a number of contracts, particularly with Australian suppliers. The prices on these contracts were adjusted upward to take into consideration increases in mining costs and the effects of changes in exchange rate.

Another metal that lacks a market place in any sense of the word is tungsten. There are different types of tungsten ores (wolframite and scheelite) and, within these types, different grades and qualities. Because of the nonhomogeneity of the commodity, and the absence of a terminal market, there is again no single "world price." A kind of substitute for such a quotation is a price published in the Metal Bulletin twice a week. When contracts are being negotiated for tungsten, this price enters into consideration as a sort of reference price.

Much the same situation applies for cobalt and manganese. With

Price (Current Dollars)

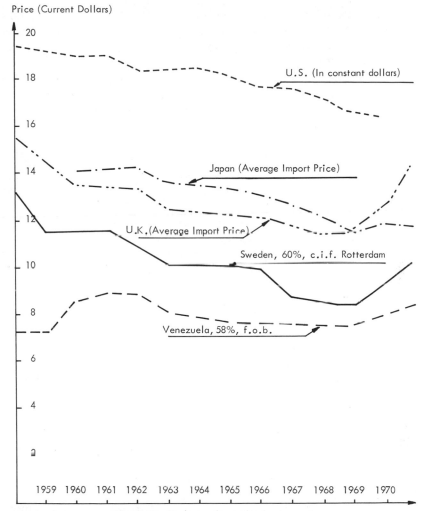

Figure 5-1. Various price series for iron ore.

cobalt, the chief producer is Zaire, and the domination by Zaire of the world market is so complete as virtually to cause all other producers to follow its lead in pricing. On the demand side, the big factor has been the United States, to include the demand of the U.S. strategic stockpile. This stockpile had an important influence on world pricing in both the 1950s and 1960s, and, since at present it may be carrying a stock equal to three-years of production for the entire world, it must still be taken into consideration when trying to predict what will happen to the price of cobalt. It is worth noticing that the steep rise in the price of cobalt during the early part of the 1970s was due to purchases by consumers of nickel who, because of the nickel shortage during this period, used cobalt as a replacement for nickel, especially in electroplating.

The manganese market is probably more distinctly a case of bilateral oligopoly than cobalt. There are some eight large producers trading with a handful of large steel companies and minerals-trading firms. Prices are determined by individual negotiation, and, since many factors enter into these negotiations, we once again cannot distinguish any representative price for the market. As with tungsten, however, the price of battery-grade manganese ore is quoted in the Metal Bulletin, and this price undoubtedly has an important role to play in negotiations between buyers and sellers all over the world.

Before continuing, the reader should be reminded that no matter how oligopolistic a market for an ore might be, it almost always contains a large tier of very small suppliers. For instance, in the United States in 1951, the mining sector showed the following:

Number of firms	Number of employees				
	0–7	8–49	50–99	100–999	1000+
36,100	27,000	7,000	1,000	1,000	100

A similar picture would have been applicable for Chile in 1970, where there were more than 3,000 small or very small copper mines.

We now come to the main topics of this section, which are producer and "exchange" pricing, and which are relevant to a large percentage of the industrial raw materials being traded in the world's markets. Producer pricing involves the following: the producers of a certain commodity set what they believe to be a long-run equilibrium price, on the basis of which they make their production decision. This price, of course, does not always clear the market. If there is excess demand, production is rationed among consumers; while, if there is excess supply, stocks are accumulated for a while, and later some capacity will go out of operation.[1]

In the United States, in 1966, the total supply of refined copper amounted to 2,409,000 metric tons. This was broken down as follows: 1,703,000 metric tons were sold at the U.S. producers' price, with 1,300,000 of these coming from producers, and 403,000 from U.S. strategic stocks. Another 168,000 metric tons were sold at a so-called "special Chilean price," or at the Canadian price. For all practical purposes these are just

[1]The basis for rationing in the U.S. copper market is apparently consumer loyalty during those periods when the market for copper is weak.

prices at which certain copper buyers bought this product when they could not obtain any "producer" copper. The two prices were, in general, greater—but not very much greater—than the U.S. producer price.

The rest of the copper sold was at free market prices. This involved 111,000 metric tons from domestic and foreign suppliers; and 430,000 metric tons from scrap. Domestic and foreign suppliers include various categories of suppliers outside the United States; small, high-cost producers inside the United States who begin to produce when the price gets high enough; and holders of inventories. This last group is the most interesting from our point of view, since, as we have tried to explain earlier, there appears to be a direct correlation between movements in stocks and movements in prices. As for the supply from scrap, that topic will be examined in the last chapter of this book, but it can be pointed out now that the amount of scrap collected and processed is a function of the price of copper—although of late this rule is working badly.

The next thing is to say something about the holders of inventories. In the United States, stocks are principally held by consumers, producers, and by merchants or dealers. These merchants buy or sell on the part of consumers and/or producers, or for their own accounts. It is these merchants who, in the U.S. copper market, determine the free market price by their activities, and the merchant (or dealer) price is often quoted alongside the producer price in many publications. In Europe the free market price of copper is generally considered to be the London Metal Exchange price. On the LME, merchants buy or sell for customers who have underestimated their requirements or who have more of the commodity on hand than they require.[2] As will be pointed out later, considerable stocks are held in London Metal Exchange warehouses, and these stocks are in many respects an excellent proxy for *all* stocks being held outside North America. (A somewhat smaller level of stocks is held by the U.S. Commodity Exchange.) Figure 5-2 shows the producer price of copper—as an average—over the period 1964–66, and the producer price of nickel, as well as the free market prices of these commodities. The free market price for copper is taken to be the LME price; and for nickel, the U.S. merchant price.

For expository reasons, all producers are not represented in Figure 5-2. The copper producers involved are those of Zambia, Chile, and Zaire

---

[2] Among the organizations that might have more than they desire are fabricators as well as producers. It is to be noted that in a perfect market there would probably be no need for merchants: everyone would correctly judge what he required or what he could sell. Markets, however, are not perfect, and merchants know this. For instance, in 1965 in the United States, merchants probably bought large amounts of copper for their own inventories, knowing that there would be excess demand in 1966.

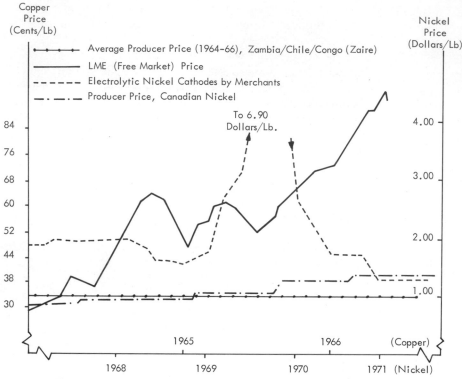

Figure 5-2. Some producer and free market prices of copper and nickel.

(Congo). It was, as a matter of fact, because of the great discrepancy between the producer price and the free market price that these producers abandoned producer pricing in 1966 and went over to "exchange" pricing. This type of pricing will be taken up below. American producers, on the other hand, still employ producer pricing, and are extremely happy with it—so happy, in fact, that in recent months a number of high-pitched attacks on exchange pricing have emanated from the executive suites of several very large North American producers.

The question that immediately comes to mind is why the producers of these—and other—commodities did not raise the producer price immediately, and thereby help themselves to the larger profits that would have resulted from a higher price. The first answer to the question is that perhaps the producers did not know what the equilibrium price was: they may have thought that the price was being held up by speculative components that would soon disappear. In waiting for this, the price was adjusted upward in small steps every six months or so. The problem here is that while speculative components can be unusually strong, speculators have a way of learning from the actual supply–demand situation after a time. Thus, while it may be considered excusable for producers to hold their price under the free market price for a short time, after six months or a year of this they should have admitted that the actual equilibrium price was in the vicinity of the free market price.

The second possibility is that although the equilibrium price might have been on the same level as the free market price, and perhaps producers even recognized this from the beginning, they reasoned that if they put up their prices, consumers would switch to substitutes. Once this happens, it is usually the case that, for technical reasons, they do not switch back. While large, diversified corporations in the industrial countries may not be so afraid of this happening, producers in the LDCs must be extremely careful. Moreover, as the record shows, they have been careful—and will probably continue to be so.

Finally, producers may have come to the conclusion that if they put their price up to the free market price, thus declaring for all the world that the equilibrium price is much higher than the actual price, then this will provide the incentive for a great deal of investment in new capacity. The producer price for copper shown in Figure 5-2 is an average price for the period shown, and in the latter part of the period the price in the three countries mentioned was increased to more than 40 cents/pound. In the circumstances, profits were quite high; and had the price been increased still further, a number of projects that were on the drawing board would have been rushed to completion.

The producer price for the United States is not shown in Figure 5-2 but it was about on the same level as that of the three countries shown, and much more stable. It was so stable, in fact, that eventually President Nixon found it necessary to commission one of his economic advisers, Professor Henrik Houthakker, to investigate the U.S. copper industry. After several years of speeches, hearings, press releases, and all the rest of it, the investigation faded away and, in due course, Professor Houthakker returned to the perfect-competition models of academic economics—probably a much wiser man. It is interesting to conjecture that had it not been for the oil crisis, which caused a general slowing down in the industrial growth of the United States, it is possible that the U.S. copper industry would have been faced with a shortage of capacity toward the end of the 1970s. Had this shortage occurred or, for that matter, should it occur, it would have its origin in the low producer prices of the 1960s. (Just as the low oil prices of the 1950s and 1960s are the principal causes of the so-called oil crisis.)

We can now begin an examination of exchange pricing. This topic is relevant for many countries and many commodities but, for the sake of simplicity, the present exposition will treat copper, with the exchange on which this copper is priced the London Metal Exchange (LME). Institutionally, exchange pricing functions somewhat as follows: a producer sells *x* tons of copper to a consumer for delivery at a future date, at a price that is the price of copper on the LME at or around the time of delivery. This price is unknown at the time the contract is drawn, and thus we have the rather unusual case of selling a *known* quantity at an *unknown* price. As mentioned earlier in this section, the price formed on the LME is established on the basis of a residual supply and demand that is, to a considerable extent, reflected in the relatively small amount of copper that is physically transacted for on the LME. Yet a large part of the copper produced outside North America is priced according to its quotations, and a strong argument can be made that the LME price—or, for that matter, the price on any exchange that functions like the LME—is about as close to a free market or perfectly competitive price as it is possible to get with this type of commodity.

The significance of exchange pricing for profits can now be examined. We start out by presenting, in Figure 5-3, the "cost" curves for two major copper producers, Chile and Peru.

These costs are for 1970, and they include administration, transport, and amortization. In that year Chile, for example, mined 690,000 tons of copper (point A in (a), Figure 5-3), and refined about 465,000 tons (point B in (a), Figure 5-3). The average world price of refined copper in 1970 was almost 60 cents/per pound or $1200 per ton. Thus, in 1970 Chile gained from the sale of copper almost 690,000 × 1200 dollars *minus* the cost of processing 690,000 − 465,000 = 225,000 tons. Some copper that was sold in 1970 cost more than 60 cents/pound to produce, but was sold for less than 60 cents/pound because long-term contracts had been signed much earlier saying that about 690,000 tons of copper would be sold during 1970 at a price that would be determined around the time of delivery.

Many readers probably feel that this method of selling a commodity involves an unacceptable degree of gambling—although, in truth, the operators of retail stores accept precisely the same kind of risk. In the short run, however, producers of copper have little choice. They cannot determine their level of production on the basis of a very conservative estimate of demand, because it is just as expensive to take capacity out of operation, and to put it back into operation later when the demand increases, as it is to sell 5, 10, or even 15 percent of the volume of commodity produced below the unit cost from time to time. In the long run, if the price trend is clearly revealed to be downward, then some high-cost capacity can be taken out of operation.

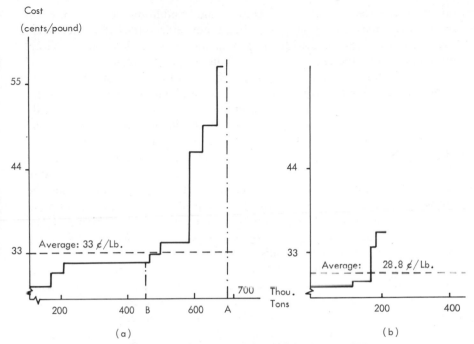

Figure 5-3. Total cost curves for Chile and Peru (1970).

The curves shown in Figure 5-3 are not supply curves—in that they are not marginal cost curves—but they are almost equally valuable for the purpose of the present discussion. There has been a great deal of speculation of late as to what is a fair price for copper and other raw materials, and various experts have come out in favor of declaring a fair price to be the cost of the last unit that the industry is capable of producing. If we continue with the case of Chile, this would mean calling a fair price—in 1970— somewhat over 60 cents/pound. This would have meant not excess profits, but superexcess profits for many installations. At this so-called fair price, however, *all* installations would have been provided with a return large enough for them to maintain their output, whether or not there was a demand for this output.[3] Whether intelligent consumers will be willing to accept this concept of fairness remains to be seen. The matter can probably best be handled by introducing some ideas from the elementary course in microeconomics. If producers feel that they have not covered, and are not

---

[3]This is so since the total unit cost includes the cost of replacement of the capacity producing that unit. Roughly speaking, we could put it as follows: as long as the producer gets enough in revenue to cover all costs, to include replacement costs, then he has an incentive to continue to produce that output.

covering, the cost of high-cost facilities, and in addition feel that they can never cover these costs, then they should not replace these facilities when they depreciate. Some consumers would then have to learn to get along without the commodity, or find a substitute, or pay a higher price for it.

At this point we can go to the mechanics of determining the price of copper on the LME. To begin, let us take a situation where the current global supply and demand of the commodity just about balance. Normally this would mean very small movements in the inventories of copper held around the world in general, and very small movements in the inventories of copper held in LME warehouses in particular. In addition, a situation of this type implies a stable price. Now let us assume an increase in demand of such an order that it could not be met merely by producers increasing the input of variable factors and/or bringing unused capacity back into operation. This would lead to a general reduction in inventories, to include LME inventories; and employing the arguments presented earlier in this book would result in an increase in price.

We can now try to get some idea of the relationship between inventories and price by examining some data from the LME. Figure 5-4 is not conclusive, in that *no* figure can be labeled conclusive for scientific purposes, but it is highly suggestive.[4] As inventories fall, price rises!

The final matter that will be considered in this section concerns some ramifications of the spread between the spot (or cash) price of copper on the LME, and the three-month price. Beginning in 1966, and continuing to 1968, the forward or three-month price of this commodity was almost always lower than the spot price. In other words, the market experienced a fairly long period of backwardation. The question must then be raised as to why stockholders did not immediately unload their inventories, since the three-month price (= the forward or futures price) must to some degree be regarded as an "expected" price.

The explanation here turns on the so called *convenience yield* of stocks. If prices should rise, a stockholder, if he is a producer or merchant, has some stocks to sell; and if he is a consumer, he has them on hand to

---

[4]Ertek (1967) has used a relation of the type $\Delta P = \alpha \Delta I$, where I represents world private stocks of refined copper, that would probably show good results with the data on which Figure 5-4 was constructed. The most satisfactory price equation that I know in most respects, however, is that of Fisher, Cootner, and Baily (1972). They have estimated the LME price of copper with an equation of the type

$$P_t = \alpha_0 + \alpha_1 \left(\frac{I_t}{C_t} - \frac{I_{t-1}}{C_{t-1}} \right) + \alpha_2 P_{t-1}$$

Here I signifies stocks of refined copper outside the U.S., while C is world consumption excluding the U.S.

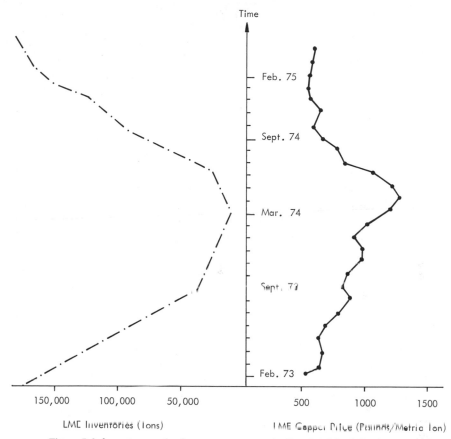

Figure 5-4. Inventory and price movements on the London Metal Exchange.

use. Moreover, backwardation is almost always associated with relatively small inventories, which in turn means that the total carrying charges are small. It is, in fact, the small carrying cost of these stocks relative to the gains that could result in the event of increases in demand or price that explains the willingness to hold stocks in the face of momentary expectations that the price of the commodity will be smaller in the future.

At the other end of the scale we find a situation where large stocks are held, and the expected price is considerably larger than the present price. Large inventories, of course, mean large total carrying charges, and stockholders are willing to hold these commodities only if they are offered a premium in the form of high yields on them in the future. A high futures or forward price is no guarantee that the price in the future will in reality be high, but some evidence exists that at times stockholders as a group employ an assumption of this type.

A SURVEY OF THE WORLD COPPER MARKET

Background

The purpose of this section is to present a nontechnical survey of the world copper industry. Readers desiring a technical exposition are referred to Fisher, Cootner, and Baily (1972), Ertek (1967), and Banks (1974).

Copper may be the first metal used by man. It is possible that rough tools or weapons made from copper existed 20,000 years before the birth of Christ; and various copper objects have been found that date from ancient Babylon and Egypt (5–4000 B.C.). The chief producers of the metal, beginning about 1500 A.D., were Hungary and Sweden, and, toward the end of the 18th century, England. By 1850, however, half the world's production originated in Chile, and this situation prevailed until about 1883, when the United States became the leading world producer. As for the African mines, their development dates from the post-World War I period, with large-scale developments in Katanga starting in 1924 and in Zambia in 1931.

Copper is highly resistant to corrosion, making it an excellent conduit for water and chemicals. It is also an excellent conductor of heat, and, above all, a superb conductor of electricity. If we want to rate conductors, using a scale of 100, if copper is rated 100, then silver is also 100, pure gold 78, and aluminum 54.2. Thus aluminum, which is copper's chief competitor in the electrical field, has only slightly more than one-half the conductivity of copper. Of course, composite cables consisting of aluminum and copper are also in the process of development, and these combine to a considerable extent the high conductive efficiency of copper with the strength and relative inexpensiveness of aluminum.

About 50 percent of the consumption of copper takes place in the electrical sector. Construction accounts for 15 percent; transport, 6 percent; and the rest is divided among foundries, electrometalurgical uses, and so on. Of the total amount of copper used, about 60 percent is primary or newly refined copper, while about 12 percent is refined copper having its origin in scrap. Approximately 28 percent of copper consumption is nonrefined scrap whose primary destination is brass mills and various alloy-producing operations.

Approximately 40 percent of the production of mined copper originates in North America (United States and Canada), 40 percent in the CIPEC countries (Chile, Peru, Zaire, and Zambia), and 14.5 percent in the U.S.S.R. About 28 percent of world *refined* production originates in North America, 17 percent in Europe, and 12 percent in Japan. The principal European refiners are the Federal Republic of Germany, Belgium, Great Britain, and Spain.

Table 5-1. Copper Imports, in All Forms, as a
Percentage of Domestic Copper Consumption, 1972[a]

Source	U.S.	Japan	OECD (Europe)
Philippines	1	20	1
Papua (Bougainville)	—	5	—
CIPEC countries	7	29	49
Chile	3	8	16
Zambia	—	16	16
Peru	4	4	2
Zaire	—	1	15
South Africa	1	2	6
Uganda	—	1	—
Socialist Bloc	1	—	4
Other OECD	6	29	15
Canada	6	23	8
Australia	—	6	3
Other countries	1	6	6

[a] Includes imports that are reexported.

Among the LDCs, the principal refiners are Zambia (with 7 percent of world refining capacity), Chile (6 percent), and Zaire (2.5 percent). Peru, which is an important producer of raw copper, only refines about 0.5 percent of the world total. Where smelting is concerned, the CIPEC countries smelt 26.5 percent of world production (Chile, 9 percent; Peru, 2.5 percent; Zaire, 6 percent; and Zambia, 9 percent). On the consumption side, Europe consumes about 31 percent of world copper; the United States, 25 percent; and Japan, 10.5 percent. Zaire exports most of its raw copper to Belgium and most of its refined copper to various other European countries. Zambia's nonrefined copper goes mostly to Japan and England, while the rest of Europe and Japan take the greater part of its refined production. Chile exports the greater part of its production to Japan and Europe; while the principal part of Peruvian production goes to the United States. Table 5-1 gives an indication of copper imports as a percentage of domestic copper consumption.

The question of price is also of interest at this point. The price of copper bounded up sharply during the 1950s and 1960s; and again after the October War in the Middle East. It was apparently the war in Vietnam and the upward trend in world prosperity during the last part of the 1960s that provided these impulses. Given the enormous amount of material being written these days about the fairness of commodity prices, it might be appropriate to make some speculations about the situation with copper over the last 10 years. In 1964 prices were on a plateau of about £ 250/ metric ton, while 10 years later they were nearing £ 1000/metric ton. If we were to make the somewhat dubious assumption that costs increased by 100 percent during the same period, there is still a great deal to suggest that profits in at least certain parts of the world copper industry were extremely healthy until about the beginning of 1975.

While theoretically it is a simple matter to get profit rates from the balance sheets of the copper-producing companies, in practice there are a number of factors prohibiting a straightforward calculation of this type. Still, I have been able to satisfy myself that the average profit rate during these years was on the order of 20 percent for the CIPEC countries. It should be remembered, however, that before the transfers of ownership that took place in some of these countries, most of these profits ended up in North America or Europe. As for the profit situation at the present time in these countries, my calculations indicate that, even in today's market, the target—and probably the realized—profit rate is somewhere around 15 percent. Figure 5-5 shows the London copper quotations from 1850 to the end of 1974.

In 1974 the growth of the gross national product in the OECD countries was almost zero. Although there was little or no decrease in the production of copper, a number of experts were inclined to assure the author that this would have no effect on the price of copper. The opinion here is that the only way for this to have been the case would have been for the law of supply and demand to go into retirement. This did not occur, however, and eventually the price fell—or crashed, to be exact. The price of wirebars was 1030 at the end of the first quarter in 1974; it rose to £ 1400/ metric ton during the second quarter; and by the end of the year it was at £528/ton. At times it was under 500, and at the moment of writing it is at 825.

This last figure deserves some comment. The last two years have featured an extremely high rate of inflation *and* the devaluation of both dollars and pounds. What this means is that the *real price* of copper is probably well under £600/metric ton. In other words, a seller of copper in the LDCs is able to buy only about 75 or 80 percent as much with his £825 today as he was two or three years ago—assuming that he is buying from the industrial countries.

Copper Cartels

Few commodities have been the object of as many attempts at price manipulation as copper. One of the first of these efforts dates from 1887, when the Société Industrielle et Commerciale des Métaux, led by Pierre Secretan, and supported by the Comptoir d'Escompte and other financial institutions, contracted for about 80 percent of the world production of

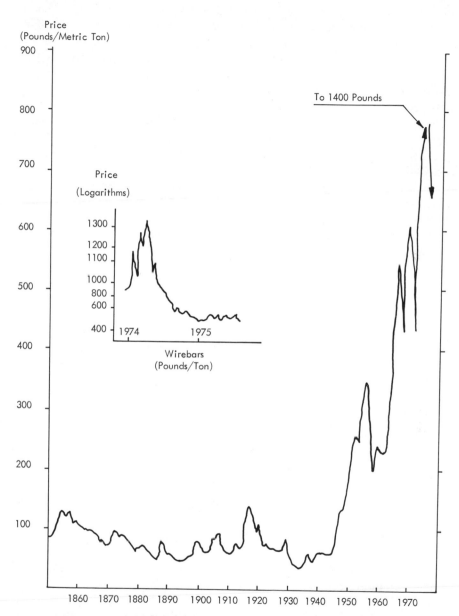

Figure 5-5. London copper quotations (Annual averages), 1850–1974.

copper. The price of copper rose from £40 to £80/metric ton in a few months as enormous inventories of the commodity were accumulated and placed out of range of the market. Considerable profits were made both in the metal and in mining shares.

This rise in price, however, caused a 17 percent increase in the production of primary copper alone. In addition, consumers hesitated to buy at the exaggerated prices.The stockpiles of copper eventually got out of hand as an increased supply had to be absorbed, and in 1889—in the face of falling demand—the Société was unable to honor its debts. The Comptoir began sliding into bankruptcy, and, when this news leaked out, copper was sold for whatever it would bring. In less than a year the price was back at the 1887 level.

The next organization of note was the so called "Amalgamated Pool." This operation was put together by Standard Oil, which for some reason took an interest in copper. A firm was formed with the name "Amalgamated Copper Company," with one of its suborganizations being the now well-known Anaconda Company. This organization eventually controlled about 20 percent of the copper production of the world, and together with some of the other large producers was able to fix the price at 17 cents/pound. Earlier, the price had been 11 cents.

Again, however, independent producers raised production to such an extent that the price could not be maintained. Fortunately for the Pool, they were able to liquidate the stocks they had built up, and this encouraged them to try another price-fixing adventure in 1906. This time the great financial panic of 1907 kept them from succeeding.

At the end of World War I, with a million tons of scrap copper covering the battlefields of Europe, and another million tons of refined copper in the inventories of various producers and governments, it was time to form another cartel. This time it was the U.S. producers, led by Anaconda, Phelps Dodge, and the Guggenheim Group (Kennecott and Asarco), and inspired by the Webb-Pomerene Act of April 10, 1918, that permitted the operation of American cartels in foreign markets. The organization that was formed was called the Copper Export Association and it functioned from about 1918 to 1923.

The purpose of this cartel was to restrict production and thus maintain the price of copper in the face of the postwar fall in demand. Some success was registered, particularly in the export market, but as the world economic situation normalized, and the producers fell to quarreling among themselves, the association gradually went out of business.

Many of the lessons learned with the Copper Export Association were put into practice with the Copper Exporters Inc. In particular, the American producers went to great lengths to ally themselves with foreign producers, and this time between 65 percent and 95 percent of world production was regulated in one way or another. Also, a great deal of time and effort went into convincing consumers that the cartel was acting in their interest against "middlemen" and "intermediaries," who were pictured as being responsible for the volatility of the price of the metal.

For almost two years the cartel functioned well, and then a wave of buying by European consumers sent the price to what the cartel directors saw as an unhealthy high—that is to say, high enough to prompt the entry of new producers. As a result, the producers established what they called a "sacred" price of 18 cents/pound. It was time, however, for the great depression to make its entry, and the problem of the cartel now became one of holding up the price. In theory, the basis on which a cartel is founded is a gentleman's agreement among its members, but, with the price accelerating downward, many of the members forgot that they were gentlemen and entered into a round of competitive price cutting that did not end until the price hit 5 cents/pound. Faced with this situation the U.S. government closed its borders to foreign producers by imposing a tariff of 4 cents/pound. Officially, this cartel went out of business in 1932.

The last prewar grouping of this kind was the International Copper Cartel. Although the idea for this cartel originated in North America, the active participants were to be the larger of the African and South American copper producers: Rhokana Corporation in North Rhodesia, Mulfulira Copper Mines Ltd. and Roan Antelope of Rhodesia, Braden Copper of Chile, Chile Exploration and Andes Copper Mining of Chile, and Union Minière of Katanga (Congo). All these corporations were linked, in various ways, to the major North American producers, and the purpose of the cartel was to establish production quotas of one type or another, harmonize commercial practices, and provide members with some statistical services. The administrative side of the last activity was to be handled by the Copper Institute of New York. Everything considered, this cartel was as much of a failure as those preceding it, and, at the time it disbanded—in 1939—world copper prices were setting out on another downward journey.

It was at this point that World War II took over. During the war new stocks were built up and a great deal of new capacity came into being. These stocks, and this capacity, were able to keep the price of copper at a moderate level until the Vietnam War and growing prosperity in Europe and Japan combined to bring about a strong upward pressure during the last part of the 1960s. Cartels, or at least overt cartels, were for the most part absent from the scene during the postwar period, but it should be remembered that from the final hours of World War II until about the middle of the war in Vietnam, a large part of the decisions concerning the world copper industry were made—or approved—in North America, and thus it might be reasoned that a cartel, at least in this industry, would have been superfluous.

Two important lessons can be culled from the above. The first is that production restrictions have not, in the entire history of the industry, succeeded in reversing a fall in price when the market is in a state of decline. This is not to say that restrictions could not work—particularly if they were very large, and maintained over long periods of time; but thus far they have not worked. Also, large price rises have a way of bringing about rapid increases in production, and perhaps even of capacity. Earlier in this chapter it was noted that certain personalities in and around the world copper industry have taken to condemning the London Metal Exchange. The reason for this is the sensitivity of the exchange where price increases are concerned: it picks up optimism early and holds it until late. Historically, optimism has meant bad news for certain elements in the industry, since optimism ultimately means competition, and competition is precisely what the major firms in most industries of this type want to avoid.

The CIPEC Countries

The ownership of the Chilean copper mines has been a bone of contention in that country since the opening of the first mine more than a century ago. It apparently became a respectable political issue—respectable to reactionaries, that is—only under the Frei government in the 1960s. Of course, even before Frei the handwriting was on the wall for all who cared to read it: the Chilean government had, for years, been attempting to accelerate the expansion and modernization of the mines, the point being that when these assets were finally nationalized neither time, energy, nor money would be necessary to put them into first-class condition. The copper producers, on the other hand, had been just as stubborn when it came to resisting or ignoring the pressure being put on them: they preferred repatriating their profits to North America, where they were either passed out in dividends or rerouted toward more politically comfortable parts of the world.

Just what Sr. Frei's actual program was is difficult to say, even now. At one time or another he announced plans for buying out the copper companies; but he also seems to have been prepared to offer investment guarantees that, evidently, were based on a long-term foreign presence in the Chilean mining sector. In attempting to judge President Frei, or for that matter previous Chilean governments, there is one thing the reader should never forget. Although the culturally advanced Chileans found foreign ownership of their most important industry intolerable, there was also the practical matter of being able to sell their copper that had to be taken into consideration. Had the mines been seized at a time when many of the political and industrial leaders of the main consuming countries were disposed to listen to Washington (D.C.), some difficulty might have been experienced by the Chileans in selling their copper.

But by the time the Allende government had come to power, things and events in the United States and in Vietnam had convinced most of the important decision-makers in the industrial world that they could get along without advice from their colleagues in the United States. As the reader probably knows, the mines were nationalized and, for that matter, they are still nationalized. Dr. Allende, however, was deposed by a putsch brought on largely by the unsuitability of the economic policies both he and his advisers insisted on following.

The new government is going ahead with a program of increasing the production of the extractive industries, although the present low prices of primary commodities must raise some doubts as to the viability of such a program. One thing, of course, is certain: it will be impossible for any government in Chile to turn the ownership of these industries over to foreigners. On this simple fact just about all shades of Chilean political opinion are agreed. It should be noted also that, since the fall of Allende, the foreign creditors of Chile have shown an unexpected generosity toward that country. The so-called "Club of Paris" has revealed a willingness to renegotiate Chilean loans, which is rather uncommon; and the U.S. government seems to have cleared the way for Chile to obtain whatever short-term credits it needs, despite the fact that at this time the Chilean economy is at least as badly off as it was under Allende.

The Central African experience was somewhat different from that described above. The British penetration of Zambia, or Northern Rhodesia as it was then known, was a relatively simple matter. The problem is that only a few people not involved in manufacturing imperialist slogans were able to figure out just what they were doing there—at least until the mining boom of the 1920s. At that time a large number of British, and some American, companies arrived to stake out claims to the rich copper, zinc, tin, and cobalt properties. Colonists arrived from the south of Africa and Europe, and the so-called "Copper Belt" became one of the richest parts of Africa.

Eventually, however, the essential laziness and lack of initiative of the mining company officials was found to be dispensable by the indigenous population—and those gentlemen departed, taking with them their colonial government. What followed was the government of Kenneth Kaunda, who is said to be a disciple of Gandhi and who had been active in the nationalist movement since the early 1950s.

Kaunda has begun a program to favor Africans in employment and commerce, and he has also negotiated the building of the Tan-Zam railroad by the Chinese. He imposed financial restrictions on foreign mining companies in 1968, and nationalized the mines in 1969 after a strike that stopped all production. Kaunda's plans call for a gradual building up of capacity, and he is said to favor economic self-reliance. He also says that he wants to avoid the "demons of development" and preserve human values. The fact of the matter is, however, that development and human values go together, although, until recently, it has been the case in countries like Sweden and England that a certain amount of television time has been available for individuals capable of formulating persuasive arguments to the contrary.

The territory covered by the state of Zaire was colonized under the Belgian King Leopold, and the Belgians administered what was known as the Belgian Congo until it became independent in 1960. A certain amount of violence went into colonizing and keeping the country pacified, and it obtained its independence amid scenes of chaos and political assassination. The former Belgian Congo provides, in most respects, a perfect example of Disraeli's remark that "colonies were a mistake because they didn't make money." There was, quite naturally, some money to be made in this large and rich country; but by the time it had been portioned out to officers and noncommissioned officers, various and sundry officials, stockholders and employees of the mining companies, and so on, hardly any made its way back to Europe in a form that would benefit the average Belgian. On the contrary, the Belgian taxpayer was, as often as not, called upon to close the gap between expenses and revenues where the management of the Congo was concerned. Of course, among the Belgian residents of Central Africa there were many who said they believed in the Congo, in the civilizing mission of the mother country, in freedom of travel, and so on; but like most Europeans with an itch to live in underdeveloped countries, what they really believed in were the privileges and luxuries that, under no circumstances, would have been available for them in their own countries.

After much coming and going by private armies, mercenaries, and the like, Zaire eventually settled down. The government of General Mobutu evidently favors private enterprise and is inclined to allow foreigners to participate in the economy to a certain extent. One of the programs of the general will be interesting to follow, since it calls for 100-percent refining of locally mined copper by 1980. Future mining ventures must also offer 50 percent ownership to the state, and all firms operating in the country had to have Zairean top management by 1975. "Le Guide," as General Mobutu is known to the faithful, is said to aspire to leadership in Africa; but, on the basis of his performance thus far, it would appear that he is not prepared to allow his political aspirations to interfere with certain economic realities.

In many respects Peru would have to be called the most interesting of the CIPEC countries, and, in fact, one of the most interesting of all LDCs. The country has a military government that calls itself "revolutionary"— as most military governments have a habit of doing these days; but, actually, it does seem to be working in the direction of a kind of welfare state.

There is, for instance, worker participation in management on a fairly wide scale; and a stiff agrarian reform law has been provided, forbidding absentee ownership. Together with this, minimum wage and profit-sharing legislation has been put through. The government's program began with the automobile industry in 1968, and continued with fishmeal, sugar, and petroleum firms. Companies that were expropriated have been compensated to a certain extent, and separate deals have been made with companies like Cerro de Pasco for its copper mines, and with ITT—which was given a hotel and an equipment company in exchange for its telephone system. It has also been the case in Peru that many firms in the extractive industries have managed to avoid nationalization by going along with government welfare and profit-sharing schemes, and helping to establish local suppliers.

In many sectors of the Peruvian economy, foreign-owned companies must set schedules for the transfer of 51 percent of the shares in their firms to Peruvians, and they are required to invest 15 percent of annual profits in employee stock. Also, in the future, the public sector will be expanded to include so-called *empresas de propriedad social,* which will be formed by groups of workers and whose profits will be used to finance other public-service enterprises. It would also appear that Peru intends to expand its refining capacity as fast as possible; and plans may also exist to raise its not inconsiderable production of copper semifabricates.

The above four countries constitute the CIPEC membership at present, and together they mine about 40 percent of the world's copper. It could happen, of course, that at some time in the future they are joined by other LDCs and even a developed country or two. Among the LDC candidates, the names of Indonesia, Iran, and Panama are most often mentioned. Huge deposits have been discovered in some of these countries—for example, the Cerro Colorado in Panama is said to contain 2,000 million tons of ore with a copper content of .80—and rumors fill the air about other discoveries about to take place in the Caribbean and Africa. Like most organizations with an international membership, CIPEC has formulated a policy that pays lip service to such things as the preservation of an orderly market and the rights of the consumer. The truth of the matter is, however, that what CIPEC wants to do—but will probably never be able to do—is to emulate OPEC. However, even if they were able to form a successful cartel and raise the price of copper by several hundred percent, the resultant sales would hardly be of a sufficient magnitude to bring health, welfare, and happiness to 40 or 50 million people; nor would it necessarily stimulate the industrial development that is quite indispensable for these things.

The Copper Producing Firms

The world of the major copper producers is a world of interlocking or partially interlocking directorships, either among the companies themselves, or among various banks and financial institutions that are associated with these companies. This is not a value judgment, or condemnation of these firms and/or banks, but merely a statement of fact. Moreover, as far as is generally known, nobody has yet to prove or disprove that the world would be a better place if these arrangements did not exist.

There is no point in using more than a sentence or two to explain why the industry takes the form it does. Deposits of copper ore tend to be contiguous and, as a result, minimum-cost exploitation requires enormous capital investments. It is in the present nature of things that these investments, and the operations they lead to, inevitably fall under a single directorate. There are, of course, some sociological problems raised by the exploitation of South American and African copper by Europeans and North Americans. Claes Brundenius (1972) has looked into some aspects of this matter where South America is concerned and drawn some conclusions that are hardly flattering to the entrepreneurs launching these enterprises, nor, for that matter, to those individuals or social groupings that made them feel so welcome for so long a time. Brundenius's work is cited here because it is well written and contains a certain irony. Most of the so-called scholarly work in this area is not well written, however, and features not irony but the intense envy of academics who take the large salaries and imagined power of the top managers of these firms as a calculated insult to their own modest place in the scheme of things.

The first step here will be to give some idea of the global reach—or lack of global reach—of some of the major copper producers. This information is presented in Table 5-2, and shows the ownership situation dating back prior to the last wave of nationalizations. One of the things the reader should appreciate is that although some of these companies have lost their most valuable properties, they are far from bankruptcy. The reason for this is that the prosperity of most of these organizations is built on organizational and technical skills: it is these skills that exploit this or that resource, and, even if the resource disappears, these proficiencies remain and can move on to another assignment.

The world copper industry has been largely dominated by North

Table 5-2. Some of the Major Copper Producing Firms

Firm	Subsidiary	Country
Anaconda	Chile Exploration	Chile
	Anaconda	United States–Canada
	Exotica	Chile
	Andes Copper Mining	Chile
	Inspiration	United States
	Cananca	Mexico
Kennecott	Kennecott	United States
	El Teniente	Chile
Anglo American	N'Changa Consolidated	Zambia
(Charter	Rhokana Corporation	Zambia
consolidated)	Bancroft Mines	Zambia
	Hudson Bay Mining	Canada
	Société Minière (Mauretania)	Mauretania
Amax	Roan Selection Trust	Zambia
	Copper Range	United States
	Heath-Steel Mine	Canada
Asarco	Southern Peru	Peru
	Asarco	United States–Canada
	Mount Isa	Australia
	Northern Peru	Peru
	Asarco Mexicana	Mexico
Phelps Dodge	Phelps Dodge	United States
Newmont Mining	Magma Copper	United States
	O'okien Copper	South Africa
	Atlas Consolidated	Philippines
	Pima Mining	United States
	Tsumob	South West Africa
	Cyprus Mines	Cyprus
	Sherritt Gordon	Canada
Cerro	Cerro de Pasco	Peru
	Andina	Chile
Rio Tinto Zinc	Palabora Mining	South Africa
	Rio Tinto	Spain
	Rio Algom	Canada
	Bougainville Copper	Papua–New Guinea

American or Anglo-Saxon firms—although at present the largest copper producing companies may be some public or state-directed companies in those countries where all production facilities have been nationalized. Prior to nationalizations, perhaps the largest producer was the Anaconda company, which controlled about 14.5 percent of the world copper producing capacity. At one time Anaconda preferred to work almost exclusively via subsidiaries, but since meeting with certain well-known reverses in Chile and Mexico, the firm has probably changed its policy. Anaconda's principal source of income from copper in the United States is the Inspiration Consolidated Copper Co. It is associated with Asarco in the development of the United Park City Mines Co., holding about 18 percent of the shares of this enterprise. In Canada, Anaconda is associated with Cominco copper in the development of a mine at Bathurst.

Another important actor in the Chilean adventure was Kennecott Copper. This firm was one of the first to sniff the winds of change, and moved much earlier to make its peace with the Allende government than Anaconda or Cerro, although later it legally seized a shipment of copper in protest against delays in the payment of compensation. Kennecott is associated with Stikkine Copper, and with the Hudson Bay Mining and Smelting Co. of the Anglo American group in a Canadian venture; and together with Amax is involved in the exploitation of some Puerto Rican deposits.

Other major North American producers are American Metal Climax Inc. (Amax), American Smelting and Refining Company (Asarco), Cerro Corporation, and Phelps Dodge. In addition to its North American properties, Amax is tied to some of the larger Anglo-Saxon firms by the intermediation of Selection Trust. This means that it was involved with Roan Selection Trust in Zambia; and is involved in Botswana, South-West Africa, and South Africa. At one time Amax controlled about 7.5 percent of the world copper-producing capacity.

Asarco has developed mines in the United States, but above all it has been active in Peru, controlling 51.5 percent of the Southern Peru Copper Corporation and 100 percent of the Northern Peru Mining Corporation. It is also involved in Canada with Newmont, in Mexico with Asarco Mexicana, and with Mount Isa Mines Ltd., in Australia. Another firm that has been extremely active in Peru is Cerro Corporation through its subsidiary Cerro de Pasco. Cerro has been active in Chile, and is also a part owner of Southern Peru Mining.

Phelps Dodge is a firm that has only minor copper-producing interests outside the United States at present, mostly in the form of a 16-percent interest in Southern Peru Mining. In 1962 an antitrust action forced this firm to break its ties with Newmont Mining, one of the most multinational of all the multinational mining firms. Newmont is active in South Africa in the O'okien Copper Co., which it manages; and also associates with Rio Tinto Zinc via the Palabora Mining Co. Newmont has a share in important properties in South-West Africa, collaborates with Asarco in Peru and Canada, and has a large share of the capital of Sherritt Gordon—which, in addition to producing copper, is the third-largest producer of nickel in Canada. It also has substantial shareholdings in Atlas Consolidated Mining and Development Corporation, which is the largest producer in the Philippines, and Cyprus Mines.

On the European scene the situation is even more complicated, since the antitrust laws are much less developed than those of North America—if they are developed at all. The major European companies seem to be holding companies as much as operating companies, with these functions combined in a complex way. The major organization here is probably Charter Consolidated Ltd., which, while commonly thought of as an Anglo-Saxon firm, also has important French connections. Principal ties are with Selection Trust, Anglo American of South Africa, Rio Tinto Zinc Ltd., and Société Minière et Métallurgique de Penarroya.

Anglo American is another highly multinational organization. Most of its African activities have centered on southern Africa, but of late it has acquired important interests in Mauretania. Selection Trust was originally a holding company, but it is, apparently, now managing operations as well. This firm is associated with the Western Mining Corporation in Australia, and is helping with the exploitation of the Sar Cheshmeh in Iran. Rio Tinto Zinc is active in Spain, in South Africa with Palabora Mining, on Bougainville, and in Canada.

The other important European producers are La Société Minière et Métallurgique de Penarroya, and Union Minière. These are associated in one way or another with such organizations as Anglo American, Rio Tinto Zinc, and, formerly, Roan Selection Trust. They are also associated with Le Nickel, mostly through the good offices of Baron Guy de Rothschild, who sits on the board of Rio Tinto.

Many of the large copper producers use the same banks. Chase Manhattan is the principal bank for Asarco and Anaconda. Manufacturers Hanover Trust Company is a banker to Amax and Phelps Dodge, and also does some work for Asarco. Morgan Guaranty Trust does business with Asarco, Phelps Dodge, and Kennecott; while First National City Bank has Anaconda and Phelps Dodge as customers. It is also not unheard of for various firms to own shares in their competitors. Phelps Dodge possesses a substantial number of shares in Amax, and Asarco has shares in Kennecott and Phelps Dodge. In Europe arrangements of this sort are much more extensive.

One final word on this subject. Despite what many people think, the U.S. government is not at all favorably inclined toward the various arrangements that the copper companies have made among themselves. The problem is, however, that antitrust litigation takes a great deal of time and, if things work in the copper field as they do with certain other commodities, the law firms defending the copper producers have the habit of hiring away from the government's antitrust department the lawyers that are prosecuting the copper companies.

6

ELEMENTARY COST THEORY

This chapter begins with an exposition of intertemporal cost theory. The intention is to provide a continuation, though at a somewhat more advanced level, of the theory of capital values introduced earlier in the book. In addition, the topic that is taken up in the following section—depreciation and depletion—should have an intertemporal setting.

The subject treated in the third section is called "synthetic oil," and it might be argued that its place is logically in Chapter 8, where some matters pertaining to energy resources are discussed. On the other hand, the last part of that section is a cost-benefit exercise having as its subject the obtaining of oil from tar sands, and that exercise requires some of the material introduced earlier in this chapter as a background.

The final section takes up the topic of productivity and wages, mostly in the light of the U.S. mining industry.

INTERTEMPORAL COST THEORY

Although the word cost has already been used quite often in this book, a greater precision will now be attached to it. Cost is the reduction in total wealth. The idea here is to make sure that the reader does not confuse cost with expenditure, which is merely an exchange of one form of wealth for another. For instance, if we purchase a machine, use it for a day, and sell it again at its original price, it has not cost us anything—assuming that interest cannot be collected for a one day loan. If we purchase a machine, use it for a day, and must sell it for $10 less because it has "depreciated," then it has cost us $10. On the other hand, if we buy a machine, use it for a year, and resell it for its original price, it *does* have a cost. The cost is the rental income we could have received had we lent out this money. Conversely, profit is the increase in wealth.

There is an important point being treated here: calculations involving profit and loss over time must be compared as of a single date. A machine is bought for 100 dollars, and sold for 100 dollars a year later. If we take a rate of interest of 10 percent, then the cost of acquiring and possessing (and presumably using) this machine is not $100 - 100$, but $100 - 100/1 + 0.10 = 8.9$ dollars. This can also be interpreted as a decrease in wealth. Similarly, if the machine is bought for 100 dollars and sold after a year for 110 dollars, there is no change in wealth. As has been expounded earlier in this book, if the rate of interest is 10 percent, there is no difference between 100 dollars now and 110 dollars a year from now.

Now we can take a closer look at the production function's place in intertemporal analysis. In the final section of Chapter 3 a production function was examined in which, among other combinations, 100 units of capital together with 100 units of labor produced 100 units of output. Let us now go over to working with value terms instead of physical units; and so we have, for example, 100 dollars worth of capital together with 100 manhours of labor—whose total income is 50 dollars—produce 100 dollars worth of output.[1] Moreover, it will be specified that these capital goods never depreciate, and demand conditions are such that the income stream they generate is unchanging over time. With only two inputs, labor and capital, capital income is the value of output, or revenue, *minus* labor income. We can thus construct the following scheme:

Period	t_0	t_1	t_2	$\ldots, t_i \ldots$
Cost of Capital Good	-100			
Revenue		100	100	100
Labor Income		50	50	50
Capital Income		50	50	$\ldots, 50 \ldots$

This capital income has a present value that depends on the rate of interest, but as yet we have no rate of interest. Thus, to begin, let us calculate a rate of interest that, if we use it to discount the capital income, will give a present value of the stream that is equal to the cost of the capital good. We would thus have:

$$100 = \frac{50.0}{(1 + r)} + \frac{50.0}{(1 + r)^2} + \cdots + \frac{50.0}{(1 + r)^i} + \cdots$$

---

[1] Take the production function used in Chapter 4 in value terms as in Klein (1962). We thus have $q = K^{\alpha}L^{\beta} = 100^{1/2} \, 100^{1/2} = 100$. The marginal product of labor is $\partial q/\partial K = w_L/p = \frac{1}{2}$ = real wage of labor. The total wage of the 100 units of labor is thus 100. We also need a marginal product of capital. This is $\partial q/\partial K = \alpha = \frac{1}{2}$, and this is also the real rental of capital. The total capital income per period is thus $\frac{1}{2} \times 100 = 50$.

If this is solved for the rate of interest we get $r = \frac{1}{2}$. This rate of interest is sometimes called the internal rate of return or simply the rate of return. As indicated in the previous footnote, it is also the real marginal product of capital.[2]

There are some other interesting aspects of the present example that should be pointed out. One hundred dollars worth of capital (a stock) produces a flow of 50 dollars of capital services a period. This can be obtained directly through the rate of interest which, among other things, enables us to turn stocks into flows (in the present case, $50 = r \times 100$). The indestructibility of the capital, and the unchanged flow of revenue is also of interest: it means that at any time in the future the capital good can be sold for its original price. This piece of equipment has no depreciation cost, only an interest charge. For instance, if the market rate of interest was 50 percent ($r = \frac{1}{2}$), which it would be in a perfect market, and the 100 dollars used to buy the machine was borrowed, then 50 dollars must be paid in interest charges per period.[3] Note what this does for profit or the increase in wealth. There is none! You start out with nothing, you borrow 100 dollars to buy a machine, you produce something every period that sells for 100 dollars, and, of this, 50 goes to wages and salaries. The rest is used to pay interest on your loan, leaving you with no income. If you get tired of this arrangement, then you can sell the machine for 100 dollars and repay the principle on your loan.

The situation would be the same if the money used to buy the machine were not borrowed. You buy a machine for 100 dollars, and each period in an indefinite future you produce something that sells for 100 dollars. From this you pay out 50 in wages and salaries, and are left with 50 as income. But remember that had you bought a bond with the 100 dollars, and the rate of interest was 0.50, then you would have obtained the same income stream. There is no difference here between having 100 dollars now and an income stream of 50 dollars per period every period in the future. Since there is no difference you do not experience an increase in wealth if you buy the machine.

The above situation corresponds to the simple textbook case. This

---

[2] If we have $a(t)$ as the capital income per period, then we can write

$$v_K = \text{cost of the capital good} = \int_0^T a(t) e^{-rt} dt$$

When $a(t) = a = $ constant, and $T \to \alpha$, we have $v_K = a/r$. In the example above $v_K = 50/\frac{1}{2} = 100$.

[3] In a perfect market the market rate of interest would be the same for physical and financial assets and, inevitably, no wealth increases. We will soon take leave of this kind of situation.

case will not, however, get us far in real life. What we need instead is an exposition in which such things as depreciation and noninfinite time horizons enter in a meaningful way. By way of introducing this discussion, let us take up the classification of costs. We start with an example where we buy a bulldozer and use it, on a contract basis, to move 25,000 cubic feet of earth a year for a mining company. We plan to do this kind of work for two years, and then to sell the bulldozer.

The first cost to be considered here is the *acquisition cost*. Let us say that we can buy the bulldozer brand-new for a price of $5,000. If, however, we immediately resell it we can only get $4,500. The acquisition cost is thereby $500. It may be possible to explain this kind of cost on the basis of a retrogression in demand for earth-moving equipment at that time. It may be the case, though, that someone will buy a bulldozer and use it to do some kind of job not always associated with this kind of equipment, such as moving scrap in an automobile disposal yard, pulling an ice cream wagon, and so on. Also, although it is not true in this case, much equipment is manufactured for a specialized purpose, and if used in any other kind of job displays reduced efficiency. This reduced efficiency results in a lower resale price even if the equipment is brand-new.

It will also be assumed that the bulldozer depreciates to the extent of 1.5 dollars per day if it is not used. Thus, the cost of acquiring the bulldozer and keeping it for one week, without using it, is 510.5 dollars. Then there are the operating costs. Two of the most important of these are the salary of the bulldozer operator and the cost of fuel. Another important operating cost might be the maintenance cost, but we will assume that maintenance is performed by the operator. Now, as in the example above, it will be possible to sell the bulldozer at any time in the future, but not at its purchase price. In the present situation depreciation reduces its value. Thus far we have assumed that the equipment depreciates at a rate of 1.5 dollars a day if it is not used, and thus the depreciation over the two-year planning horizon is approximately 1100 dollars, if the bulldozer is not used. If it is used to move 25,000 cubic feet per year, there is additional wear and tear and it will be assumed that the resale price is only 2,500 dollars.

The cost of possession with use can now be computed. Remember that the 2,500 dollars is obtained two years after purchase of the equipment. This 2,500 must therefore be discounted before it can be compared with expenditures on the purchasing date. Assuming a rate of interest of 10 percent, the discounted value of 2,500 becomes $2,500/(1.1)^2 = 2,070$ dollars. The cost of possessing *and* using the equipment over two years is 4,500 *minus* 2,070 = 2,430. Similarly, the cost of acquiring, possessing, and using the equipment is $5,000 - 2,070 = 2,930$ dollars.

The other cost that we will take into consideration here is the cost of

Table 6-1. Some Entries in a Two-Period Cost-Benefit Scheme

Item	Period		
	t_0	t_1	t_2
Purchase price	5000		
Resale value			2500
			(2070)
Fuel and lubricants		500	500
		(455)	(414)

fuel and lubricants. This will be taken as 500 dollars a year, and will be paid—as if on a credit card basis—at the end of the year. Discounted to the initial date this gives $500/1.1 + 500/(1.1)^2 = 869$ dollars. The 869 dollars is added to our previous cost of 2,930 to give $2,930 + 869 = 3,799$ as the total cost. Labor cost is still absent, and will be inserted when we come to profits. We can sum up the proceedings thus far in Table 6-1, where the discounted values of the entries are in parentheses.

Two cost effects can now be noted, the first dealing with volume and the second with rate of production. The question of volume turns on the total amount of earth to be moved over time. In the program being described above, 50,000 cubic feet is to be moved in two years, or 25,000 cubic feet per year. It might thus be interesting to ask what kind of equipment would be appropriate if, instead, the total amount to be moved was 500 cubic feet or 500,000 cubic feet, still assuming that the rate at which this was to take place was 25,000 cubic feet per year. In the above discussion we have implied that to move a total of 50,000 cubic feet requires a certain type of bulldozer. Where 500,000 cubic feet are concerned, a least-cost solution might call for a larger bulldozer; or more than one bulldozer used sequentially, with each bulldozer sold after 1½ years of operation, etc.

To move 500 cubic feet at a rate of 25,000 cubic feet per year might call for renting instead of buying a bulldozer. Remember that in the example above, if a bulldozer was bought, its resale value was appreciably less than its purchase price even if it was resold immediately. Thus, even if the bulldozer has a trivial operating cost for the period concerned, the acquisition cost obviously makes purchase uneconomical.[4] Figure 6-1, below,

---

[4] At a rate of 25,000 cubic feet per year, moving 500 cubic feet would take $500/25,000 = \frac{1}{50}$ of a year, or about 7.3 days. Fuel and lubricant costs would be approximately $500/50 = 10$ dollars. If we assume labor costs are 5,000 dollars/year, this would make labor costs for moving the 500 cubic feet about 50 dollars. Thus, total operating costs are about 60 dollars.

Now look again at the acquisition and depreciation costs for the owner of a bulldozer. These have been shown to be 2,930 dollars for 2 years. One way of handling this cost is to turn it

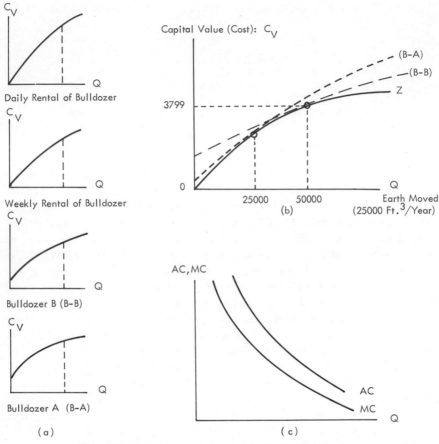

Figure 6-1. Cost curves: cost vs. total volume of production.

shows the cost curves for some equipment possibilities, where bulldozer *B* represents the bulldozer in the example above.

In the figure, *Q* is the total volume of earth moved, and for each value of *Q* at a given rate *q*, there is an optimal arrangement in so far as the kind of equipment is concerned, and perhaps also the conditions under which it is obtained (rented or bought outright). For a given *q* and the total amount Q_a, bulldozer *A* is best. At Q_b bulldozer *B*, which is larger and has a larger

into an annuity for 2 years. By doing this we get a yearly cost of 1,690 dollars/year. If we were to rent this bulldozer and pay operating costs, this would mean that we would have as a total cost $(1,690/50) + 60$. On the other hand, if we were to buy this bulldozer and sell it after 7.3 days, the cost would be the acquisition cost + the operating cost + the depreciation cost = $500 + 50 + 10 +$ depreciation cost. Obviously it pays to rent the bulldozer.

fixed cost, is the optimal machine.[5] A reason for this might be that a smaller bulldozer depreciates faster than a larger one under the pressure of moving 25,000 cubic feet of earth a year, and thus the total cost for using bulldozer A to move 50,000 cubic feet would probably be greater than for B. At the same time, notice that while the total cost does rise as we go from Q_a to Q_b—though not so fast as it would have had we used bulldozer A at Q_b— the average or unit cost and the marginal cost decreases.[6] Alchian and Allen (1964) have called this the economy of mass, or volume, production, and they have also given an important exception to this situation. It is when, at a production site, supplies of inexpensive raw materials are used up and resort must be had to more costly resources. In some areas in the United States this is true with the production of oil and natural gas. There are undoubtedly some other exceptions; and so, rather than call this a rule, say it is something that happens most of the time.

The next cost effect has to do with *rate*, or *q*. Rate is the speed at which a given volume is produced. In our above example this was 25,000 cubic feet per year. Moreover, with the equipment we chose we were able to produce this for a total cost of 3,799 dollars. If we increase the rate at which a given volume is to be produced, we increase the total, average, and marginal costs. Alchian and Allen explain this on the basis of having to bring in more resources at the same time, and thus having to resort to less efficient resources. However the mere fact of having to use quantitatively more resources in a given time period should, by itself, suffice to increase the total cost. As for the average and marginal costs, we can reason as follows: if increasing the rate of production meant a lower average or marginal cost, then by increasing it enough we could get these costs down to around zero. This is a situation which, in the light of reality, is eminently unrealistic. Thus with an increase in *q*, Figure 6-2 shows the most likely cost situation.

These two concepts of costs may now be combined by considering proportional increases in volume and rate. In addition, something can be said about varying the time horizon. We have discussed in the above example moving 25,000 cubic feet per year of earth for two years—or, we

---

[5] At first sight the fixed cost appears to be the acquisition cost and a part of the possession cost; but if there was no acquisition cost there would still be a fixed cost. Suppose that one bulldozer costs 3,000 dollars and a larger machine 5,000 dollars, and after two years they can be sold for the same price. However remember that in two years 5,000 dollars is $5,000/(1.1)^2 = 4,130$, and 3,000 is $3,000/(1.1)^2 = 2,470$. The fixed cost of the larger bulldozer is thus $5,000 - 4,130 = 870$ dollars, and that of the smaller is $3,000 - 2,470 = 530$. It could be said that in this example the fixed cost is a pure possession cost caused by tying up money in a machine.

[6] The average cost can be taken from (b), Figure 6-1. It is simply the cost, as shown on the vertical axis, divided by the volume Q. Marginal cost is the slope of the envelope curve.

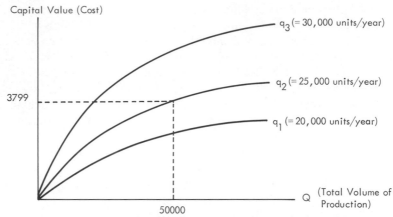

Figure 6-2. Cost as a function of the rate of production in units time period.

could say, producing 25,000 units per year—for a total of 50,000 cubic feet. We might instead be interested in 50,000 per year over a period of two years, for a total of 100,000. Essentially we have two effects here: the volume effect that, if there were no change in rate, would reduce unit costs; and the rate effect that, by itself, tends to raise unit costs. These two effects can be combined on a diagram similar to the type constructed in Figure 6-2. On the horizontal axis we have total volume; while on the vertical, capital value costs for a number of rates (e.g., 25,000 cubic feet per year, 37,500 cubic feet per year, etc.). We can then draw Figure 6-3.

The reader should note the similarity between one of the dashed curves in this figure and the total cost curves discussed in Chapter 4. Fundamentally these have the same shape, but in the present figure the time element must be taken into consideration, and each of the dashed cost curves is only valid for a specific output period. If we take the above example we might want to consider the possibility of moving the 50,000 cubic feet in three years instead of two. Generally this would mean smaller labor costs per year; less annual wear and tear on machinery, and thus smaller depreciation costs in addition to smaller maintenance costs; and, of course, smaller fuel and lubricant costs per year. Or take the case of a mine where we decided to remove 50,000 units of reserves in three years instead of two. Certainly almost all of the direct operating costs would be lower, and the same would probably be true for the indirect and capital costs. This does not mean, however, that it is wiser to remove the 50,000 units in three years instead of two, since there might not be a market for the product after the second year.

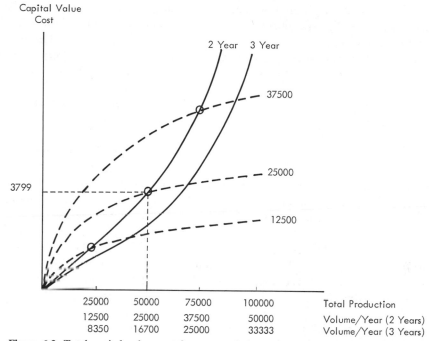

Figure 6-3. Total capital value cost for two- and three-year programs with proportional increases in total production and rate of production.

A sample calculation here might go as follows: we plan to move 50,000 cubic feet of earth in three years instead of two. Suppose that we take the same bulldozer, and total fuel and lubricant expenses are still 1000 dollars, but this time they are stretched out over three years and so they are 333 dollars per year. Since the bulldozer is not being used so intensively, the assumption will be made that it is in better condition at the end of three years, and can be resold for 2800 dollars. Total cost now becomes, with $r = 0.10$, $5000 - 2,800/(1.1)^3 +$ discounted fuel costs $= (5,000 + 2,100) + 333/1.1 + 333/(1.1)^2 + 333/(1.1)^3 = 2,900 + 302 + 275 + 250 = 3,727$, as compared to the earlier cost of 3,799.

TAXES, DEPLETION, AND PROFITS

Some gaps will now be filled in the exposition of the previous section, and the important topics of taxes and depletion can be broached. The first thing to look at is wages and revenues. In the last example of the previous section it was perhaps implied that the purchaser of the equipment would also operate it. For the purpose of our analysis this would not provide a problem where imputing a wage to the purchaser–operator was concerned, since this wage would simply be equal to the income per time period that the purchaser would have to give up if he left some other job to operate the bulldozer.

Certain complications might be introduced when we come to the subject of taxes, however, and so, to keep the discussion as simple as possible, an assumption will be made that the purchaser takes the title of President, Director, Chief Operating Officer, or something like that, and employs someone else to operate the bulldozer. Let us say that the operator receives a salary of $5,000/year, which, for purposes of our exercise, he gets at the end of the year. The Director, on the other hand, does not assign a salary to himself. There is also the matter of revenue. Let us say that the revenue from moving 25,000 cubic feet of earth a year is $8,000 in each of the two years. We now have in Table 6-2 the data for our two-year cost-benefit scheme. The capital value of profit is 1405.

This 1,405 dollars represents a wealth increase for the purchaser of this equipment. Put another way, the purchaser enjoys a yield higher than the 10 percent he used as a discount factor. In fact, the yield, or internal rate of return as we called it in the previous section, is approximately 27 percent, as the reader can check by discounting the net receipts at a rate of interest r, and setting this equal to the cost of the equipment. Solving for r gives 0.27.

We now come to the matter of taxes. The gross revenue is 8,000, but

Table 6-2. Some Costs and Benefits in a Two-Period Scheme

	Period		
Item	t_0	t_1	t_2
Revenue		+8000	+8000
Purchase price	−5000		
Resale value			+2500
Fuel and lubricants		−500	−500
Wages or salaries		−5000	−5000
Net receipts	−5000	+2500	+5000
Present value (r = 10 percent)	−5000	+2275	+4130

Capital value of profit = Sum of present values = 1405

Table 6-3. Some Costs and Benefits in a Two-Period Scheme

Item	t_0	t_1	t_2
		Period	
Revenue		+8000	+8000
Purchase price	−5000		
Resale value			+2500
Fuel and lubricants		−500	−500
Taxes		−300	−800
Wages or salaries		−5000	−5000
Net receipts	−5000	+2200	+4200
Present value	−5000	+2000	+3471
($r = 10$ percent)			

Capital value of profit = − 5000 + 2000 + 3471 = 471

the revenue for tax purposes—or what can be called the net revenue—is defined here as gross revenue *minus* expenses for tax purposes; but in the calculation of these expenses there is another element that must be considered that we have not taken up earlier. This is the depreciation cost, which is a portion of the cost of the equipment that the tax authorities permit the firm to deduct from gross income each year as a compensation for the "using up" of the equipment. One of the depreciation techniques often used is straight line depreciation, by which we mean that the cost of the equipment is divided by some sort of arbitrary "length of life" or "write-off time" to obtain the amount of the deduction. In the present exercise, if the write-off time for the bulldozer is taken as five years, then 1,000 dollars/ year can be charged as depreciation when calculating taxable income, and this can be done for five years. Again it must be pointed out that there need be no relation between the actual life of the equipment and the write-off time.

Continuing with our example, we see that during the first year total expenses for tax purposes are the sum of wage costs, the cost of fuel and lubricants, and the depreciation cost, or 500 + 5,000 + 1,000 = 6,500; and during the second year also 500 + 5,000 + 1,000 = 6,500 dollars. Net receipts for tax purposes are thus 8,000 − 6,500 = 1,500 dollars during the first year; and during the second year 8,000 + 2,500 − 6,500 = 4,000 dollars. The next step is to assume a tax rate on net receipts. For our purposes this will be taken as 20 percent, and thus taxes for the first year are 300 dollars, and 800 dollars for the second year. In Table 6-3, costs and benefits now take on the following form.

Because of the tax the profit, or increase in wealth, has fallen to 471 dollars. The internal rate of interest is now 16 percent.

The next item is depletion. Depletion provides for the recovery of the investment in a wasting asset, such as a mine or oil well, in the same way that depreciation does for a fixed asset. In most countries, when calculating taxable income, depletion is also deducted from gross income. In the United States the formula for determining depletion for any given year, which is known as depletion by cost, is:

$$\text{Depletion for year} = \text{Depletion Rate} \cdot \text{Units Sold} = \left(\frac{\text{Cost of Property}}{\text{Total Units in Property}} \right) \cdot \text{Units Sold}$$

Oil, gas, and mineral properties can also be depleted for tax purposes by employing a percentage of gross income, providing that the amount allowed for depletion is less than 50 percent of the taxable income of the property before depletion. In general, percentage depletion will be used if it results in less tax than depletion based on cost. In the United States some typical depletion allowances are:

Oil, gas wells, sulfur, uranium, bauxite, cobalt, lead, manganese, nickel, tin, tungsten, vanadium, zinc	22 percent
Gold, silver, copper, iron ore	15 percent
Coal, lignite	10 percent

To see how this works, we can construct an example similar to the one given above. Instead of a bulldozer, let us take a property that was bought for 2,500 dollars, together with a package of mining equipment that also cost 2,500 dollars, and was unused. Assume that the property contains 50,000 units of ore that will be extracted in two years, at a rate of 25,000 units per year. The revenue per year is taken as 12,000 dollars; and the operating expense is 5,000 dollars/year in wages and salaries, and 500 dollars/year for other inputs.

As specified above, the depletion rate for this example is the cost of the property divided by the total units of ore in the property, or 2,500/5,000 = 0.50. The depletion during the first year is then 0.50 × 2,500 = 1,250 dollars, and the same for the second year. If we take depreciation on the package of equipment to be 500 dollars/year, then the taxable income for the first year can be determined as follows:

Gross income		+12000
Wages, salaries, other inputs	−5500	
Depreciation	−500	
Depletion	−1250	
	−7250	−7250
Taxable Income		4750

If the tax rate is 20 percent, taxes are 950 dollars. On the other hand, if the 22-percent rule is used, we have for the first year

Gross income		+12000
Wages, salaries, other inputs	−5500	
Depreciation	−500	
	−6000	−6000
Taxable income before depletion		+6000
Depletion allowance = 0.22 × 12000 (This is 22 percent of gross income, and since it is less than 50 percent of taxable income before depletion, this method of depletion may be used)		−2640
Taxable Income		3360

If the tax rate is 20 percent, taxes amount to 672 dollars. In the present case the 22 percent depletion rule is more favorable for tax purposes. At this point it might be instructive to look at the income statement of an actual mining company. This is given in Table 6-4.

Most of these entries are self-explanatory. Amortization and interest is repayment of part of the money borrowed by this firm, together with the interest on the outstanding debt. Sales Costs are "the cost of selling," and includes such things as advertising, the salaries of sales personnel, the various expenses they incur for travel, the rent and maintenance of their offices, etc. Net Profit, as expressed here, is Total Sales *minus* all costs, to include depreciation and depletion. Cash Flow, on the other hand, is the excess of in-payments over out-payments during a certain period. Remember that depletion and depreciation are not sums of money specifically set aside to pay for new equipment or develop new mineral properties, but a part of the increase in liquidity accruing to the firm.

Table 6-4. Cost Structure of the Southern Peru Copper Company for 1969, in Millions of Dollars[a]

Entry	Amount	Amount (percent)
Wages	5.95	3.6
Salaries	6.64	3.8
Materials and equipment	20.60	12.2
Energy	5.50	3.3
Peruvian taxes	47.5	28.2
Amortization and interest	3.46	2.0
Sales costs	3.22	1.9
Other costs	2.50	1.5
Total costs	95.37	
Other deductibles		
Depreciation	11.50	6.8
Depletion	22.70	13.5
Costs + "deductibles"	129.57	76.7
Gross revenue	169.00	100.0
Net profit	39.43	23.3
Cash flow	73.63	43.6

[a] Exchange rate—1 dollar = 38.7 soles.

SYNTHETIC OIL

The place of oil in the building of the prosperity of the industrial world is too obvious to require elaboration in this book. Thus only a few comments on the international oil economy will be offered as a prelude to a short discussion of the production of synthetic oil in general, and the extraction of oil from tar sands in particular.

The oil reserves of the Middle East amount to more than half of the entire world's reserves. The unit cost of this oil, dockside in the Middle East, is about $0.10/barrel. It seems likely that in a decade or two this cost will not be higher than $0.20 dollars/barrel.

On the other hand North American oil is among the most expensive. But, according to Fisher (1974) and Hottel and Howard (1971), the supply price of U.S. oil is declining. The argument here is that technical progress has kept the real cost of oil falling over the past century or so, and this is reflected by a price that has been decreasing in respect to such things as the wage of labor. Put more simply, the hours of work necessary to buy a barrel of oil have been steadily falling in the United States. Be this as it may, we should still remember that, as exhaustion approaches, the price of traditional oil will have to rise, and by this we mean the real price as well as the market price.

After the October War in the Middle East, the market price of oil climbed in a series of steps from about $1.50 per barrel to about $12. As is well known, at a price of $12 a barrel, a great deal of fossil fuel from other than OPEC sources becomes attractive. First and foremost among these sources are the North Sea, Alaska, and perhaps the continental shelf of North America. The so-called "synthetic fuels" such as the production of oil from coal, the production of gas from coal, and the extraction of oil from shale and tar sands are also of interest when we get into this price range.[7]

The question mark is: how long will the price of oil from traditional sources stay at, or above, this level? Many experts, in particular Professor Adelman (1972), have convinced both themselves and, unfortunately, a sizable amount of influential opinion in the industrial countries that there are inherent strengths in the existing world economic system, and weaknesses in the structure of OPEC, that will eventually cause the price of oil to fall. Alas, the issue in the case is not the world economic system but the laws of basic arithmetic. Unless the OPEC members forget how to add and subtract, and thus to compute the financial losses they would experience if they were to reduce the price of oil just because a few outstanding economists think they should, then the price of OPEC oil will continue to rise until there is an immense augmentation in the world supply of non-OPEC oil. In the circumstances, anybody interested in bringing down the price of oil should be concerning himself with altering the world supply–demand pattern. This will involve, among other things, large-scale investments in exploration and in increasing the production of existing oil fields, as well as a comprehensive and sustained effort to expand the production of synthetic fuels.

The most expensive of these synthetic products at the present time is oil produced from coal. During World War II, Germany produced aviation gasoline, motor oil, diesel oil, and heating oil and lubricants from coal. The largest German plant produced 10,000 barrels/day; and the entire German synthetic oil industry produced 100,000 barrels per day. Immediately after the war the synthetic oil program was dropped, but some semiofficial reports have it that if the price of conventional crude oil reaches $14/barrel the program might be reactivated. On this point the reader should remember that due to the realignment of exchange rates that has been taking place over the last two years, the price of oil has gone up much less for the Germans than for most other consumers.

At the present time synthetic oil is being produced in South Africa employing the process developed by the Germans during the war and improved later by technologists in the United States and South Africa. The

[7]The average price of oil in the United States at present is about $9.50 per barrel; 38 percent of U.S. oil is from OPEC, and sells for $12.50; 37 percent is so-called "old oil" and sells for a price slightly under that of OPEC; and the rest is price-controlled "new oil" that sells for $5.25 per barrel.

South African plant at Sasolburg—which employs what has now come to be known as the Sasol process—converts two million tons of coal a year to 160 million gallons of gasoline *and* large quantities of gaseous fuels, petrochemicals, and so on at a cost believed to be considerably under the World War II cost. The cost of oil, for instance, is said to be well under $10 per barrel. One of the reasons for this comparatively low cost is the inexpensiveness of coal in South Africa, since in that country the production cost is approximately $2.50/ton, as compared to an average of $15.70/ton in England and $6/ton in the United States. Of course the real explanation behind the South African capability to manufacture oil from coal has nothing to do with cheap coal, or even the inexpensive labor that produces the coal, but the absence of a domestic crude oil industry. This means that there is no one present to convince the South African government that what the oil companies like to claim is impossible is, in truth, eminently possible.

Where other countries are concerned, Fisher has come to the conclusion that the optimal strategy consists of allowing the Sasol installation, and pilot installations now under construction in various parts of the world, to get the unit cost of producing oil from coal down a little further, and then to take advantage of economies of scale by constructing production facilities several times as large as any in existence. The logic here, as indicated earlier in this chapter, is that if huge and contiguous coal deposits are available, and very large volumes can be planned, then high yearly outputs may also be possible at low unit costs. Fisher has based his argument on so-called "learning effects," plus an almost mystical faith in economies of scale, but what it comes down to is expecting the same decreasing cost phenomena to prevail here as we have observed in the lead and aluminum industries.

Another source of refined products is shale. Shale is mined and then subjected to intense heat to distill off the kerogen or shale oil that it contains. Shale oil is less expensive at present than producing oil (and natural gas) from coal, but it is more expensive than oil from tar sands. The big advantage of shale is its abundance: shale deposits are found in every inhabited continent. Perry (1975) estimates the amount of oil to be found in high-grade shale at 720 billion barrels, while the total oil supply from this source could amount to 17,000 billion barrels, or 25 times the current estimates of the ultimately recoverable petroleum resources of the world. If lower-quality shale is considered, then Perry's contention is that the last figure above can be multiplied by a factor of 20. These estimates may be overoptimistic, but even if they were halved it is apparent that this is an extremely important source of energy. The disadvantage with shale is that a certain air pollution is involved, and most recovery processes require a great deal of water. In addition shale mining produces large amounts of an unsightly waste that, environmentalists say, cannot be beautified later.

Whether this last statement is true or not remains to be seen, since similar statements were made several decades ago about the slag heaps in the coal mining districts of England, and yet modern landscaping techniques eventually turned many of these eyesores into virtual oases in an otherwise drab countryside.

It is interesting to note that by practically stopping the exploitation of shale, and by using similar arguments against tar sands, Alaskan oil, coal gasification, North Sea Oil, and so on, the environmentalists played a major role in paving the way for the introduction of nuclear power—in the long run probably the cheapest, cleanest, and most efficient source of energy. In the *short run,* however, nuclear power may turn out to have a number of disadvantages, particularly when employed on the scale that is being planned. Interestingly enough, techniques for producing shale oil are being developed that use very little water and involve almost no environmental deterioration: the so-called *in-situ* process is one of these. However the "powers that be" have made their decision, and thus such things as coal and shale—which are not only safe but economical—are being passed over for nuclear power, despite the fact that the present reliability of nuclear power may well leave something to be desired.

The final topic treated in this section involves the recovery of oil from shallow oil fields. A typical shallow oil field is one in which the oil is found in various strata underground in a form ranging from seeps and pools containing almost pure petroleum to rock in which petroleum residue fills a fraction of the pore space. These fields are, in fact, merely downward extensions of bituminous rock deposits, with an average depth of less than 500 feet. The term "bituminous rock," as it is used here, includes tar sand, which is an oil-bearing sand and a major component of most shallow oil fields.

Because of their relatively limited depth, it is not particularly costly to reach and expose the oil-bearing strata in this type of field. The problem is that the oil recovery percentage from these sources, if ordinary wells are employed, is very low; as a result a great deal of special equipment of a mining rather than a drilling nature is necessary to get the recovery level up to 95 percent, which is a level that can and should be achieved for long-run efficiency. As time passes, however, and the winning of oil from traditional sources becomes more difficult, governments and mining companies will undoubtedly become more inclined to see that this equipment is provided.

The ideal characteristics for a shallow oil field include the following: (1) a high oil content for the oil-bearing material. By that it is meant that every ton of material (sand, rock, etc.) processed should have an oil content, by weight, of at least 13 percent. This amounts to almost one barrel of oil per ton. (2) The density and sulfur content of the oil should be of a commercially satisfactory grade. These two factors are probably the most important in determining market value. (3) The overburden (or covering) of the deposit should not, as a rule of thumb, exceed the thickness of the oil-bearing formation, and should be removable without extensive drilling and blasting. (4) The mining site is located in an area that facilitates the disposal of overburden. Here it should be mentioned that strong objections to the open pit mining of oil have also been registered by environmentalists.

An area in which many of these prerequisites are fulfilled is the Athabasca tar sands area in Canada, about 250 miles northeast of Edmonton. The estimated reserves in this area are about 270 billion barrels, and there are about 70 billion more in surrounding areas. To get an idea of how much this is it can be pointed out that before the energy crisis, the North American consumption rate for oil was said to be heading for about 25 million barrels per day in 1980. Very large shallow oil fields have also been discovered in the Orinoco region of Venezuela and the Soviet Union.

Most of the terrain around the Athabasca tar sands takes on the appearance of a swamp. The overburden, or covering, of the oil bearing strata runs from about a meter to almost 650 meters. The deposits themselves are mostly in the form of sand, with some water; but there is often a certain amount of bitumen present that must be thinned before pumping can take place from these deposits.

The actual mining and the first stages of processing go as follows. In the summer the land is cleared of brush and trees, and dynamite is used to get to the minable strata. Oil recovery, however, can only take place during the winter, when the ground is solid enough to support the huge vehicles used in mining. First bulldozers push the overburden aside, and then giant trucks that are larger than many houses, and that mount 1,800-ton bucket wheels at the end of huge arms, scoop up the sand and drop it onto a conveyor belt that takes it to an extraction plant. At the plant, the first step is to strip the tar away from the sand. Depending upon the process, a number of things can then happen, but in the end a flow of synthetic crude is released that can be refined into the entire range of petroleum products.

Herkenhoff (1972) has provided an interesting case study of the present topic. The example provided below will not duplicate his data, since much of this is inapplicable at the present time, but will employ some figures more in line with present conditions. The purpose of this exercise, however, is not to say anything meaningful about investment practices in the Athabasca tar sands area, but to give further insight into profitability calculations of a type related to those discussed in the previous section.

The assumption here will be that a plant having a feed rate of 44,500 tons per day costs $125 million. This plant can produce 13.2 million barrels of oil per year, which will sell for $6.50/barrel. The total revenue for the plant is thus $85.8 million per year. The operating cost has been estimated

Table 6-5. Calculation of Cash Flow for a Tar Sands Project

Item	Amount (millions of dollars)
Annual gross revenue	85.80
Less operating cost	−18.20
Less royalty (2.37 dollars/barrel)	−31.30
Less depreciation	−8.30
Less interest	−5.00
Income	23.00
Less depletion	−4.05
Income before tax	18.95
Less income tax (52 percent)	−9.90
Net income	9.05
Add depreciation + depletion	+12.35
Cash flow	21.40

at \$18.2 million per year, and there is a royalty of \$2.37 on each barrel of oil. This makes a total royalty charge of \$31.3 billion per year. Depreciation is on a 15-year basis, and so the yearly depreciation charge is 125/15 = \$8.30 million.

The interest rate is taken as 8 percent, and the assumption here will be that the \$125 million needed to build the plant is borrowed. The interest charge per period is taken as an average over the 15-year period, and is 125/2 × 0.08 = \$5 million.[8] The next matter is the depletion. According to Herkenhoff the rule that is to be followed is 23 percent of gross income, or 50 percent of net—whichever is less. Twenty-three percent of gross income came to 0.23 × 85.8 = 19.7, and the assumption was that this was higher than the 50 percent of net. For instance, by the U.S. depletion rules this amounted to more than 50 percent of taxable income before depletion, and thus it would not have been allowed. What was done instead was to use the 50 percent of net income that, unfortunately, had to be estimated from the data provided by Herkenhoff. The figure that was settled on was \$4.05 million per year.

A summary of the above is provided in Table 6-5. It should be noted that the concept of "income" employed here may not correspond to general usage.

[8] One way of looking at this is as follows. Assuming some kind of straight-line debt repayment scheme over 15 years, then 125/15 = \$8.3 million would be paid back per year. The amount on which interest was being paid would thus decrease by \$8.3 million per year. Thus, after the first year, interest would be paid on \$125 million at 8 percent, and this would amount to \$10 million. After the second year interest would be paid on (125 − 8.3) = 116.7, and at 8 percent this would result in an interest charge of approximately 9.3, etc.

Before finishing with this topic, it might be interesting to look at a concept called the "pay back" period, or sometimes the "payoff" period. For the purpose of the present analysis this can be defined as Cost of the Investment/Cash Flow, and with the figures that we have been using gives 125/21.40 = 5.84 years. Gordon (1955) has shown that the reciprocal of the payoff period gives a rough estimate of the rate of return in those cases where the "life" of the investment is considerably longer than the payoff period, and where the payoff period has been adjusted to take discounting into consideration. As the reader can easily check, if discounting is used, it takes 8 years to recover the original investment. Assuming that the life of the equipment is much longer than 8 years, this would make the approximate rate of return $\frac{1}{8}$ = 12.5 percent.

The basis for this last calculation was merely a discounting of cash flows. Cash flow for the first year was taken as 21.40. Cash flow for the second year was then 21.40/1.08 = 19.80, assuming an 8 percent discount rate. For the third year it was $21.40/(1.08)^2$ = 18.3, and so on. After approximately 8 years these entries add up to 125. Undiscounted revenue by this time is approximately 170.

All this is, of course, very rough. In the above example the reasoning might be that the 12.5 percent estimated rate of return seems like a safe minimum figure. Whether it is close to the rate of return that would have been obtained using a more exact method of calculation is quite another matter. Most textbooks, in fact, go to a great deal of trouble to warn their readers against using this technique to evaluate investments if they have the time and the ability to use the discounted cash flow method. The same warning can be repeated here.

PRODUCTIVITY AND WAGES

Productivity in the raw materials industries can be largely explained by two factors. The first is the increased level of training and skill of the human element working in the industry; the second is the replacement of labor by capital or, what amounts to the same thing, increasing the capital-labor ratio. These things, in fact, go together: complicated machinery requires a high level of competence on the part of cooperating labor.

The practice of increasing the amount of capital per unit of labor is not confined to the industrial world. This is also happening in the mining industries of the LDCS. In the bauxite industries of Surinam and Guyana, for example, a large-scale introduction of such devices as bulldozers, draglines, large trucks, huge rotary excavators, and the like has been going

Table 6-6. Some Productivities and Wages in the U.S. Lead Mining
Industry, 1956–62

Units	1956	1958	1960	1962
Man-hours worked per ton of recoverable lead plus zinc	36	26	24	20
Labor cost per ton of recoverable lead plus zinc[a]	78.83	60.97	58.45	53.10
Average wages paid per hour to production workers[a]	2.19	2.33	2.43	2.63

[a] In U.S. dollars.
Source: U.S. Tariff Commission.

Table 6-7. Employment and Average Hourly Earnings, in Dollars, of Workers in
Three Mining Industries, 1972, in the United States

Employment	Iron ore mining		Copper ore mining		Lead and zinc ore mining	
	E	AHE	E	AHE	E	AHE
Bulldozer operators	386	4.23				
Change room attendants	141	3.54	52	3.64		
Conveyor operators	161	3.75				
Crusher operators	192	4.14	345	4.32	118	3.45
Electricians (maintenance)	496	5.01	794	4.80	161	4.09
Furnace operators	111	4.49				
Laborers (Non-underground)	1078	3.52	1760	3.66	149	3.23
Mechanics (maintenance)	1452	4.83	843	4.68		
Miners (underground)	854	5.42	1547	4.94	1642	5.26
Truckdrivers	1079	4.30	2575	4.61		
Welders (maintenance)	743	4.82				
Laborers (underground)			683	3.89	369	3.42
Machinists (maintenance)			408	4.81		
Mechanics, heavy duty			1472	4.78	190	4.25
Power shovel operators			424	5.25		
Welders			632	4.70		
Hoistmen					178	3.69
Shuttle car operators					156	3.65
Underground serviceman					175	3.63

Notes: Total production workers: 1. Iron ore mining: 13,128; 2. Copper ore mining: 27,046; 3. Lead and
zinc ore mining: 6,586. Average hourly earnings: 1. Iron Ore Mining: 4.41 dollars/hour; 2. Copper Ore
Mining: 4.43 dollars/hour; 3. Lead and Zinc Ore Mining: 4.20 dollars/hour. E = Employment; AHE =
Average hourly earnings in dollars/hour.
Source: U.S. Bureau of Labor Statistics.

on for some time. The overall result of this will undoubtedly be to put a brake on the expansion of employment opportunities, while raising productivity and wages in this industry. A similar phenomenon has been noted in the copper mining industry in Chile. The average number of workers at Kennecott's El Teniente mine declined from 8,114 in 1931 to 6,978 in 1959, although production increased by 70 percent. Just what this tendency will mean for aggregate economic development remains to be seen.

The student of microeconomics and growth has almost certainly been introduced to the concept that, as the capital–labor ratio increases, wages also tend to increase. Most likely, however, he has not bothered to analyze any empirical evidence to this effect, although such evidence is easy to obtain. If we take the lead industry in the United States we see in Table 6-6 a situation where the labor cost of lead (and zinc) production has steadily decreased, but wages have increased. This is clearly the effect of an increased mechanization in this industry.

It is interesting to note that in the United States underground miners— the employees who drill and blast the ore body—are among the highest paid personnel in the metal mining and processing industries. In fact, the composition of the work force by type of work is extremely important in determining the average wage in a given branch or industry. Some indication of earning in three different branches of mining are given in Table 6-7,

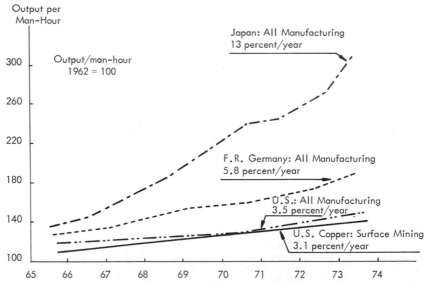

Figure 6-4. Productivity in U.S. surface copper mining and all manufacturing activities in Japan, West Germany, and the United States.

Table 6-8. Output per Man-Hour in Several Industries in the United States, 1968–72, and Percent Changes, 1971–72 and 1960–72

Industry	1968	1969	1970	1971	1972	Percent change 1971–72	Average annual percent change 1960–72
Iron mining, crude ore	110.0	117.8	118.0	123.4	139.1	12.8	5.2
Iron mining, usable ore	105.1	109.6	108.7	110.6	121.5	9.8	3.0
Copper mining, crude ore	109.6	116.2	126.9	137.2	141.1	2.9	5.1
Copper mining, recoverable metal	103.4	106.9	112.8	114.6	110.9	-3.2	2.2
Coal mining	105.1	105.4	103.2	101.6	100.1	-1.3	3.5
Petroleum refining	103.0	107.0	107.6	113.2	120.3	6.3	5.3
Steel	104.2	104.8	101.9	105.6	111.8	5.8	2.2
Grey iron foundries	107.1	113.2	108.4	113.6	118.5	4.3	2.4
Steel foundries	97.7	99.5	96.0	100.3	104.6	4.4	1.2
Primary copper, lead, zinc	118.3	120.9	117.0	122.3	135.2	10.5	1.7
Primary aluminum	94.9	105.1	108.9	119.6	126.6	5.8	3.1
Aluminum rolling and drawing	104.7	107.2	109.1	119.0	139.9	17.6	5.3

Source: U.S. Bureau of Labor Statistics.

which also shows numbers employed. It should also be pointed out that shift differentials of 10 cents/hour are applied to the second shift; and 15–20 cents to the third.

The question can now be asked as to how productivity in the mining industries compares with productivity in other industries. This seems like a valid inquiry, since one of the problems in mining is the lower ore grades that are encountered over time and that must, of necessity, be matched by productivity increases of at least the same order of magnitude if the world mining industry is to continue to function in a satisfactory manner. If we take the period 1965–73 we can compare in Figure 6-4 productivity increases in copper mining with those in all manufacturing in the United States, Germany, and Japan.

From a productivity point of view, mining does not present an encouraging picture. Yet, there are some mitigating factors behind these curves. The great slowdown in productivity increases is to be found in the older mines that, numerically, dominate the industry. As pointed out by Michaelson (1974), there is a 250-percent difference in productivity between mines opened in the pre-1950 period, and those opened in the 1970s.

The main reason for this difference is to be found in the use of larger shovels and much larger truck capacities in the newer installations. What this has done is to break a productivity bottleneck caused primarily by an extremely low haulage efficiency. By introducing larger and more modern equipment it becomes possible to take advantage of the relatively high productivities that are to be found in other components of mining. This also explains why, at the present time, investment in the world copper industry has not turned down: the proprietors of new mines can introduce high productivity equipment *en masse,* and thus press unit costs down under those of older installations whose rationalization and mechanization possibilities often are severely constrained by their existing layout and practices.

In comparing productivity between continents, it has been reported by a large copper company operating in both North and South America that, in 1968, productivities in North American mines were generally in excess of 200 tons of material per manshift, while those in South America were less than 200 tons per manshift. This particular difference simply says something about the investment policy of this firm where these two continents are concerned. In North America this corporation practiced one of the highest levels of mechanization in the world; while in South America new investment was generally neglected in favor of more repatriated profits.

This section will conclude by presenting in Table 6-8 some data on output per man hour in several industries for the period 1968–72. As the reader will see, changes over 1971–72 were quite pronounced in several industries as compared to what the 1960–72 trend has shown.

COMMODITY POLICIES; IRON AND STEEL; SUBSTITUTION AND RECYCLING

7

In the past year or so a certain note of urgency has finally been injected into various high-level discussions of the primary commodity markets, in particular the markets for the major nonfuel minerals. What these discussions have in common is the recognition that it is in the interest of both the producers and consumers of these commodities that the producers are insured against calamitous shortfalls in revenue caused by the vagaries of this or that market force. There is as yet, unfortunately, no consensus on how this is to take place, although it must be obvious even to laymen that certain proposals are distinguished by their obvious lack of workability. The first part of the present chapter addresses itself to these matters. This is followed by an examination of some of the more important aspects of the world iron and steel industry; and the chapter is concluded by a brief discussion of substitution and recycling.

PRICE- AND INCOME-COMPENSATION SCHEMES

A price-compensation scheme is an arrangement for reimbursing, to one degree or another, a primary producing country whose products are selling under a certain price. What is supposed to happen is that the producing and consuming countries agree on some sort of reasonable price for the product and, when the actual price falls under this price, compensation is transferred to the producers. This arrangement may also include a provision for the producing countries to make a transfer to the importing countries in the event of the actual price exceeding the target price, although a scheme that resulted in a net transfer from producers to consumers could hardly be taken seriously.[1]

---

[1] If C is the compensation and A the repayment (by the producing country to the country making compensation), and if we also have $\bar{p}_t$ as the target price and p_t the actual price, then we might have

$$C_t = \alpha(\bar{p}_t - p_t)q_t$$

Price compensation schemes have been designed that can be operated on either a bilateral or a multilateral basis. Multilaterally, of course, this would mean the formation of yet another "international agency," and given the fact that most of the existing agencies have the unfortunate and apparently incurable tendency to confuse grandiose rhetoric and crass self-interest with elementary economic logic, the only rational arrangement would appear to be direct contact between producer and consumer countries. This might conceivably function as follows.

Most industrial countries have regular suppliers of primary commodities from among the LDCs. Each consuming country would then direct the major part, but not all, of its compensatory payments toward just these supplier countries, leaving other countries having a production and trade potential with an incentive to play a more active part on the market in question. This would also seem to indicate that the compensatory payments should be generous. In addition, in those years in which the actual price was below the target price, but the industrial country in question was experiencing full employment, compensation would mostly be paid in cash. In a year in which the industrial country was experiencing a high unemployment, the compensation would be for the most part paid in goods.

There are perhaps some controversial elements in the above paragraph. The idea of generous compensation payments may not make a great deal of sense to certain categories of readers, but the general idea behind this proposition is that such things as compensatory measures, preference schemes, and the like would be at the expense of the conventional "unbound" cash transfers that have gone under the misnomer of development aid up to now. As for substituting payments in goods for cash payments, it should be remembered that any government composed of sensible men would insist upon the flexibility to cancel or reduce development aid when the domestic employment rate began to rise and balance of payments considerations prevented the application of an expansionary

---

and

$$A_t = \beta (p_t - \bar{p}_t) q_t$$

if

$$\sum_{t-\phi}^{t-1} (p_i - \bar{p}_i) q_i (1 + r)^i > 0$$

Compensation here depends upon the actual price being lower than the target price, with the total amount of the compensation also being a function of the amount sold during the period. But note that repayment only takes place if actual exports exceed some kind of norm over a contingency period ϕ. We also have α and β constants, q_t is the amount sold, and r the rate of interest.

economic policy to the domestic economy. Of course, opposition to trans-fers of goods is quite strong on both sides of the aid setup. Aid agencies are opposed to it because it infringes on their prerogatives, and the scope of the careers of the people working within these agencies depends upon these prerogatives rather than the effectiveness of the agency in question. Simi-larly, it has been observed on a number of occasions that LDCs have insisted on being allowed to purchase certain types of equipment instead of receiving it as a gift, because it is only when large amounts of cash are changing hands that "rakeoffs" and "skimming" can take place.

One of the well-known shortcomings of price-compensation schemes is that the stabilization of price is not the same thing as the maintenance of income. It is quite conceivable that the actual price can be held above the target price for a considerable period, but the income of producers will still be low. This type of situation might come about in the event of a crop failure or if an extractive facility had to close because of a strike or an accident.[2] We are thus led to consider income-compensation measures.

A number of international organizations are already involved in this kind of compensatory financing. Producing countries have drawn about one billion dollars from the IMF, and schemes have also been proposed by the EEC, the World Bank, and so on. The problem with most of these schemes is that they do not encourage producers to restructure their economies along more efficient lines. The opinion here is that what must be done is to introduce compensatory arrangements that reward success. One possibility is to introduce repayment provisions, and to make these provisions regres-sive: if compensatory transfers over a period of time improve the export performance of a country, then that country need not repay the transfer. A variant on this device would make the transfer payments proportional to export success over a certain period, where success would be measured by a system of indicators.

A possible objection to this kind of proposal is that it does not take into consideration the least developed of the underdeveloped countries. This is, of course, precisely the point. Many of these least developed countries have proved over hundreds, or even thousands, of years that they are incapable of making the effort required to transform their economies into workable propositions, and it is probably time that the rest of the world accepted this inertia at face value.

There is also the problem that might be introduced by large increases in the output of certain goods, which would press down the price even in

---

[2]This should be clear just be examining $\bar{v} = \bar{p}q$, where $\bar{v}$ is income. If compensation is for price, and thus price $= \bar{p}$ at all times, $\bar{v}$ might still show considerable volatility if q has a high variance. This would not be the case if income were the object of a stabilization policy.

years in which the demand for the product was high. This is not a new dilemma however, and the remedy is still the same: the bulk of new investment in these primary-commodity-producing countries must be directed away from traditional sectors or industries. Instead it should go into labor-intensive manufactures that, in turn, must be allowed access to the markets of the industrial world. If this happens, then it might be conceivable that the rather embarrassing predicament caused by the periodically recurring oversupply of this or that primary commodity can eventually be brought under control. But it must be emphasized that the success of this type of arrangement depends first and foremost upon the unconditional opening of the markets of the industrial countries to the non-primary-commodity exports of the LDCs. Without this assistance, these countries cannot possibly hope to improve their standard of living.

In addition to a simple opening of markets, a comprehensive scheme of preferences may also have to be established to compensate for the present low productivity of most LDCs outside their primary commodity sectors. With a little luck it might be the case that, in the long run, these preferences can be eliminated or reduced. To begin with, the industrial countries might even go so far as to consider buying everything, or almost everything, that the LDCs can produce. Some readers might think that this is asking a great deal, but, to be truthful, this attitude is difficult to understand, particularly when many of these same readers view with complete serenity the misuse of a substantial part of the so-called development assistance being provided the Third World.

BUFFER STOCKS

The purpose of a buffer-stock system is to stabilize the price of a product by buying when the price is low and selling from the buffer stock when the price is high. In other words, it keeps the price from falling through a "floor" or rising above a "ceiling." The interesting aspect of the buffer-stock discussion at the present time, however, is the way that the concept of "price stabilization" has been linked with economic growth and development, even though it is in the nature of things that these two matters are completely unrelated. It should be noted, however, that this mistake is largely characteristic of economists having a strong theoretical orientation and little or no interest for what goes on in the real world. The representatives of the LDCs, on the other hand, view the role of buffer stocks as one of establishing a lower limit to the price of their products, although, for purposes of the record, they too have been known to bemoan the excessive discomfort caused consumers by unexpected drastic rises in price.

At the present time several buffer stocks are in operation. One of them, the tin buffer stock, has managed to attract a good deal of attention as a model of what a buffer stock should be, even though, in actuality, it would be extremely difficult, if not impossible, to prove that what might be called pure buffer-stock operations have produced any noticeable effect on price formation in this market. The short run price has in no way been made less volatile; nor have the floor or ceiling prices been defended with any appreciable degree of success on those unfortunate occasions when the buffer-stock management was unable to establish those limits in such a way that a defense would not be necessary. On this point, it should be appreciated that the buffer-stock management accepts little or no responsibility for moderating short-run fluctuations in tin prices, even though many people have come to believe that this is one of the main functions of a buffer stock.

There is also a general tendency among many students of the tin buffer stock to overlook the role played by the U.S. government's strategic stockpile of tin. Movements in and out of this very large inventory generally tended to be in phase with those of the tin buffer stock, although quantitatively there was hardly any comparison. During many of the post-war years the annual acquisitions of tin by the U.S. strategic stockpile were larger than the average total size of the tin buffer stock over this period. Given the various slumps to which this market was susceptible during this period, it seems clear that had the purchasing power of the strategic stockpile been absent, the price of tin would have descended to some very low levels.

There is also the matter of the various "tin agreements" calling for the tin-producing countries to support the tin buffer stock with export quotas in the event of the price falling through the floor. In reality, however, the situation works precisely the other way. Export quotas can, in theory, always be successful in maintaining a floor price, while the same can be said of a buffer stock only if it were possible to finance and set one up several times larger than any private buffer stock that has been contemplated to date. If we ignore the problem of maintaining the ceiling, and examine the success with which the floor price has been supported, it is hard to avoid the conclusion that the key factors have been heavy buying or restrictive selling on the part of the U.S. strategic stockpile, threats of invoking export restrictions—which in themselves inevitably cause buying for inventories, and, of course, the actual invocation of export quotas on several occasions.

A constant complaint of the buffer-stock management is that it never seems to have sufficient money to fulfill its aims. This is only natural since, in response to changes in costs, the floor price is being continually negotiated upward by producers, thus reducing the real resources at the disposal of the buffer-stock management. Under the Fourth Agreement (dating from July 1, 1971) the buffer stock was provided with funds equivalent to 20,000 tons at the existing floor price of £1,350/ton. Even allowing for profits gained when the buffer stock was holding surplus money, the present buying capacity is around 12,000 tons, depending on exchange rates and the cost of storage.[3]

Present hopes are that the International Monetary Fund will be drawn into the financing of the buffer stock; or that the buffer stock will become a part of the multicommodity scheme proposed by UNCTAD. There is also talk of bringing some "oil money" into the financing of these stocks. A better idea than all these, however, is simply to drop entirely the idea of a buffer stock, and for the tin-consuming countries to guarantee the tin-producing industry in the less developed countries a certain level of profitability or income, even though the calculation of a "fair" level of profitability might prove to be a complicated exercise. There are, however, several reasons why this type of scheme is not of interest to the producing countries, the most important being that these countries—like most primary-commodity-producing countries—want somewhat more than a fair level of profitability. What they want is a price that, while it might not allow workers and technicians in the production end of these industries to attain a decent standard of living, will permit the maintenance of a great deal of luxury consumption and socially unproductive investment outside these industries. Unfortunately, as yet, it is not widely understood that a buffer stock will not provide this kind of price.

Perhaps the ultimate in buffer-stock schemes is the newly proposed multicommodity arrangement that UNCTAD and others seem intent upon launching. In structure, this amounts to no more than the amalgamation of a number of buffer stocks under a central management. Just what this will mean for "price stabilization" is unsure at the present time, but there is little doubt that in certain circumstances this kind of scheme would be useful as yet another instrument of confrontation between the Third World and the industrial countries. Still, various influential personalities in the great world of international diplomacy have come to believe that a buffer stock has great promise as a "price stabilizing" device since, ostensibly, it does not interfere with the price mechanism. Even if this were true, which it probably is not, or, for that matter, it were possible to resurrect Adam Smith himself to serve as the manager of this operation, the opinion of the author is that the weight of both experience and common sense—as well as the skillful theoretical evidence produced at UNCTAD by Dr. John Cuddy

[3]Dr. M. J. Colebrook of UNCTAD, perhaps the leading expert in the world on these matters, has assembled an astonishing amount of information on the cost of storage of various commodities.

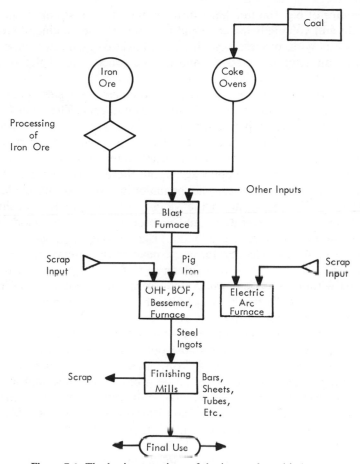

Figure 7-1. The basic operations of the iron and steel industry.

and others—is firmly on the side of direct compensatory payments. But whether this will suffice to place buffer stocks in their proper perspective remains to be seen.

THE IRON AND STEEL INDUSTRY

The technology of the iron and steel industry is shown in bare outline in Figure 7-1. The purpose of this figure and the next few paragraphs is to give the reader a short introduction to how steel is made.

The three principal stages of production shown in the figure are (1) the manufacture of pig iron in a blast furnace, with the most important inputs by weight and volume being coke and iron ore; (2) the making of steel in a furnace employing processes such as the basic oxygen, Bessemer, open hearth, or an electrical process; and (3) the processing of the steel in a finishing mill.

Earlier in this book we mentioned so-called mini steel plants. The electric arc furnace shown above fits into this category. The other furnaces have as their main input pig iron, and they also take some scrap; while the main input for the electric arc furnace is scrap, with only a small amount of pig iron. Mini steel plants are of considerable interest for LDCs because of the relatively low cost of shipping scrap, but there is also considerable and growing electric furnace capacity in the major industrial countries. Much of this capacity is to be found in the vicinity of "integrated" steelmaking installations, where integrated signifies processing the commodity from iron making (to include coke production) right through to finishing. The big advantage in having electric furnaces near these integrated operations involves their being able to take advantage of the large amount of scrap generated within the cycle of integrated operations. Another point in favor of electric furnaces is that they permit a high degree of control over the grade and composition of the steel produced.

Some terminology is of interest at this stage of the discussion. The iron ore is *reduced* in a blast furnace whose output is called *pig iron.* There are other technologies for obtaining pig iron, but as yet their expense—primarily in terms of energy—has proved to be prohibitive. Important inputs for the blast furnace are limestone, fuel oil, pulverized coal, and natural gas. These are generally called *fluxes.* The form in which most steel leaves the furnace is that of an *ingot,* although it is sometimes cast directly into *molds* for shapes that are very large or complex.

Finishing involves working steel ingots into their final shape via *hammering, pressing,* and *rolling;* and all these operations require very high temperatures. (Rolling requires up to 1200 degrees centigrade.) For the rolling stage the ingot is first passed through a cogging mill, and then sheared into blooms or slabs. These are then rolled into *billets, small sections, bars, plates, rods,* and *wide strips* and *sheets.*

Billets, rails, bars, and some rods are usually cut into standard lengths, while plates are cut to specification. Billets can be used for the manufacture of tubes or pipes through being rerolled as bars and "pierced." They can also be made into such things as motor axles by forging or drop forging. Nuts and bolts, parts for automobiles, bicycles, machinery, shafts and gears, and seamless tubes are made from bars. Rods are turned into such things as wire, rivets, needles, springs, and so on. Plates are employed as such in many heavy industries, and are also used in the making of tubes.

Wide strip is sheared, and after further processing, to include tinning, is turned into tinplate. It is also used for car bodies. Pipes are manufactured from such items as strip, sheets, and plates. They can also be rolled from pierced or solid billets and bars.

The creation of scrap begins at the instant pig iron is tapped from the blast furnace, and from that point on scrap is generated by almost every operation in the steelmaking process: the pouring of ingots, the rolling and cropping of slabs, the trimming of bars and sheets, etc. Most modern steelworks generate internally about 50 percent of their input of scrap, and additional scrap is generated in the various plants in which steel is used. Finally, it should be mentioned that while coke is made from coal, not all coals have the requisite properties. Those that do are called *coking coals*.

The international trade in iron ore, coking coal, semifinished and finished steel products, and the like, involved the transportation in 1974 of 1.1 billion tons of products per year, with a value of about $70 billion. Everything considered, the products of this industry would have to be judged the most valuable ingredient of modern industry. According to UNIDO estimates, the direct value of the products and by-products of the iron and steel industry corresponds on the average to between 3 and 5 percent of the GNP of a mature industrialized country; but can reach 6–10 percent for an industrial or semiindustrial country that is still expanding at a high rate of growth (such as Japan, Brazil, or perhaps Spain). If the direct and the indirect impact of steel production on GNP is considered, this might involve as much as 20 percent of GNP.

The iron and steel industry is a very capital-intensive industry, with a specific requirement (in January 1975) of about $600 of investment for each ton/year of steel ingot production capacity. In addition, when carrying out major increases in steel production capacity, substantial investments in infrastructure are almost always necessary, particularly in LDCs. The reader can get some idea of the magnitude of various flows within the world iron and steel industry in 1973 from Figure 7-2.

As seen in Figure 7-2, 8 percent of the world output of steel was accounted for by the LDCs, which also delivered about 28 percent of the total world input of iron ore. The direct input of raw materials into this industry came to 1,760 million tons in 1974, where this figure includes fluxes, ore, coking coal, and scrap. The combined value of these particular inputs was somewhat over $50 billion. As for the by-products of the steelmaking process, many of these are of great value in their own right: pig iron by-products that are needed for cast iron foundries; coke by-products that are important inputs in the chemical industry; slag, which is used for the production of cement and some other materials, etc. Here it should be noted that only 200 million tons of the scrap shown in this diagram is

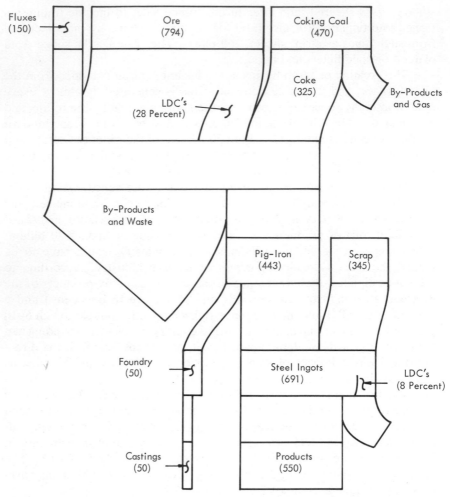

Figure 7-2. Simple flow diagram of the iron and steel industry: total world figures, 1974.

purchased from external sources. The remainder, or $345 - 200 = 145$, is generated within the various production processes of the industry itself, and is known as "home" or "prompt" scrap.

In steelmaking the principle innovation of the post-World War II period has been the shift from the conventional open hearth furnace, which dominated the steelmaking process during the first half of this century, to the basic oxygen furnace (BOF) and the electric arc furnace. In Table 7-1 we have the composition of the world steel output by process.

Table 7-1. Percentage Composition of the World Steelmaking Processes

Year	Open hearth	Electric	Oxygen	Other[a]
1955	74.7	7.7	—	17.8
1960	68.5	10.3	3.8	17.4
1965	59.0	12.0	16.4	12.6
1970	38.8	13.8	41.5	5.9
1975	30.7	14.4	52.7	2.2
1980[b]	17.1	20.0	62.0	0.9
1985[b]	6.5	28.0	65.0	0.5
1990[b]	3.8	34.0	—	—

[a] Mostly Bessemer.
[b] Estimated by simple nonlinear regression.
Source: British Iron and Steel Federation; also UNIDO documents.

The basic oxygen process, which is also called the LD (Linz–Donowitz) process, features the injection of oxygen, at a very high velocity, onto molten iron in a specially designed furnace. Among other things this burns out impurities, and accelerates the speed of reaction. In the electric furnace a charge of nearly 100 percent scrap is melted by means of electric heat. In recent years improvements of the electric furnace have made them extremely useful for small-scale operations (such as mini steel plants) serving local or specialized markets. The economies realizable by this type of equipment when operated on a larger scale is largely a matter of the availability of ample supplies of energy.

In the case of ironmaking, technology has mostly worked to economize on the use of raw materials, principally coke, and to increase the productivity of blast furnaces. Where the latter is concerned, the principle gains have resulted from improved raw material blending and *beneficiation*. Beneficiation principally covers enriching or concentrating the ore, which in turn means increasing its iron content while eliminating many impurities. It also has to do with *agglomerating* the ore through *sintering* and *pelletizing*.

Ore enrichment through crushing, grinding, and screening has been standard practice in the iron-ore-mining or iron-ore-using industries for years, but of late the economics of blast furnace operations has tended in the direction of requiring an even higher iron content for ore, uniform particle sizes, and so on. This in turn has necessitated more sophisticated processing operations. Sintering consists of agglomerating—or lumping together—the fines of an ore; while pelletizing involves reducing the ore to small ball-shaped particles, or pellets, having a uniform size and composition. These processes have facilitated the exploitation of poorer quality ore; and in addition have made extensive economies possible where blast furnace operation and the transportation of blast furnace inputs are concerned. Ten years ago very fine ores, or ores with a size of about 10 mm, were generally considered unsalable. At present there is an extremely high demand for this kind of ore. Similarly, the percentage intake of the world's blast furnaces of sinterized and pelletized ore has increased from one-half to three-fourths in the last dozen years, while the use of iron ore at a lower stage of processing has declined accordingly.

Due to the rising cost of coke—which is manufactured from coal—strenuous efforts have been made to increase the efficiency of coke usage. The ratio of oven coke production to raw steel output declined from 0.81 in 1960 to 0.59 in 1970, and is expected to reach 0.48 in 1980. Where this commodity is concerned, the reader should take note that there are enormous supplies of coal available, but technological change in this industry has lagged considerably, and in recent years productivity has occasionally declined.[4]

World Steel production has been expanding at a rate of about 6 percent a year since 1965. A poll of most prognoses would seem to indicate that the average expansion over the next 5 years may be slightly greater than 40 million tons per year, with a total cost that could reach 50 billion dollars per year, where this cost includes iron ore production and steelmaking. In addition, extensive replacement and modernization investments are going to be necessary.

The interesting thing about these forecasts is that they presume no global income realignment such as that envisaged in programs like the "New World Economic Order." If, however, the New World Economic Order is to be taken seriously, then notice should be given as soon as possible that the amount of new steel and iron ore producing capacity that will be necessary is not just huge, but astronomical. As a result it seems appropriate to suggest that while the New World Economic Order may continue as a popular and, to a certain type of person, exciting idea, the chances are that it will not amount to much outside those conference rooms and seminars where well-spoken people with high ideals and incomes come together to manufacture illusions.

[4]World coal reserves of all types have been estimated (in 1970) as being in excess of 4.7 trillion tons, with over 3.9 trillion tons bituminous, anthracite, or subbituminous. Nearly 50 percent of the world reserves are in Asia, with about half of these in Russia, and the rest in China. It is also thought that there are huge undiscovered deposits of coal in China. The United States has about ⅓ of the world's total reserves of coal; and the balance is in Europe. Given that production in 1970 was about 2.1 billion tons, and the growth rate of production was 2.1 percent/year, the global reserves of coal, measured in years, is on the order of 1500.

Table 7-2. Flow of Funds Account for the World Steel Industry, 1961–71

	Source of funds	Percent		Use of funds	Percent
(1)	Net earnings depreciation	53.6[a]	(1)	Expenditure on fixed assets	66.5
(2)	Increase in current liabilities	15.3	(2)	Increase in current assets	16.2
(3)	Increase in long term debt	21.3	(3)	Reduction in long term debt	0.9
(4)	Increase in capital stock	5.0	(4)	Dividend payments	11.7
(5)	Other income	4.8	(5)	Other outpayments	4.6
		100			100

[a] Without France this figure would have been 18.8 from net income, and 34.9 from depreciation.
Source: International Iron and Steel Institute.

The International Iron and Steel Institute has gone into the problem of how investment in the steelmaking industry has been financed in the past. Most of this financing appears to have come from the net earnings and depreciation allowances of the steel companies. The rest came from an increase in current liabilities, or short-term debt; an increase in long-term debt—mostly in the form of bonds; and an increase in equity (stocks or shares). Other sources include such things as subsidies, income from financial investment, etc. These items can also be referred to as "sources of funds."

In the macroeconomic literature sources of funds can be used both to purchase assets and to reduce liabilities. The assets that interest us here are real assets, but it must be granted that steel companies can use their net income to purchase financial assets as well, or for that matter can simply hold cash. They can also reduce debt, pay dividends, make various business transfers, and so on. For the period 1961–71 the International Iron and Steel Institute lists in Table 7-2 the following sources and uses of funds, by percent, for the world steel industry.

It seems to be the case that in periods when a great deal of investment activity is taking place, there is a fairly low percentage of self-financing. Depreciation has undoubtedly been the most important factor for financing new equipment, and in 1971 about 30 percent of new capacity was financed via depreciation. At the present time the general "feeling" within the steel industry is that funds for expansion are going to be more difficult to obtain in the future than was previously the case. Still, it may be possible to maintain the historic rate of expansion if no further explosion of energy prices takes place.

We can now go to the iron ore industry. As indicated earlier, price in

Table 7-3. World Iron Ore Reserves, 1970

Region	Reserves			Potential ore			Total
	Total	Iron content ≥60%	Iron content ≤60%	Total	Iron content ≥60%	Iron content ≤60%	
Eastern Africa[a]	1,144	384	760	10,839	382	10,457	11,983
Western Africa[b]	2,134	1,900	234	8,625	11	8,614	10,759
Asia[c]	27,425	7,990	19,435	32,307	15	32,292	59,732
Europe, Africa (North) and Middle East	24,048	34	24,014	19,086	1,006	19,080	43,134
Latin America and the Caribbean	34,789	657	34,132	58,562	116	58,446	93,351
Sub total	89,540	10,965	78,575	129,419	1,530	127,889	218,959
United States and Canada	41,245	0	41,245	184,287	0	184,287	225,532
Centrally Planned Economies (Total)	120,671	14	120,657	224,021	0	224,021	344,692
(of which U.S.S.R.)	110,483	0	110,483	193,818	0	193,818	304,301
World total[d]	251,456	10,979	240,477	537,727	1,530	536,197	789,183

[a] Including Mozambique and Namibia.
[b] Includes Angola and Spanish Sahara.
[c] Includes New Caledonia.
[d] Present world total considerably higher.
Source: U.N. documents (Survey of World Iron Ore Resources, 1970).

Table 7-4. Iron Ore Procurement Arrangements: Selected Countries and Regions

Area (1968)	Percent		
	Captive mines	Long-term contract	Free market
United States	96	—	4
Japan	—	96	4
U.K. and E.E.C.	31	—	69
Eastern Europe	—	87	13
World	30	36	34

this market is closely tied to the grade of the ore. Here a certain amount of optimism on the part of consumers is probably justified, since with present demand known reserves would last several hundred years, while they will last 100 years if consumption continues to expand at present rates. Equally as important, listed world reserves have expanded by a factor of seven in the past 25 years, which would indicate that we are far from diminishing returns where exploration is concerned. Table 7-3 shows the world reserve situation as of 1970.

In 1960, 42 percent of all ore traded originated in captive mines, or mines that are controlled to one degree or another by steel companies. Nineteen percent was traded through the medium of long-term contracts; and the remainder sold on what has been called the "free" market. In 1968 these proportions were 30, 36, and 34. The problem here is that free market sales are contract sales where the price is negotiated once a year, and in some circles this type of arrangement is regarded as analogous to trading on the London and New York metal exchanges — which is quite untrue.

Different countries employ these three trading arrangements to different degrees, as Table 7-4 shows.

Contracts fix the quality, quantity, and price of ore, sometimes over very long periods. It often happens that when new iron ore producing capacity is being established, long-terms contracts are arranged by investors as a guarantee that they have access to the ore at favorable prices. Special consortia or large trading companies are also active in negotiating contracts. Where this subject is concerned it should be noted that many steel companies also control or share control of the facilities for transporting ore and other inputs.[5]

[5] Two-thirds of the world's steel output is produced by about 20 companies. The top 12 are Nippon Steel, U.S. Steel Corporation, British Steel, Bethlehem Steel (U.S.), Nippon Kokan Kabushiki Kaisha, August Thysson Hutte Group (F.R.G.), Sumitomo Metal Industries, Kawasaki Steel Corp., Finsider (Italy), Republic Steel (U.S.), Wendel-Sidelor (France), and USINOR (France). Each of the top three produces more steel than *all* the LDCs.

Table 7-5. Some Self-Sufficiency Ratios, 1950–70

Area	1950	1960	1970
United States	95	75	69
United Kingdom	61	58	38
E.E.C.	79	69	44
Japan	39	11	1
All developed market economies	95	81	69
Eastern Europe	42	33	24

An important feature of the past 25 years has been the growing trade in iron ore. From 1950 to 1970 world exports of iron ore increased at average annual rates of 14 percent by value and 11 percent by volume, as compared to an average annual rate of increase in steel consumption of about 5.8 percent/year. One of the big reasons for this was the decline in the iron ore self-sufficiency ratio in many of the large consuming countries, where a self-sufficiency ratio gives the percent of consumption of an item that is satisfied out of domestic supplies. Table 7-5 shows these ratios over the period 1950–70 for certain countries.

As to be expected, there has not only been an increase in the amount of ore moved, but in the pattern. For instance, over the period treated in this table, several new sources of ore appeared. The country that deserves special attention among these is Australia, which between 1965 and 1970 emerged as the world's largest exporter: in 1970 it supplied 12 percent of world exports. A trade matrix giving some approximate figures for 1975 is shown in Table 7-6.

It need hardly be mentioned that the sale of iron ore has provided a nice income for producers in those LDCs fortunate enough to possess supplies of ore. Once again, however, it is necessary to question whether these countries intend to accept an indefinite relegation to the status of suppliers of unprocessed materials. As with other primary commodities, the cost of transporting iron ore is highly dependent upon the form in which it is shipped. Thus there should be enormous incentives for the local beneficiating of the ores of many LDCs, and shipping these in the form of sinter and pellets. It might also be the case that the processing of the ore can be done in adjacent countries—that is, a country without ore can process the ore of another LDC if it happens to be in a more favorable situation in regard to energy, trained manpower, etc.

A similar argument can be made with regard to steel. The structure of the world steel market is changing, and changing rapidly. In the United States a higher level of steel imports is already being taken for granted; and while nobody wants to say just where these imports will originate, it is no

Table 7-6. Approximate Iron Ore Trade Matrix, 1975

	Imports into				
Exports from	United States	Japan	West Europe	Other	Total
Canada	22	7	13	—	42
Sweden	—	—	30	1	31
Republic of South Africa	—	1	3	—	4
Australia	1	62	9	—	72
Brazil	2	25	24	6	57
Venezuela	16	—	4	—	20
Chile and Peru	3	12	1	—	16
Liberia	3	—	19	2	14
Mauritania/Angola	—	4	9	—	13
Other Africa	—	3	7	1	11
India	—	18	3	5	26
Other Asia	—	3	—	2	5
Total	47	135	122	17	323

longer unthinkable that they will come from closer to the source of the iron ore, where labor also may be less expensive and pollution standards less rigid. At the present time the LDCs, taken as a group, are heavy importers of steel but, according to UNIDO forecasts, they should be net exporters by the year 2000. Where the world pattern of steel exports is concerned, Table 7-7 shows the ratio of exports to total steel production.

It is hard to imagine these trends continuing and not involving a higher level of exports from the LDCs. In addition, as some of the LDCs expand their production to cover their own needs, they may find that the economies of large-scale production require that they produce more steel than they can use, and so they will tend to become aggressive in seeking out foreign markets. Most likely they will find them.

SUBSTITUTION AND RECYCLING

It is one of the commonplaces of economic theory that if the price of most commodities increases by a large amount, substitution will take place. If the price of butter becomes outrageous, for example, toast eaters will cultivate a taste for margarine, or perhaps imitation caviar.

We often see the same phenomenon in action where minerals are concerned. Several prominent cases of substitution have been referred to earlier in this book—synthetic rubber for natural rubber, various silicate ores for bauxite, and so on. Attention in this section will be concentrated on the substitution of aluminum for copper, but first a few general remarks are

Table 7-7. World Steel Exports as Proportion of World Steel Production

Year	Exports	Total production	Export ratio	Year	Exports	Total production	Export ratio
1950	20.5	192.0	10.7	1961	52.3	354.3	14.8
1951	20.3	208.8	9.7	1962	56.0	358.7	15.6
1952	24.3	211.6	11.5	1963	60.0	384.7	15.6
1953	24.1	233.3	10.3	1964	69.3	434.2	16.0
1954	24.4	222.8	11.8	1965	78.5	456.9	17.2
1955	34.0	270.5	12.6	1966	77.6	473.1	16.4
1956	35.8	284.3	12.6	1967	85.0	497.2	17.1
1957	40.0	293.5	13.6	1968	98.5	529.9	18.6
1958	38.0	274.5	13.8	1969	110.1	574.2	19.2
1959	42.1	306.3	13.7	1970	116.1	595.3	21.4
1960	52.7	345.5	15.3				

in order. For instance, concerning aluminum and copper, it is usual that when aluminum has replaced copper there is no switch back to copper. The reason for this cannot be explained completely by the fact that different types of machinery are used to process the two metals and, for obvious economic reasons, the machinery cannot be replaced on a short-run basis; that type of problem could undoubtedly be solved in time. Instead, we must realize that there is a general feeling among many users of copper that, because of its relative abundance, aluminum may be the metal of the future.

The mechanics of substitution are not always easy to grasp, much less quantify. The belief here is that there is insufficient evidence to claim that the relative price of copper to aluminum has moved in such a way as to justify the rather strong displacement that we have witnessed from copper to aluminum. In those uses where aluminum displays a similar efficiency to copper, the market share of copper as compared to aluminum has fallen from 90 to 50 percent over the last 50 years. The reasons often cited for this sort of thing taking place are the lower price *and* price volatility of aluminum; however, in point of fact, the price of copper has been very low until recent years, and it is still too early to determine whether the upturn of this price experienced in the late 1960s was a onetime event or the beginning of a new trend.

One of the ways of thinking about substitution is to postulate some kind of optimal substitution pattern. For instance, let us look at the use pattern of aluminum in the United Kingdom and France for the rather broad category "electric cables," as quoted in a recent CIPEC report. Figures given here are in percents.

	1965	1966	1967	1968	1969	1970	1971
United Kingdom (Electric cables)	9.0	14.3	15.8	16.0	15.5	17.8	20.4
France (Insulated lines and cables)	7.2	13.7	16.1	16.4	19.3	20.7	22.8

A possible interpretation of this data is that a certain amount of substitution could take place that has not taken place. Even if we were to assume different qualitative standards in these two countries, it seems clear that one is either lagging behind with its substitution or, at a much lower level of probability, moving too fast. Moreover, this is an important observation, since if each of the copper-consuming countries were to substitute aluminum for copper at a rate corresponding to the country exhibiting the fastest rate of substitution for all the various uses of copper, then the world copper industry would find itself facing a severe drop in demand.

The cable industry is of particular interest for this discussion since various branches of that industry have experienced a particularly rapid rate of substitution. Given the relative densities of the two metals, even if copper and aluminum were the same price per ton, an insulated copper conductor would cost twice as much as an aluminum conductor being used for the same purpose. Given existing price levels, copper conductors cost somewhere in the range of five times as much as aluminum; and thus, regardless of certain structural advantages possessed by copper over aluminum (such as better vibration and fatigue strength, better contact resistance performance, smaller cable size per unit load, etc.), cable manufacturers are being compelled to press ahead with substitution as fast as possible. Naturally, at the same time, a great deal of research is being directed toward overcoming the various shortcomings of aluminum. A composite copper-aluminum cable can be cited here.

Unfortunately, when we speak of something like cables, we actually mean a very large range of cables and wires, each with different technical and economic characteristics. Thus it becomes extremely difficult to say at just what price copper cable gives way to aluminum. If we consider the wires in distribution transformers, Swarbrick (1974) has quoted a change-over price of £750/ton. On this point we see that in the United Kingdom only one percent of transformer winding wires are of aluminum, while the corresponding figure for the United States is 15 percent. Obviously it is to be expected that the U.K. shift to aluminum in this particular use will be considerable in the next few years.

Aluminum is not the only substitute for copper. Plastics are also extremely important, but at the present time plastics are less popular because of the high price of oil, one of their most important inputs. It is also interesting to note that in such things as automobiles, a considerable amount of substitution will probably come about because the final product—in this case the automobile—might experience radical changes. For instance, given the expected increases in the price of fuel, extensive alterations will have to take place in the design of vehicles in order to achieve a higher energy efficiency. One of the first things that comes to mind here is a reduction in weight, which in turn means that some of the 35 pounds of copper used in the average automobile will be replaced by aluminum.

SCRAP AND RECYCLING

One of the more attractive spillovers of the energy crisis is the emphasis being placed on the recycling and reusing of natural resources. Materials such as oil, coal, and natural gas fall outside the scope of this part of our discussion, since the reuse or regeneration of these items is not economically feasible at the present time; but a large and increasing amount of recycling is taking place of such important industrial inputs as aluminum, copper, and steel.

The basic scheme where recycling is concerned has already been shown in Figure 2-2. At various points in the production-use cycle scrap (or secondary materials) is generated and, after collection and, quite often, some processing, finds its way back into the production input stage of the cycle. The amount of material being recycled varies considerably. No more than 21–22 percent of the total present consumption of aluminum has its origin in scrap, while as much as 45 percent of the world consumption of copper has been of unprocessed or processed secondary copper.

Needless to say, the amount of consumption that could be based on secondary material is much higher than that realized today. Wakesberg (1974) has cited a study claiming that only 61 percent of potentially recyclable copper is exploited, maintaining, in an important analysis, that the principle problem is one of insufficient tax incentives, in addition to a badly functioning market. There may well be something to this point of view, since the stock of copper eligible for recycling is probably somewhere in the neighborhood of 25 million tons at the present time in the United States alone, and yet it appears that the percentage of copper being recycled is independent of the price of primary copper. From a "social" point of view this is not exactly an ideal situation for the consuming countries, since this stock of secondary material is a domestic asset that is free of those rather tiresome political implications that seem to surround many minerals at the present time. Still, some recognition of this fact may be dawning, since both the French government and aluminum industry have announced that the use of secondary materials shall increase in France; while in the United States the number of aluminum cans being recycled increased from 185 million in 1970 to 1.6 billion in 1973.

The incentive for the "mining" of scrap is plain and simple profit maximization. Presumably, if scrap collectors and processors could earn more for their efforts, the supply of scrap would be larger. In comparing the cost of primary copper with secondary, it appeared that in 1973 the cost of converting secondary copper into refined copper that was almost indistinguishable from primary refined was between 3 and 6 cents per pound, or approximately 10 percent of the price of refined copper originating from copper ore (primary refined). At the same time, it should be realized that only a minor part of the scrap collected goes to the refinery: in the developed market economies this amounts to about 23 percent. Instead, most of this secondary material is alloyed with zinc and tin and turned into such things as brass and bronze.

The next step here will be the construction of an accounting exercise dealing with the flow of primary and secondary metal through the first part of the production–consumption cycle in the Unites States in 1965. One of the advantages of this exercise is that it clarifies movements in and out of the system due to exports, imports, and inventory changes. The exposition below will be organized so as to break the cycle into three parts: the first considers flows between the mining stage and the smelter; the next between the smelter and the refinery; and finally between refinery and consumption input. The figures used here are all "copper equivalent," and are in thousands of metric tons in the diagrams, and metric tons otherwise. For the first part we have

(1) Mine Production − Exports + Imports ± Stock Changes
 − Direct Use of Concentrates + Secondary Blister
 = Smelter Input = $(O_T - O_E + M_{OS} \pm \Delta O_L - O_I + I_S)$

O_T is mine production, O_E is exports, and so on. In this expression the direct use of concentrates indicates that part of the output of copper concentrate that can be employed as a direct input in an industrial process. Secondary blister is scrap that must, because of some undesirable properties, be processed before it can go to the refinery. Diagrammatically we have in Figure 7-3 this phase of the cycle.

It should be noted that the direct use of concentrates (O_I) was equal to zero during this year. Expression (1) can now be rewritten to give

$$S_{ST} = I_S + M_{OS} + (O_T - O_E - O_I \pm \Delta O_L) = I_S + M_{OS} + O_S$$

The term in the parentheses is the output of the mining industry that continues to the smelter. Note that an inventory increase results in a minus sign, since it signifies a flow out of the system. If we use the figures shown we get $S_{ST} = 85{,}200 + 33{,}400 + (1{,}229{,}000 - 9{,}700 - 0 - 8{,}300)$. Observe here that the scrap supply consists of new or "current" scrap generated in the production process, as well as old scrap that comes from discarded automobiles, cables, pipes, etc.

We can now go to the smelter–refinery phase. Our accounting relationship is

(2) Smelter Production − Exports of Smelter Products
 + Imports of Smelter Products ± Stock Changes
 + Scrap Input to Refinery − Direct Use of Blister
 = Refinery Input = $S_{ST} - S_E + M_{SR} \pm \Delta S_L + I_R - S_I$

In this expression the "scrap input to the refinery" gives the amount of old and new scrap that is refined. Percentagewise this amounts to 318.7/

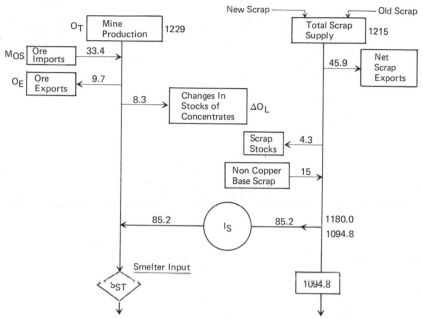

Figure 7-3. Flow of primary and secondary metal between mining stage and smelter.

$1215 \times 100 = 26.2$ percent of the total supply of scrap. The remainder of the scrap is not refined and goes directly into foundries, powder mills, brass mills, and so on. Similarly the direct use of blister signifies blister copper (unrefined copper of a high purity) that is used in industrial processes without refining. Figure 7-4 shows this phase of the cycle.

We can rewrite expression (2) to give

$$R_{RT} = I_R + M_{SR} + (S_{ST} - S_E - S_I \pm S_L) = I_R + M_{SR} + S_R$$

In this expression S_R is the output of the smelter reaching the refinery *plus* the decrease in blister stocks. R_{RT} is refinery input and, if losses are negligible, also refinery output. Remembering that all values are in copper content, if we put in the figures in the diagram we get $R_{RT} = 318,700 + 301,700 + (1,329,600 - 4,400 - 0 + 11,200) = 1,956,800$. Observe that the positive value for ΔS_L means a movement out of inventory.

Finally we have the refinery–consumption input stage. Here we write

(3) Refined Production − Exports of Refined + Imports of Refined
± Changes in Private and Official Inventories of Refined
= Total Consumption of Refined = $R_{RT} - R_E + M_{RI} \pm \Delta R_L \pm \Delta R_G$

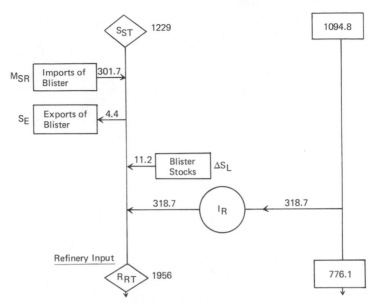

Figure 7-4. Flow of primary and secondary metal between smelter and refinery.

This expression is self-explanatory, and so we can go directly to Figure 7-5.

Expression (3) can be rewritten $R_{RT} = M_{RI} + (R_{RT} - R_E \pm R_L \pm R_G) = M_{RI} + R_I$, and, when the figures are put in, we have $124{,}700 + (1{,}956{,}800 - 294{,}900 + 6{,}900 + 46{,}300) = 1{,}839{,}800$ as the consumption of primary refined copper.

Among the advantages of recycling can be mentioned the possibility to save large amounts of energy. Recycled steel, for example, uses 75 percent less energy than primary steel, while 12 times as much energy is used to produce primary aluminum as to recover secondary aluminum. There are also enormous environmental advantages to be gained when the recycling system has been built up to an optimal extent since, among other things, this will mean that definite economic incentives are created for everyone to assist in providing input for the system. Just as, at the present time, certain types of used containers possess a monetary value and thus, to a high degree, are recycled, it is not inconceivable that the same arrangement may eventually apply to all containers.

It should be realized, however, that recycling materials does not make exhaustible resources inexhaustible. As Solow (1974) has pointed out, the laws of thermodynamics ensure that we cannot recover a pound of secondary copper from a pound of primary copper, nor a pound of tertiary from a pound of secondary: there are bound to be processing losses that can be

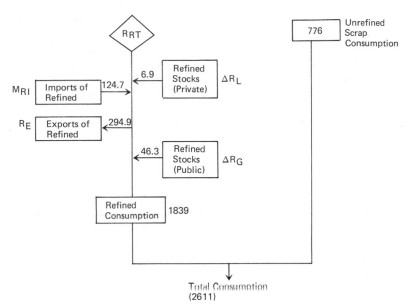

Figure 7-5. Flow of primary and secondary metal between refinery and consumption.

regarded as "leakages" from the recycling system. Here we have a concept similar to that of the multiplier in elementary macroeconomic theory. If ϕ is the percentage that is recoverable of a particular material (and thus $1 - \phi$ is the leakage, processing loss, or simply the amount that cannot be recovered for various technical reasons), then one pound of primary metal can be multiplied up through recycling to $1 + 1\cdot\phi + 1\cdot\phi^2 + \cdots + 1\cdot\phi^i + \cdots = 1\cdot(1 + \phi + \phi^2 + \cdots + \phi^i + \cdots) = 1/(1 - \phi)$.

Although this last expression may be of interest, unfortunately it does not say anything about *when* this metal will be available. Determining when is a matter of the durability of the goods in which the metal is used, as well as the amount of the metal that is being used. If, for instance, the durability of such things as automobiles, houses, etc., were to double, then we would expect—with everything else the same—that we would have to wait twice as long to obtain the recyclable material in them.[6] Of course, as the reader

---

[6] Let us take Y_t as income at time t, and postulate an income–output relationship between copper and income; this means that we have, for example, $C = \alpha Y$. We shall also take g as the growth rate of income, L the average durability of goods containing copper, and β the percentage of copper recoverable from these goods. We can then write

$$C_t = \alpha Y_t = \alpha Y_0 e^{gt}$$

This is the amount of copper being used in year t. If durability is L, then the copper available

probably realizes, if durability is increased then it might also be possible to decrease the amount of new production, and thus less recyclable material will be demanded.

One of the best examples of a high-efficiency recycling system is to be found in the German Democratic Republic (GDR). In every county in the GDR there are recycling firms responsible for the purchase of all usable waste. On the supply side, almost every firm or production unit has an employee, responsible to the manager, who takes charge of the collection and storage of scrap.

Households are also organized to supply scrap. All individuals can take recyclable materials to a place where they are bought by the personnel of any of the several hundred trucks, driving fixed routes to a fixed timetable, that are a part of the scrap-collecting organization in each county. Then, too, there are regular collections made by youth organizations, who sell the collected materials. The prices they receive are generally set at such a level that there is a real incentive to collect as much scrap as possible.

During 1975 it is calculated that about 517,000 tons of used paper will be collected in the GDR, which corresponds to paper from about four million trees. A target also mentioned is the collection of 345 million bottles and 190 million tin cans during the year. Among other things, this will save 90 million kilowatt-hours of energy. A research institute called the "Institute for Secondary Materials" has been started, and technicians employed

---

for recycling is the amount used L years earlier, or

$$C_{t-L} = \alpha Y_0 e^{g(t-L)}$$

Given that β percent of this can be recovered, we have as the amount recovered

$$R_t = \beta \alpha Y_0 e^{g(t-L)}$$

We can now determine the ratio of the amount of copper recovered, and presumably recycled, to the total consumption of copper. This is

$$\gamma = \frac{R_t}{C_t} = \frac{\beta \alpha Y_0 e^{g(t-L)}}{\alpha Y_0 e^{gt}} = \frac{\beta}{e^{gL}}$$

If we take as approximate values $L \approx 20$, $g \approx 0.03$, and $\beta \approx 0.80$, then we get $\gamma \approx 0.50$. In other words, about 50 percent of the copper being used can have its origin in scrap. It should be appreciated, however, that this is a "steady state" figure. Up to now, for instance, recycling percentages have generally been under the maximum percentage, and thus a very large stock of potentially recyclable material has been built up. Thus, for a short time, it may be possible for most of the consumption of copper to originate from scrap.

by this institute have distinguished 350 separate waste products. Of these, 65 can be reused fully; 200 partially; while, at the present time, the remainder are considered to be without scrap value.

Programs of this sort have also been considered by other countries. The problem is that they do not bother to implement them. W. M. Ruckelshaus, the former director of the U.S. Environmental Protection Agency, has pointed out that the metal in a single can could be used three or four times a year. In addition, he emphasized that the use of more aluminum in automobiles would reduce the weight of a car in such a way as to enable the driver to obtain an increased mileage per gallon of fuel. Moreover, the scrap value of the vehicle would be greater. Automobiles in the United States had an average content of 80 pounds of aluminum per vehicle, but it might be possible to increase this to 420 pounds. At present there are only 1,300 recycling centers in the United States, most of them relatively small, but these have shown that substantial savings in energy—with a measurable increase in economic benefits for all Americans—would be possible if the recycling effort in the United States could be made comparable to that in the GDR.

Professor Glenn Seaborg (1974) envisages a society where the present materials situation is reversed, with secondary materials becoming the principal reserve of resources, and primary commodities relegated to a backup role. There is no doubt but that this is an ideal situation; however, unfortunately, it has a no growth implication. The goal, instead, must be the maximum amount of recycling possible, together with the kind of technological progress that will permit a higher efficiency in both the obtaining and use of natural resources. As for the long-run solution of the mineral supply problem, this may involve an extensive alteration of consumption patterns, with sport and culture   to include education—playing a more important role in the scheme of things.

ENERGY PROBLEMS

8

The first two sections of this short chapter examine some aspects of the supply of energy resources. The treatment is nontechnical in the extreme, and is designed mainly to provide an easily read survey of these matters.

The third section of the chapter is what I call a "closing statement," which is followed by four appendixes and a list of references. The four appendixes will probably not interest the general reader; but the introduction to the reference list is supposed to convey some idea of the kind of literature that I consider to be most important when dealing with this subject. As for the list itself, I have attempted to include most of the literature that I have had occasion to consult either for this book or in my other work with natural resources. It will undoubtedly be the case, however, that, by the time this book reaches the reader, the list will be quite incomplete.

SOME ENERGY RESOURCES

Perhaps the best way to describe the present period from an energy standpoint is as a transition from an era of scarce, but low-cost, resources, to one of copious—or perhaps even unlimited—supplies that will be very expensive, at least if present calculations hold. *The* low-cost resource has been fossil fuel, although recently both its price and, to a somewhat lesser extent, its cost have increased considerably. For the purposes of the present chapter, with its limited time span, the fast breeder reactor probably represents the ultimate source of energy. The word "probably" should be noted very carefully, however, since, regardless of the advantages of the breeder from the point of view of efficiency of fuel utilization, there are technical problems concerning safety and the environment that still must be solved before such equipment should be introduced on a mass basis. Beyond the breeder there are such things as fusion and solar energy that, when they become available, should remove energy from the list of mankind's worries. But this will take time. The technical feasibility of fusion may not be established before the next century; while the economics of solar energy are still slightly on the unfavorable side.

At the present time coal supplies 32 percent of the world's energy needs, gas supplies 19.2 percent, and oil 44.2 percent. All other sources provide only 3.9 percent. Just how this situation will change is difficult to say, but change it must since it seems unlikely that the complete exhaustion of oil, coal, and gas can be delayed for more than several centuries. On the other hand, while uranium is also exhaustible, the reserves of this material can be greatly extended by introducing the breeder, since this reactor may permit extraction of up to 100 times as much energy from a given amount of uranium as is possible with today's reactor technology. Looked at in another perspective, one ton of uranium consumed in a fast breeder is equivalent to about 2 million tons of coal burned in a coal-fired power station. Thus it should become economically feasible to exploit very low quality uranium, which in turn will mean that, for all practical purposes, natural resource constraints upon energy supplies no longer exist.

Before surveying the world inventory of energy supplies, it should be emphasized that if nuclear resources are going to supply more than a small fraction of primary energy supplies, it will not be possible to rely upon electricity alone as the secondary energy carrier, since electricity is an uneconomical source of energy for transport and for heat. What will have to happen instead is that nuclear power be used as an input to produce other energy carriers such as hydrogen, methane, or methanol. Apparently it is not well known that hydrogen would be a superb fuel for aircraft, possessing as it does a high heating value per unit of weight; and, as a fuel for automobiles, it is nonpolluting. Moreover, on these and other counts, methanol may be even more satisfactory.

Some estimates of coal reserves were given in the previous chapter, and on the basis of those figures it is probable that enough coal is available for the next few centuries even if, at some time in the near future, large amounts of coal go into the production of oil or gas. In fact, if coal became the *only* source of energy for the United States, there would be enough for between 50 and 100 years. The type of coal that is of primary interest in energy matters is bituminous, or hard, coal. Brown coals and lignites have only about one-half the calorific value of hard coals; but even so, in the long run, these should not be overlooked. About 38 percent of the measured reserves of these soft coals are in energy-poor Europe, and it may be that sufficiently large gains in the thermodynamic efficiency of systems employing soft coal can be achieved to make the use of this commodity economically attractive.

The next item on our list is natural gas. World reserves at present are 52,532 cubic kilometers, with 32 percent of these in Europe, 23 in Asia, 20

Table 8-1. Estimated Percentage of Energy Supplied by Coal, Oil, and Gas for 1980, 1985, and 2000

Source	1980	1985	2000
Coal	12.5	10.8	5
Oil	66.0	63.0	14
Gas	13.0	14.5	20

in North America, 11 in Africa, and 9 in Europe. World consumption of natural gas was 1,202 cubic kilometers in 1972, and so known recoverable reserves can last slightly more than 40 years if consumption continues to grow at the present rate. Expectations are that the discovery rate for gas, which is quite high, will be maintained for some years in the future, which, for Europe, would mean a slight increase in the part played by gas in the total energy picture. The estimated figure for the total recoverable reserves of natural gas come to 300,000 cubic kilometers.

A number of forecasts are available for energy consumption in Europe to the year 2000. Table 8-1 shows a simple average of some of these forecasts. As can be seen, only coal, oil, and gas are considered in these forecasts, with the remainder of energy supplied being attributed mainly to nuclear power.

The figures presented above are far from definitive, and at least one of the investigators rocketed into the spotlight by the energy crisis, Professor Odell (1974), has an entirely different point of view as to how energy usage will develop. He sees gas supplying 32 percent of the total in 1998; oil, 40 percent; and coal, 14 percent. As much as I would like to believe Odell's vision, the problem is that he has placed too much reliance on such things as rumors about the total amount of exploitable resources of natural gas in the North Sea and elsewhere, while at the same time ignoring the influence of the nuclear lobby in the United States and Western Europe. In the same vein, he and others forget that the accelerated exploitation of a wasting energy asset will force the pace at which new technologies have to be introduced if a given level of energy use is to be maintained. Inherently there is nothing wrong with this, except that in the present case the new technology is characterized by the mass deployment of nuclear reactors. For instance, given estimated supplies of natural gas, and assuming a 7-percent depletion rate, de Vries and Kommandeur (1975) have calculated that by the end of this century, one 1000-MW nuclear power plant would have to be put into operation every two days if the energy level existing at that time is to be maintained. Needless to say, unless certain well-known technical problems connected with nuclear technology have been completely solved, nobody in his right mind would want to be a party to this kind of arrangement.

On the other hand, Odell is completely correct in so far as his scenario for energy use encourages a delay in the introduction of unsafe or uneconomical techniques. The important thing, however, is to choose the correct energy medium for the future; and with this in mind there is no sense in overemphasizing the importance of natural gas while underemphasizing—or ignoring—the economic and technical advantages of synthetic oil and the gasification of coal. But most of all it is necessary to increase by a quantum amount the exploration and investment required to expand conventional energy reserves; and also, if necessary, to interrupt the premature introduction of nuclear technologies. At the same time, politicians, ecologists, and technologists must unite around a strategy that calls for pressing ahead with the scientific and engineering work necessary to create a safe nuclear alternative.

From here we go logically to petroleum oil. Total proved economically exploitable reserves at the present time are about 91.5×10^9 tons, with 54 percent of this in the Middle East, 14 percent in Africa, 9 in the U.S.S.R., 8 in North America, 7.5 in South America, and 1.5 in Europe—to include 0.55 in the United Kingdom. Known measured reserves, as compared with what are called recoverable reserves, are three times as large; and with increases in the price of petroleum there will be an upgrading of reserves, with a certain amount being reclassified that previously were considered as not worth exploiting for economic reasons. In terms of years, economically exploitable reserves amount to about 35 years at the present time; however this has been the case for at least the last 15 years, even though petroleum use during this period has doubled.

It might therefore be suspected that a considerable amount of the pessimism associated with petroleum forecasts is unjustified. Moreover, if we consider speculative or hypothetical resources, a paper issued by the U.S. Department of the Interior in 1973 estimates that probably world resources run for between 70 and 700 years. Which of these figures we take hardly makes any difference, since it almost certainly is the case that the technical and environmental problems connected with such things as the breeder will not defy solution for much longer than another half century.

Even so, it must be reiterated here that a powerful economic argument exists for beginning the conversion of shale and coal into synthetic fuels as soon as possible, and on a fairly large scale. (Nordhaus [1973] sketches a kind of strategy for energy-resource utilization during the next 200 years, basing his calculations on existing cost data as well as assumptions as to how these costs will change.) The cost of a barrel of oil from high-grade shale was about $6 per barrel in 1972, and from low-grade shale about $12.

Given the quantities of high-grade shale available at the present time, most processing during this century would involve only high-quality resources; and thus, even if large costs are invoked by the need to meet environmental standards, it may be possible at the present time to obtain a certain amount of oil from shale at less than the price of conventional oil. Of course, if the *in-situ* process for mining shale could be perfected, then the environmental problems associated with shale would cease to be relevant.

The same thing is true for coal. The techniques for gasifying coal underground have been available for at least 15 years, although little has been done to perfect them until recently. In general, these techniques call for the creation of enough permeability in the coal so that a stream of air can flow from one point in the seam to another without a great loss of pressure. The coal is then ignited, and gasification commences. Part of the coal burns with the injected air, producing a mixture of carbon monoxide, carbon dioxide, and heat. In an efficient process the hot carbon dioxide is continuously reduced to carbon monoxide by a reaction with the hot coal. The product is a gas that can be used for industrial purposes.

The main problems that have arisen here have to do with obtaining the necessary permeability of the coal and maintaining the constant heating value of the gas generated underground. Some new approaches have been suggested for solving these problems. These include breaking up the coal with explosives, and using lasers for various drilling operations. If these methods succeed, then it will be possible to extract energy from coal in the ground with almost no requirements for underground manpower. In addition, it might be possible to obtain energy from coal seams that are presently classified as unexploitable for economic reasons.

Wind, Geothermal, and Tidal Energy

The future for wind energy is uncertain, even though, in many respects, this medium must rank with solar energy as an ideal source of power. The main problem here is that the wind is very variable and unpredictable, and a great number of installations would be necessary if a large percentage of power requirements were to be met using energy from the wind. Of course, if there were some economic method of storing large amounts of electricity generated by wind machines, the entire energy picture might undergo a drastic change.

Saab-Scandia of Sweden has made some projections concerning the economics of wind power. According to its calculations, which were made in 1974, the cost of electricity from wind power was slightly more expensive than from most oil-fueled power plants. It was also reckoned that it would take about 3,000 wind-power plants to provide 14 percent of the Swedish electricity production in 1970. This is no small amount, and if the balance of payments effect was included in the cost calculation—and the calculation was otherwise correct—then, where Sweden is concerned, wind power is a paying proposition today.

On the other hand, the use of wind power, with its 50- and 60-meter-high towers, causes a rather tricky environmental problem. Depending upon where they are put, these towers could have a somewhat unaesthetic effect on the line of the horizon. It might be argued, however, that the lack of emissions of sulphur or radioactivity into the atmosphere more than compensates for any visual pollution that might result.

The American experience with wind power is also interesting from a number of points of view. Experimentation with the generation of electricity by wind machines began well before World War II. Until the 1950s it was generally considered that, because of the cheapness of fossil fuels, these machines came within a factor of two of being economical. Given that oil is now more than five times the price it was at that time, and that the intention in the United States is to reduce the imports of energy as much and as fast as possible, then it seems likely that the economics are now favorable.

Some interesting suggestions have also been made concerning the use of this medium. It is true that adequate storage systems are not as yet available, but there are, in fact, a number of uses that do not require continuity of power. By and large, at the present time, wind generators should be used in conjunction with other generating systems: when the wind is blowing, power generation could originate with wind equipment, thus saving fuel and reducing the power drain from other types of plants.

W. E. Heronemus (1972) has made some estimates for an offshore wind-power complex for the United States consisting of 13,600 floating wind machines of 6 megawatts each clustered about 82 submerged hydrogen generating stations. The total generating capacity would thus be about 82,000 megawatts, and Heronemus has put the cost, in 1975 dollars, at 26 billion. Due to the vagaries of the wind a capacity factor must also be introduced, and Inglis (1975) has established this as 35 percent for wind machines enjoying a favorable wind situation. Nuclear stations, by contrast, appear to have a demonstrated capacity factor of at most 60 percent, although it is almost certain that this will be improved.

Thus 82,000 megawatts of wind power should be compared with 82,000 × 35/60 = 48,000 megawatts of nuclear capactiy. This is equivalent to approximately 44 of the 1,100-megawatt nuclear stations contemplated in the official U.S. nuclear plan, or about 12 percent of the 400,000 megawatts of electric power consumed yearly in the United States. The $26 billion estimate of Heronemus then reduces to about $600 million for the wind equivalent of a large nuclear plant, or about $550 per nuclear-installed kilowatt. If these figures are correct, then it means that in the United States at the present time the cost of power from the wind is less than the cost from a nuclear power plant, and this situation is reinforced when the balance of payments effect is taken into consideration.

The next item in our survey is geothermal energy, which is probably the most economically attractive of all the energy sources. Its principal drawback is that it is available in only a relatively few locations in commercially feasible amounts.

By 1980, in the United States, it may be possible to have an amount of thermal energy available that is equal to four or five of the large 1,100-megawatt nuclear power plants. At the present time geothermal energy is being used for space heating on a fairly large scale in Oregon and Idaho; it is also the primary energy source on Iceland; and in Japan geothermal energy is the prime energy source at one lead-zinc plant. This last example is interesting in that it indicates the possibility of using relatively small geothermal fields for individual projects. Geothermal energy can also be used in hothouses, swimming pools, therapeutic centers, and for refrigeration purposes.

The temperature of hot-water geothermal sources is different for each location. The largest deposits in the United States are in the Imperial Valley of California, and these have a temperature range of 350° Fahrenheit to 600°. These sources can be utilized, essentially, in two ways. The first is to flash steam from the hot water, and to use this steam to generate electricity in a low-pressure steam turbine. One of the disadvantages of this method is that, because of the low steam temperatures, the turbines must be very large per unit of electricity generated. In addition, serious erosion damage to turbine blades often takes place.

The other method employs a heat exchanger to transfer heat to another liquid, which in conjunction with a special turbine generates electricity. This avoids most of the problems of the steam-flashing method, but requires additional equipment. Even so, the average capital cost for geothermal power plants is considerably lower than that for most other systems. The approximate figures, as of July 1974, are given in Table 8-2.

Just how much geothermal energy can eventually be developed is uncertain. In the long run it may not amount to more than a few percent of the total power requirement of those countries with geothermal sources. This, of course, is irrelevant, since every kilowatt that finds its origin in an environmentally superior source means a kilowatt less that must be obtained from nuclear or, for that matter, fossil fuels.

The final source of energy that will be mentioned here is tidal energy.

Table 8-2. Capital Cost of Various Types of Power Plants

Power plant	Capital cost (dollar/kilowatt)
Geothermal	170
Oil and Gas	260
Gas	270
Coal and Gas	300
Coal	325
Oil	370
Nuclear	600

In order to be able to utilize this resource, it is necessary to have a situation where the total range of the tide is large. Perry (1975) has pointed out that along most of the coasts of the world the range between high and low tide is too small to be useful for generating electricity. His estimate of the total potential of these sites is about 50 billion kilowatts per year. Everything considered, the time, energy, and engineering talent involved in investigating this source of energy would probably be better employed elsewhere.

Solar Energy and Fusion

The advantages of solar energy are so well known that they hardly need to be repeated here; and the same is nearly true of the problems that need to be solved before this almost ideal source of energy can be fully exploited. First of all it requires large collecting surfaces if reasonable quantities of energy are to be trapped. This by itself implies very large capital investments. Then, too, in a large part of the industrial world, the supply of sunshine is unpredictable; and thus energy collected when the sun is shining must be stored in such a way that it can be used when there is no sun. Although the purely technical problems associated with this difficulty have been solved, it will be years—if not decades—before the solutions have been perfected to a point where they are economically feasible.

Solar heating has already been developed on a pilot scale, and demonstration units are even in operation in sun-poor Scandinavia. Solar cooling still features a number of unsolved technical problems, but indications are that within the decade the state of solar cooling technology will almost be on a level with solar heating. Among the things needed to accelerate the introduction of these technologies is the establishment by governments of building-design criteria and tax incentives that will encourage the installment of solar heating and cooling systems in residential and industrial structures. An example of these incentives can be found in present-day

French and Swedish subsidies to the owners of residential housing who invest in energy-saving devices and materials.

Fusion is supposed to be the source of energy of the sun and stars, but thus far on earth has been demonstrated only in the form of a hydrogen bomb. So, if it is to be used for peaceful purposes, it must be packaged in modules of a reasonable size, and controlled. Essentially this requires duplicating, on earth, conditions that are similar to those found in the sun, to include a temperature of 100 million degrees.

Just when this can be done defies saying. Intensive research is at present under way in the U.S.S.R., the United States, Western Europe, and Japan. A number of physicists claim that studies indicate that a fusion reactor can be built, and the cost of electricity generated would be comparable to that obtainable from a fast breeder. The target date for presenting the first fusion reactor now seems to be about the year 2000; however it would hardly matter if it were 2100—as long as such a construction is possible in fact as well as theory.

The fuel that would be used in such a reactor is deuterium, or a combination of deuterium and tritium. Deuterium is found in nature in almost unlimited quantities, and can be extracted from seawater at a very low cost. Tritium, however, exists only in trace quantities in nature, and must be obtained by reacting a neutron with lithium. As for the energy obtainable from fusion, Perry (1975) claims that 30 pounds per hour of fusionable material is equivalent to the energy needed by all the U.S. electric generating capacity. The corresponding amount of coal would be 280,000 tons of coal per hour. The safety and environmental problems that would be met in the operation of this equipment are thought to be minor as compared either to those of the fast breeder or the light water reactor; but a certain amount of radioactive waste materials would have to be disposed of when a fusion plant was dismantled, since some of the materials from which the reactor is constructed would become radioactive as a result of exposure to the neutrons produced by fusion reaction.

URANIUM

If the construction of nuclear reactors continues at the present pace, it is estimated that about 4 million tons of U_3O_8 (uranium) will be needed during the remainder of this century. Against this requirement, the present catalogue of reserves shows about 1.2 million tons at a cost of up to $10/pound; and an estimated 1.1 million tons of undiscovered reserves in the same cost range. Another 920,000 tons of "reasonably assured" reserves can be found in the $10–$15 range, together with about 780,000 tons of

Table 8-3. The Geographical Distribution of Uranium Reserves in the Cost Range 0–30 dollars/pound[a]

Area	0–10	10–15
United States	340	180
Sweden	—	350
Southern Africa	260	80
Canada	240	160
Australia	210	80
France and French-speaking Africa	130	—
Other	60	70

[a] Source: U.S. Bureau of Mines.

probable or undiscovered reserves. The geographical distribution of these reserves is given in Table 8-3.

These resources, and for that matter those at double these costs, are inadequate to support the number of reactors that have been projected for the year 2000. Even if the breeder can be introduced in the 1980s, the demand for uranium will continue to climb for some years. In fact, estimates are available that indicate that the total reserves that must be identified to support the level of power generation that will be taking place at the end of this century amount to 12 million tons.

Just how and when these reserves will put in an appearance is uncertain today. The present picture of uranium resources has resulted after 25 years of intensive exploration, and it must be asked if another 25 years will see the tripling of today's level of reserves. One of the major difficulties that must be faced is that there is a short-run limit on the acceptable minimum ore grade of uranium. This limit is in the neighborhood of 50 to 100 parts per million, and corresponds to a cost of recovery of $100/pound. In the United States the only large deposits in this category are in the uranium-bearing shales of the Southeast; but mining these deposits will call for milling and disposing of several million tons/day of overburden. As a result, if *in-situ* methods cannot be developed that will handle this enormous amount of material, it can easily happen that these shales will not be transformed into nuclear fuel. In fact, the opinion of Robert Nininger of the U.S. Atomic Energy Commission seems to indicate that the cut-off grade imposed by environmental constraints is somewhere on the order of 100 to 500 parts per million.

If we go over to nuclear technology, we see that expectations are that there will be between 200,000 and 400,000 megawatts of nuclear generating capacity by 1983–85. Most of this is scheduled to be of the American light water reactor type. At present there are eight principal types of reactors, to include the fast breeder, but about half of the capacity on order in the nonsocialist countries involves American manufacturers. In Europe, France and Germany seem to have decided to buy American technology, and the same is true of Japan. The United Kingdom, on the other hand, has generally expressed a preference for the lower-capacity, but perhaps safer, Magnox and Advanced Gas Cooled Reactor.

As expressed earlier in this chapter, the breeder reactor is probably the short-run key to the energy future of the world. Given this situation it seems clear that considerably more effort must be put into obtaining a safe—a perfectly safe—breeder. If we consider that the energy potential of 3.5 million tons of uranium is sufficient to fuel 800 conventional reactors over their 40-year lifetimes, but that these same reserves will be adequate to run 800 breeders for 37 centuries, then it becomes pointless to carp at the estimated $10-billion development cost of the breeder. The United States, for instance, has already spent several times that much on a space program whose eventual benefits, while they conceivably might be considerable, can at present hardly be compared to what would be the first step in the definitive solution of the energy problem, since by the time fuel for the breeder is exhausted solar or fusion power should be available in unlimited amounts.

One of the more interesting aspects of the breeder is its ability to make use of the uranium "tailings" that in the United States are stored at places like Oak Ridge, Tenn. These tailings take the form of more than 200,000 tons of discarded uranium, or uranium that is not useful at present as a nuclear fuel. However, as Lapp (1975) has noted, if the breeder becomes a reality, the energy in these tailings are the equivalent of 400 billion tons of coal, which, at present prices, carries a value of $20 trillion. In the circumstances, opponents of the breeder in the United States would do well to promote the virtues of some of the other sources of energy, instead, simply, of giving the impression that they would not be unhappy if this $20 trillion was excluded from the U.S. energy scene.

CLOSING STATEMENT

For reasons given in the opening paragraphs of this book, a cloud of gloom has settled over much of the industrial world. Journalists and television commentators of various descriptions attempt to outdo each other as prophets of an impending disaster, and sensitive souls from every layer of society race to get on the bandwagon.

The trouble is that this bandwagon is not going anywhere. Most of the readers of this book certainly know deep down in their bones that although the Club of Rome and Limits to Growth documents are invaluable as warning signals, they constitute at best a travesty of the scientific method. Still, as with econometrics, it may be possible to use them without believing them.

To begin, it must be understood that *the* problem of our time is population. If the population explosion can be brought under control, then everything is possible, including the so-called New Economic World Order. It is, however, hard to believe that such will be the case. In this event the reader can rest assured that even if the rate of growth of the flow of raw materials could be doubled, the experience called development, or industrialization, will only be shared by a small percentage of the poor countries.

But even if the patently impossible goals hatched by this or that commission of eminent persons cannot be achieved in the near—or even the distant—future, some changes for the better are within reach. First, financial aid to the LDCs must be transformed into real aid. Put another way, what now goes under the name of aid must be replaced by trade and, for this to happen, some schemes must be designed and put into operation that will compensate, to some degree, for the low productivities that are found in LDCs outside the primary commodity sectors. The suggestion here is a comprehensive system of preferences involving products that can be produced by the LDCs, as well as a complete dismantling of tariffs that affect these countries.

As for the developed countries, they will have to do something about their consumption in any case. The happiest of all possible solutions will see them making some changes in its structure, with things like sport and culture, including education, achieving a much larger place in the scheme of things. Concerning the energy problem—this is already on the way to being solved in an environmentally acceptable form; hopefully, not just because it makes sense to those veterans of the ecology crusades, but because there is no economic reason to settle for less.

A COMMENT ON "DYNAMIC" DEMAND CURVES

In the third footnote of Chapter 1 it was pointed out that in the short run the demand for an industrial raw material is price-insensitive, where by demand, in this case, we mean the demand for the commodity to be used as a current input. But price changes can, *ceteris paribus,* cause changes in the demand for a commodity that is to be used in the future. In other words, it can cause changes in the buying of commodities for inventories. If we then define demand as the demand for current inputs *and* inventories, we can get a downward-sloping demand curve of the conventional type.

It may also be the case that, even if we cannot talk of a great deal, or for that matter any, short-run price sensitivity, there may be a sort of long-run price sensitivity that is independent of inventory demand. Take a case where the price of an industrial raw material falls and stays at a much lower level for a long time. Purchasers might eventually be willing to make modifications in their product to the extent that they can use more of that raw material. It is also probably so that by long-run we must specify *very-long run*. Moreover, the logic of demand curves indicates that where there is an increase in the demand for a commodity, given a price fall, there must also be a decrease given a price rise. The problem is that empirical data, as well as simple observation, would seem to indicate that this type of back-and-forth movement does not take place for industrial raw materials. On the other hand, a tendency toward this type of movement may well exist, but, given factors such as an autonomous growth in demand and the secular substitution of one commodity for another, this tendency may be overwhelmed.

Diagrammatically the arrangement mentioned above is shown in Figure A-1 for the case of a fall in price. The original price is P_0, and the long-run demand curve is D_0. If demand adjusted immediately to a fall in the price to P^*, then we would move to C^*. Instead, in the very short run, with price P^*, demand increases only to C_1. Gradually, however, we get an asymtotic movement to C^*. What might be called an intermediate demand curve is shown by D_2, in that C_2 is an "intermediate consumption" on the way to C^*. This asymtotic movement is shown in (b), Figure A-1.

241

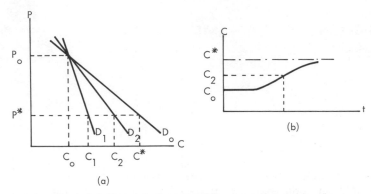

Figure A-1. Demand adjustment following a decrease in price.

It is simple to show that the law of adjustment for this model is $C_t = C_{t-1} + \lambda(C^* - C_{t-1})$, where C^* is the equilibrium value of demand, and $0 < \lambda < 1$. When $C_t = C^*$, there is no further change in the variable. If, as in (a), Figure A-1, long-run demand is related to price by $C^* = \alpha + \theta P_t$, and put into this expression, we get $C_t = \lambda\alpha + (1 - \lambda)C_{t-1} + \lambda\theta P_t$. When $C_t = C_{t-1} = C^*$ we have an equilibrium, and are back on D_0. This can be verified by substituting $C_t = C_{t-1} = C^*$ into the last expression given for C_t. As a result of this substitution we get $C^* = \alpha + \theta P_t$.

Another way of looking at this is to recognize that the adjustment equation can be written as a difference equation, or $C_t - (1 - \lambda)C_{t-1} = \lambda C^*$. If $C = C_0$ when $t = 0$, the solution for this simple first order equation is $C_t = (C_0 - C)(1 - \lambda)^t + C^*$. Since $0 < (1 - \lambda) < 1$, we see that as t increases, the first term goes toward zero, and C_t approaches C^*.

The above analysis, which began by a fall in the price, is sometimes called the "adjustment hypothesis." It might happen, however, that instead of an actual change in price, we might have an expected change, with demand a function of this expected price. This approach involves what might be called the "expectations hypothesis." One of the attractions of this type of hypothesis is that it fits in with the concept of a gradual change in consumption, since it is reasonable for consumers to be cautious until reality coincides to some degree with their expectations.

We can begin the algebraic part of our discussion by postulating that $C_t = \alpha + \theta P_e^t$, where P_e^t is expected price. The next step is to form expectations. A widely used assumption is that expectations are "adaptive," which means that we have $P_e^t = P_{t-1}^e + \lambda(P_{t-1} - P_{t-1}^e)$, where P_{t-1} represents the actual price in period $t - 1$. We then get

$$C_t = \alpha + \theta[P_{t-1}^e + \lambda(P_{t-1} - P_{t-1}^e)]$$

Next, lag C_t by one period to get $C_{t-1} = \alpha + \theta P^e_{t-1}$, and multiply this expression by $(1 - \lambda)$. This gives $C_t(1 - \lambda) = \alpha(1 - \lambda) + \theta(1 - \lambda)P^e_{t-1}$.   If this is subtracted from the above expression for C_t we get

$$C_t = \alpha\lambda + (1-\lambda)C_{t-1} + \theta\lambda P_{t-1}$$

What we see here is that this expression differs from that obtained via the adjustment hypothesis only through the presence of P_{t-1} instead of P_t. If, however, we take for expectations $P^t_e = P^e_{t-1} + \lambda(P_t - P^e_{t-1})$, where P_t in this case should be considered as some kind of "normal" price, then we get the same expression for C_t as we did employing the adjustment hypothesis. It should perhaps be added that the expectations hypothesis employing this latter formulation of expectations probably makes more sense for production rather than consumption, since production usually involves more than a simple forecast.

SOME ASPECTS OF SUPPLY ELASTICITIES

B

If we remember the contents of Appendix A, it soon becomes clear that we are dealing with two elasticities when we have a "dynamic"-type situation. Naturally, these are designated a short-run elasticity and a long-run. Before examining this matter more closely, we note that the usual textbook definition of elasticity is

$$p = \frac{\partial X}{\partial P} \frac{\bar{P}}{\bar{X}}$$

In the above expression $\partial X/\partial P$ is the slope of a demand or supply curve, and $\bar{P}$ and $\bar{X}$ refer to the point at which the elasticity is to be measured or, if we are calculating elasticities from an equation that has been fitted econometrically, these can be taken as the mean of the time series for P and X.

Just as the adjustment equation for consumption, as derived in the previous appendix, was $C_t = \lambda\alpha + (1 - \lambda) C_{t-1} + \lambda\theta P_t$, similar equation can be postulated for supply. As an example take $S_t = \phi\beta + (1 - \phi)S_{t-1} + \phi\pi P_t$. In certain respects the adjustment hypothesis seems much more appropriate for supply than for consumption, since changes in production inevitably take time.

It also happens to be so that this type of equation permits us to regard supply as a function of a weighted average of present and former prices. The easiest way to see this is to lag the equation for S_t, and use it to replace S_{t-1} in the same equation. The result is

$$S_t = \phi\beta + (1 - \phi)[\phi\beta + (1 - \phi)S_{t-2} + \phi\pi P_{t-2}] + \phi\pi P_{t-1}$$

Repeated application of this procedure gives

$$S_t = \beta + \phi\pi \sum_{}^{\infty} (1 - \phi)^i P_{t-i}$$

245

As for the calculation of elasticities, the short-run elasticity can be obtained directly from $S_t = \phi\beta + (1 - \phi)S_{t-1} + \phi\pi P_t$, since $\partial S_t/\partial P_t = \phi\pi$, and thus

$$\varepsilon_{sp} = \phi\pi\frac{\bar{P}}{\bar{S}}$$

For the long-run elasticity, we know that in the long run $S_t = S_{t-1}$, and so $S_t = \phi\beta + (1 - \phi)S_t + \phi\pi P_t$, or $S_t = \beta + \pi P_t$. As a result we get, as before, $\partial S/\partial P_t = \pi$, and thus

$$\varepsilon_{Lp} = \pi\frac{\bar{P}}{\bar{S}}$$

Since $\phi < 1$, $\epsilon_{sp} < \epsilon_{Lp}$, as is to be expected.

Some typical long- and short-run supply elasticities for newly mined copper can be found in Banks (1974). The U.S. Bureau of Mines has computed supply elasticities for several of the more important minerals, and these are as follows:

	Price range (cents/pound)	Implied elasticity
Aluminum	27–37	1.15
Copper	52–75	0.77
Nickel	128–200	2.03
Lead	14–20	1.84
Zinc	16–25	1.75

EXHAUSTIBLE RESOURCES—A NONLINEAR PROGRAMMING APPROACH

C

The purpose of this appendix is to reexamine the topic taken up in the last section of Chapter 4: that of choosing a program for the extraction of a given amount of an exhaustible resource over a time horizon T. This is to be done in such a way that the profit from this program is maximized. To begin, we know that the removal of q_t in each period involves a unit cost c_t, and in addition each unit commands a price p_t. For each period, with the exception of the present period, p_t and c_t are estimated values. Also, to keep the discussion as general as possible, both p_t and c_t will be taken as functions of q_t. The expression for the discounted profit that we will want to maximize is then

$$\sum_{t=1}^{T} \frac{p_t(q_t)q_t - c_t(q_t)q_t}{(1 + r)^t} = \sum_{t=1}^{T} \bar{B}_t(q_t) = \text{Max}$$

$\bar{B}_t(q_t)$ means the discounted value of $p_t(q_t)q_t - c_t(q_t)q_t$. The summed expression is then the same as

$$\bar{B}_1(q_1) + \bar{B}_2(q_2) + \cdots + \bar{B}_T(q_T) = \bar{B}(q_1, q_2, \ldots, q_T)$$

In mathematical programming terminology this is called the objective function. The constraint on the maximization results from the presence of a finite and given amount of the resource, or $\bar{K}$. This means that we must have

$$q_1 + q_2 + \cdots + q_T \leq \bar{K}$$

We also have

$$q_1, q_2, \ldots, q_T \geq 0$$

The above expressions constitute a simple nonlinear program. The next step is to write the dual of this program. We get

$$\text{Min: } Z' = \lambda \overline{K}$$

subject to

$$\lambda \geq \frac{\partial \overline{B}}{\partial q_1} = \overline{B}'(q_1)$$

$$\lambda \geq \frac{\partial \overline{B}}{\partial q_2} = \overline{B}'(q_2)$$

$$\vdots \qquad \vdots$$

$$\lambda \geq \frac{\partial \overline{B}}{\partial q_T} = \overline{B}'(q_T)$$

and

$$\lambda \geq 0$$

Remember that we have $\overline{B}'(q_t) = B'(q_t)/(1 + r)^t$. We can now examine the expression $B'(q_t)$. Since $B(q_t) = p(q_t)q_t - c(q_t)q_t$, we must have $B'(q_t) = p(q_t)'q_t + p(q_t) - c(q_t)'q_t - c(q_t) = MR(q_t) - MC(q_t)$. This is so since the marginal revenue (MR) is $p(q_t)'q_t + p(q_t)$, and the marginal cost (MC) is $c(q_t)'q_t + c(q_t)$. In general terms the above condition is

$$\lambda \geq \overline{B}'(q_t) = MR(q_t) - MC(q_t)/(1 + r)^t$$

The expression $MR(q_t) - MC(q_t)$ can be termed the marginal profit, or $MP(q_t)$.

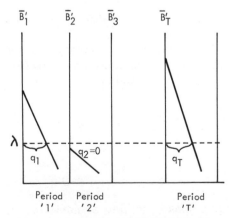

Figure C-1. Intertemporal production program from an extractive resource.

We know from Kuhn–Tucker theory that if $\lambda > \bar{B}'(q_t)$ then production in period t is zero, or $q_t = 0$. We also know that if we have $K > \Sigma q_t$, then $\lambda = 0$, and the shadow price—or scarcity value—of the resource is zero. Diagrammatically we have Figure C-1.

As was pointed out earlier, we are away from the familiar $MR = MC$ of elementary microeconomics. The reason for this is that we must add a component to the cost to take into account the scarcity value of the resource. In other words, what we have is $MR = MC + \lambda$. Of course, if the resource is not scarce over the planning period or time horizon T, then $\lambda = 0$. This is the meaning of $\Sigma q_t > \bar{K}$. It should also be noted that $\lambda_t = \lambda_{t-1} = \lambda_{t+1}$, and so on. If the resource has a greater scarcity value (discounted) in one period than in another, then units are transferred into that period until we get an equality across periods. This arrangement is patently Ricardian, but with an intertemporal twist.

Finally, we can write λ in continuous form, or $\lambda = B'e^{-rt}$, and take advantage of the constancy of λ to get a result referred to in the first part of the first section of this chapter. We have

$$\frac{d\lambda}{dt} = -rB'e^{-rt} + e^{-rt}\frac{dB'}{dt} = 0$$

Thus

$$\frac{1}{B'}\frac{dB'}{dt} = r$$

This is an equilibrium condition, and it indicates indifference between extracting a resource and using the profit from selling it to buy a financial asset, or leaving the resource to appreciate in the ground. On the other hand, if the left-hand side of this expression is larger than the right-hand side, then the marginal profit is appreciating faster if the resource is left in the ground than it would be if the resource were extracted and the marginal profit put in a bank and left to grow at the bank rate of interest or, identically, the marginal profit were used to buy some other type of financial asset.

NEOCLASSICAL INVESTMENT THEORY— AN OPTIMAL CONTROL APPROACH

A few of the ideas in this book that involve investment will now be looked at with the help of some elementary neoclassical investment theory. The first part of the discussion follows Banks (1975). As a beginning, assuming only capital and labor as production factors, we can write as our expression for discounted cash flow over an infinite time horizon

$$W = \int_0^\infty \left[PF(K,L) - wL - GI \right] e^{-rt} \, dt$$

P is the price of the product being produced, w the wage of labor, and G the price of the capital good. Note that, as expressed here, the capital good is being paid for in the initial period, while there revenues PF, and payment for the current input wL, in every period from $t = 0$ to $t = \infty$. Of course we could replace G by a yearly payment, or annuity, of $A = rGI$ if we have an infinite time horizon. This is so since

$$\int_0^\infty rGI \, e^{-rt} \, dt = GI$$

On the other hand, if we had a finite time horizon, or $t = 0$ to $t = T$, the yearly payments would amount to $rGI/(1 - e^{-rT})$, and once again

$$\int_0^T \frac{rGI}{1 - e^{-rT}} e^{-rt} \, dt = GI$$

As for net investment, this is taken as $\mathring{K} = I - uK$, where u is a depreciation rate. The neoclassical characteristics of the production function imply that the bordered hessian of the production function is positive,

251

or

$$\begin{vmatrix} 0 & F_K & F_L \\ F_K & F_{KK} & F_{KL} \\ F_L & F_{LK} & F_{LL} \end{vmatrix} = 2F_{KL}F_LF_K - F_{KK}F_L^2 - F_{LL}F_K^2 > 0$$

We can now write as our Hamiltonian

$$H = [PF(K,L) - wL - GI]e^{-rt} + \lambda(I - uK)$$

The discount factor being used here is the market rate of interest. The state variable is K, while the control variable is I. On this point, it should be noted that we are drawing on an interpretation of the calculus of variations in which the control variables are rates of change of the state variables, and are also unrestricted in value. We then get from the Hamiltonian

$$-Ge^{-rt} + \lambda = 0$$

or

$$\lambda = Ge^{-rt}$$

and

$$\overset{\circ}{\lambda} = -rGe^{-rt}$$

$$PF_Ke^{-rt} - \lambda u = -\overset{\circ}{\lambda}$$

In the last expression F_K is the physical marginal product of capital. Combining these expressions we get

$$G(r + u) = PF_K$$

This is an equilibrium condition. When it is satisfied (in conjunction with $w = PF_L$) we have an optimal stock of capital. Observe also that both sides of the above expression can be defined as the rental of capital. In elementary textbooks we usually have $R = rG = PF_K$, since depreciation is assumed away for simplicity; but, in the present case, the rental of capital includes not only the rental charge rG, but also the decay uG, since this is a part of the good that the owner will not get back. Also, note carefully that u here is physical depreciation. We also see from the last equation

$$G = \frac{PF_K}{r + u} \equiv \int_0^\infty PF_Ke^{-(r + u)t}\,dt$$

This is essentially the same expression that we have in the second footnote in Chapter 6. Now, for simplicity's sake, let us assume that we have a capital good that is reproducing itself, in which case we have $G = P$. If taxes enter the picture, then the rental on a machine becomes $R = (r + u)G + T$. Where taxes are concerned these are figured on the basis of net income minus depreciation, where depreciation in this case is called D, and thus distinguished from physical depreciation or an actual using up of the equipment. We also know that in equilibrium net income should equal the rental rate. Thus we have

$$R = (r + u)G + t(R - D)$$

or

$$R = \frac{G(r + u) - tD}{1 - t}$$

In these expressions t is the tax rate. As long as realistic assumptions are made about D, then an increase in t will increase the rental cost of capital.

REFERENCES

A NOTE ON THE LITERATURE

I think it is perfectly clear that a book of this sort could not be written without referring to a great deal of literature. First, the economist interested in industrial raw materials—and particularly nonferrous metals—will read the *Engineering and Mining Journal,* which is a monthly based in New York. My advice is for the newcomer to get all the issues of this journal for the past 10 years, and to pay particular attention to the investment and prospecting information. There are also two new journals that are growing in importance and that definitely should be followed. These are *Resources Policy* and *Energy Policy,* both from the IPC Science and Technology Press, London. I also strongly recommend the journals *New Scientist,* the *London Economist,* and the daily *London Financial Times.* In addition, it is valuable to keep up with the American periodicals *Business Week, Fortune,* and *Industry Week.* The special issues of the *Metal Bulletin* (e.g., 1965 and 1974) are important documents, and I also recommend the journal *World Mining.*

For the reader shopping for an economics background I recommend the well-known elementary textbook by Paul Samuelson (1975). This should be followed by the textbooks of Alchian and Allen (1964), and Clower and Due (1974). There are, of course, many other superb microeconomics textbooks (Dorfman, Lancaster, B. Moore, Lipsey and Steiner, etc.), but when I was preparing this book I particularly had in mind the approaches of Alchian and Allen and of Clower and Due.

Where the economics of specific commodities are concerned, I recommend for copper the paper by Fisher, Cootner, and Baily (1972), and, if the reader can overlook a few "slips," my own earlier book on the world copper market. For tin, M. Desai (1966) should be looked at and also, if it can be obtained, his Ph.D. thesis from the Wharton School of Economics. I would also advise the reader to examine the Ph.D. thesis of W. Witherell if he is interested in a first-rate attempt to construct an econometric model of an important market. The Charles River Associates do econometric model-

255

ing and analyses of the various commodity markets, and some of their work can be obtained at a low price from the U.S. government. On this point, the U.S. Bureau of Mines publishes a great deal that the economist in this field will find valuable, and most of this material is free. Extensive references to the publications of this agency, and to similar types of publications, conferences, etc., can be found in *Resources Policy*.

Some of the international organizations publish material that can be useful. The Economics Analysis Department of the World Bank comes first to mind, and in particular the work of Kenji Takeuchi, Bension Varon, and Irfan Ul-Haq. These economists have done excellent work on such items as iron ore, copper, rubber, and aluminum. The Commodities and Research divisions of UNCTAD are also important sources of material. They have prepared a number of papers on manganese, cobalt, copper, tin, lead, and zinc, and on commodity policies over the past few years. Where UNIDO (The United Nations Industrial Development Organization) documents are concerned, I can recommend without hesitation the papers presented at the Brazilia Conference on the Iron and Steel Industries (1973). Other material on this subject is available from the Economic Commission for Europe (Iron and Steel Division), and the International Iron and Steel Institute, Brussels. I can also mention that the ECE-UNCTAD Reference Room at the Palais Des Nations, Geneva, publishes, on a weekly basis, a bibliography in which both new and old publications on commodities are listed.

The scientific literature is not particularly extensive at the present time, but it is growing. In my recent course at the University of Stockholm I was able to satisfy myself that among the best literature available at an elementary level is Solow (1974), Nordhaus (1974), and, at a slightly advanced level, Nordhaus (1973). The Nordhaus (1973) paper deals with energy resources, but the techniques he uses are applicable to almost all exhaustible resources. A recent book edited by D. W. Pearce (1975), with the assistance of J. Rose, is also very timely and contains contributions at a number of levels of difficulty. I also suggest that the reader capable of following a fairly advanced treatment of the theory of resource exhaustion examine Appendix C above if he plans to attack some of the recent material in the scientific journals.

It should also be emphasized that a great deal of important material is to be found in the French, German, and Swedish languages (and, for all I know, half a dozen others). The periodical *Annales des Mines* comes first to mind. I also recommend the research publications of the major German research institutes, in particular the HWWA Institute at Hamburg, and the Institute for World Economics at Kiel. Finally, I would like to remind the reader of the importance of the statistical sources. I mention in particular the *World Metal Statistics* of the World Bureau of Metal Statistics; *Metal Statistics* of Metalgesellschaft A.G. (Frankfurt), and the *International Wrought Copper Council Statistical Reports*.

Adams, F. G. "The Integration of World Primary Commodity Markets into Project Link: The Example of Copper," Paper Prepared for the Annual Meeting of Project Link, Stockholm, September 3–8, 1973.
———. "A Model of the Nickel Market," Department of Economics, Wharton School of Finance and Commerce, Philadelphia, 1974.
Adelman, M. A. *The World Petroleum Market*. Baltimore: The Johns Hopkins Press, 1972.
Agostini, Barbara. "The Comeback of Natural Rubber," *Ceres*, Nov./Dec. 1974.
Alchian, A., and W. Allen. *Exchange and Production Theory in Use*. Belmont, Calif.: Wadsworth Publishing Co., 1964.
Alexander, W. O. "The Competition of Metals," *Scientific American*, 1967.
Anderson, K. P. "Optimal Growth When the Stock of Resources is Finite and Depletable," *The Journal of Economic Theory*, April 1972.
Arrow, K. J. "Applications of Control Theory to Economic Growth," Mimeograph Report, Stanford University, 1967.
Baldwin, R. E. *Economic Development and Export Growth*. Berkeley: University of California Press, 1966.
Banks, Ferdinand E. "An Econometric Model of the World Tin Economy: A Comment," *Econometrica*, 1972.
———. "An Econometric Note on the Demand for Refined Zinc," *Zeitschrift für Nationalökonomie*, 1971.
———. "Elementary Investment Theory: An Optimal Control Approach," *Jahrbüchern für Nationalökonomie und Statistik*, 1975.
———. "A Note on Some Theoretical Issues of Resource Depletion," *The Journal of Economic Theory*, October 1974.
———. *The World Copper Market: An Economic Analysis*. Boston: Ballinger Publishing Co., 1974.
Barger, H., and S. H. Schurr. *The Mining Industries, 1899–1939*. New York: National Bureau of Economic Research, 1944.
Barkman, Kerstin. "The International Tin Agreements," *Journal of World Trade Law*, 1975.
Barnet, H. J., and C. Morse. *Scarcity and Growth: The Economics of Natural Resource Scarcity*. Baltimore: The Johns Hopkins Press, 1963.
Beckerman, W. "Economists, Scientists, and Environmental Catastrophe," *Oxford Economic Papers*, November 1972.
Bohm, Peter. *The Pricing of Copper in International Trade*. Stockholm: The Economic Research Institute, Stockholm School of Economics, 1968.
Bottelier, J. C. *A Case Study of the World Copper Industry*. Study prepared for UNCTAD, 1968.
Bradley, P. G. *The Economics of Crude Petroleum Production*. Amsterdam: North Holland Publishing Company, 1967.
Brundenius, Claes. "The Anatomy of Imperialism: Multinational Mining Corporations in Peru," *Journal of Peace Research*, 1972.
Burt, O. R., and R. G. Cummings. "Production and Investment in Natural Resource Industries," *American Economic Review*, September 1970.

Bushaw, D. W., and R. W. Clower. *Introduction to Mathematical Economics.* Homewood, Ill.: Irwin Publishing Co., 1957.

Carlisle, D. "The Economics of a Fund Resource with Particular Reference to Mining," *American Economic Review,* September 1954.

Clower, R. W. "An Investigation into the Dynamics of Investment," *American Economic Review,* 1954.

——— and J. F. Due. *Microeconomics.* Homewood, Ill.: Irwin Publishing Co., 1972.

Cummings, R. G. "Some Extensions of the Economic Theory of Exhaustible Resources," *Western Economic Journal,* September 1969.

Desai, M. "An Econometric Model of the World Tin Economy, 1948–1961," *Econometrica,* 1966.

———. "An Econometric Model of the World Tin Economy: A Reply to Mr. Banks," *Econometrica,* 1972.

Ertek, Tumay. *The World Demand for Copper, 1948–63: An Econometric Study.* Ph.D. Dissertation, Wisconsin University, 1967.

Fisher, F. M. *Supply and Costs in the U.S. Petroleum Industry.* Washington: Resources for the Future, 1964.

———. P. H. Cootner, and M. N. Baily, "An Econometric Model of the World Copper Industry," *Bell Journal of Economics and Management Science,* 1972.

Fisher, John C. *Energy Crisis in Perspective.* New York: John Wiley, 1974.

Gaffney, M. *Extractive Resources and Taxation.* Madison: University of Wisconsin Press, 1967.

Gordon, R. L. "A Reinterpretation of the Pure Theory of Exhaustion," *Journal of Political Economy,* June 1967.

Grillo, H. "The Importance of Scrap," *The Metal Bulletin,* Special Issue on Copper, 1965.

Habeler, G. *A Survey of International Trade Theory.* Special Papers in International Trade Theory, Princeton University, 1961.

Herfindahl, O. C. *Copper Costs and Prices: 1879–1957.* Baltimore: Johns Hopkins Press, 1959.

Herkenhoff, E. C. "When Are We Going to Mine Oil?," *Engineering and Mining Journal,* June 1972.

Heronemus, W. E. "Pollution Free Energy from Offshore Winds," 8th Annual Conference and Exposition of the Marine Technology Society, Washington, September 13, 1972.

Higgins, C. I. "An Econometric Description of the U.S. Steel Industry," in L. R. Klein, ed., *Essays in Industrial Economics,* Vol. II. Philadelphia: Wharton School of Finance and Commerce, 1969.

Hobson, Simon. "Mining Costs and Inflation," *The Metal Bulletin,* Special Issue, 1974.

Hottel, H. C., and J. B. Howard. *New Energy Technology—Some Facts and Assessments.* Cambridge, Mass.: MIT Press, 1971.

Hotelling, H. "The Economics of Exhaustible Resources," *Journal of Political Economy,* April 1931.

Hufbauer, G. C. *Synthetic Materials and the Theory of International Trade.* London: Duckworth, 1966.

Inglis, David R. "Wind Power Now," *Bulletin of the Atomic Scientists,* October 1975.

Johnson, H. G. *Economic Policies Toward Less Developed Countries.* Washington: Brookings Institution, 1967.

Johnston, J. *Statistical Cost Analysis.* New York: John Wiley, 1960.

Klein, L. R. *An Introduction To Econometrics.* Englewood Cliffs, N.J.: Prentice Hall, 1962.

Kolbe, H., and H. J. Timm. "Die Bestimmungsfaktorn der Preisentwicklung auf dem

Weltmarkt für Naturkautschuk—Eine Ökonometrische Modellanalyse," Nr. 10, HWWA Institut für Wirtschaftsforschung, Hamburg (1972).

Kuller, R. G., and R. G. Cummings. "An Economic Model of Production and Investment for Petroleum Reservoirs," *American Economic Review*, March 1974.

Labys, W. C., H. J. B. Rees, and C. M. Elliott. "Copper Price Behavior and the London Metal Exchange," *Applied Economics*, 1971.

Lapp, R. E. "We May Find Ourselves Short of Aluminum Too," *Fortune*, October 1975.

Lanzilotti, R. F. "Pricing Objectives in Large Companies," *American Economic Review*, December 1958.

Leontief, W. "Environmental Repercussions and the Economic Structure," *Review of Economics and Statistics*, August 1970.

Lovesay, G. "Forecasting Inflation Effects on Prices of Primary Products," IBRD Working Paper, Washington, 1973.

Macavoy, P. W., and R. S. Pindyck. "Alternative Regulatory Policies for Dealing with the Natural Gas Shortage," *Bell Journal of Economics and Management Science*, 1972.

Manne, A. S. "Waiting for the Breeder," *Review of Economic Studies*, July 1975.

Maple, J. H. C. "Power From Nuclear Fusion," *Energy World*, April 1975.

Meadows, D. H. *The Limits to Growth*. New York: Universe Books, 1972.

Nerlove, M. *The Dynamics of Supply: Estimation of Farmers' Response to Price*. Baltimore: Johns Hopkins Press, 1958.

Netschert, B. C., and H. H. Landsberg. *The Future Supply of the Major Metals*. Washington: Resources for the Future, 1961.

Newhouse, J. P., and F. Sloan. "An Econometric Study of Copper Supply," Unpublished Report, Rand Corporation.

Nordhaus, W. D. "The Allocation of Energy Resources," *Brookings Papers*, 1973.

———. "Resources as a Constraint on Growth," *American Economic Review*, May 1974.

Odell, P. R. "European Alternatives to Oil Imported from OPEC Countries: Oil and Gas as Indigenous Resources," Paper presented at the John F. Kennedy Institute Colloquium, May 1974, Eindhoven, The Netherlands.

Paterson, N. R. "Geophysics Leads Mineral Exploration," *World Mining*, Catalog, Survey, and Directory Number, 1974.

Pearce, D. W. *The Economics of Natural Resource Depletion* (edited with the assistance of J. Rose). London and Basingstoke: MacMillan Press, 1975.

Perlman, Louis. "Copper Smelting: Some Commercial Considerations," *The Metal Bulletin*, Special Issue, 1974.

Perry, Harry. "The Gasification of Coal," *Scientific American*, March 1974.

———. "Developing Alternative Energy Sources," *Current History*, July/August 1975.

Plourde, C. G. "A Simple Model of Replenishable Natural Resource Exploitation," *American Economic Review*, June 1970.

Radetski, M. "Koppertillgångarna—Ett Fallstudie i Resursuttömning," *Ekonomisk Debatt*, 1974.

Rayment, Paul B. W. "On the Analysis of the Export Performance of Developing Countries," *The Economic Record*, 1970.

Rowe, J. W. F. *Primary Commodities in International Trade*. Cambridge, England: Cambridge University Press, 1965.

Samuelson, Paul A. *Economics, An Introductory Analysis*, 9th ed. New York: McGraw Hill, 1975.

Scott, A. D. *Natural Resources: The Economics of Conservation*. Toronto: University of Toronto Press, 1955.

Seaborg, Glenn T. "The Recycle Society of Tomorrow," *Futurist,* June 1974.

Shaw, Joseph. "Manganese Model II." Miscellaneous Paper, UNCTAD, Geneva, 1973.

Silberston, A., and A. Cockerill. *The Steel Industry: International Comparisons of Industrial Structure and Performance.* Cambridge, England: Cambridge University Press, 1973.

Smith, V. K. "Re-Examination of the Trends in the Prices of Natural Resource Commodities, 1870–1972," Economic Growth Institute, State University of New York at Binghamton, Working Paper No. 44, 1974.

Smith, V. L. "An Optimistic Theory of Exhaustible Resources," *The Journal of Economic Theory,* December 1974.

Solow, R. M. "Richard T. Ely Lecture: The Economics of Resources or the Resources of Economics," *American Economic Review,* May 1974.

––––––. "Intergenerational Equity and Exhaustible Resources," *Review Of Economic Studies,* July 1975.

Somerset, G. S. "Economic Aspects of Copper Production and Marketing Possibilities for Developing Countries," UNIDO, ID/WG/74/4, 1970.

Spendlove, Max. "Opportunities in the Production of Secondary Non-Ferrous Metals," UNIDO, 4 September, 1969.

Stewardson, B. R. "The Nature of Competition in the World Market for Refined Copper," *The Economic Record,* 1970.

Swarbrick, P. "Cable Makers and Substitution," *The Metal Bulletin,* Special Issue, 1974.

Takeuchi, Kenji. "CIPEC and the Copper Export Earning of Member Countries," *The Developing Economies,* 1972.

Tilton, S. E. "The Choice of Trading Partners: An Analysis of International Trade in Aluminum, Bauxite, Copper, Lead, Manganese, Tin, and Zinc." Ph.D. Dissertation, Yale University, 1966.

Treadgold, M. L. "Bougainville Copper and the Economic Development of Papua-New Guinea," *The Economic Record,* 1971.

Varon, Bension. "The International Market for Iron Ore: Review and Outlook," IBRD Working Paper, November 30, 1972.

––––––, and K. Takeuchi. "Developing Countries and Non-Fuel Minerals," *Foreign Affairs,* April 1974.

de Vries, Bert, and Jan Kommandeur. "Gas for Western Europe: How Much For How Long," *Energy Policy,* March 1975.

Wakesberg, Si. "Scrap: Myths and Realities of the U.S. Market," *The Metal Bulletin,* Special Issue, 1974.

Weinstein, M. C., and R. J. Zeckhauser. "Use Patterns for Depletable and Recycleable Resources," *Review of Economic Studies,* 1975.

Wilson, T., R. P. Sinha, and J. R. Castree. "The Income Terms of Trade of Developed and Developing Countries," *Economic Journal,* December 1969.

Witherell, W. "An Econometric Model of the World Wool Market." Ph.D. Dissertation, Princeton University, 1967.

Wohlin, L. "Kommer Industrisektorn att gå Tillbaka i Sverige," *Ekonomisk Debatt,* 1974.

ABOUT THE AUTHOR

Ferdinand E. Banks attended Illinois Institute of Technology and Roosevelt University (Chicago, Illinois), graduating with a B.A. in Economics. After military service in the Orient and Europe, he worked as an engineer and systems and procedures analyst. His graduate work was done at the University of Stockholm, from which he received the M.Sc. and Fil. Lic. He also has the Fil. Dr. from Uppsala University. He taught for five years at the University of Stockholm, was Senior Lecturer in Economics and Statistics at the United Nations African Institute for Economic and Development Planning, Dakar, Senegal, and has been consultant lecturer in macroeconomics for the OECD in Lisbon, Portugal. From 1968 until 1971 he was an econometrician for the United Nations Commission on Trade and Development in Geneva, Switzerland. At present he is Associate Professor and Research Fellow at the University of Uppsala, Sweden, and Lecturer in the Economics of Natural Resources, the University of Stockholm.

INDEX

263